S... GUIDE TO

Sewing Home Furnishings

Expert Techniques for Creating Custom Shades, Drapes, Slipcovers and More

Photograph courtesy of Calico Corners—*Calico Home*

ILLUSTRATED GUIDE TO

Sewing Home Furnishings

Expert Techniques for Creating Custom Shades, Drapes, Slipcovers and More

Distributed By
Fox Chapel Publishing

Photographs on cover and pages 6 and 7 courtesy of Calico Corners—Calico Home, www.calicocorners.com.

Fox Chapel Publishing would like to thank Calico Corners for their support on this project.

Published and distributed in North America by Fox Chapel Publishing Company, Inc.

Illustrated Guide to Sewing Home Furnishings is an original work, first published in 2010.

Portions of text and art previously published by and reproduced under license with Direct Holdings Americas Inc.

ISBN 978-1-56523-510-6

Library of Congress Cataloging-in-Publication Data

Illustrated guide to sewing home furnishings : expert techniques for creating custom shades, drapes, slipcovers and more.

p. cm.

Includes bibliographical references and index.

ISBN 978-1-56523-510-6 (alk. paper)

1. House furnishings. I. Fox Chapel Publishing.

TT387.I44 2010

646.2'1--dc22

2010025535

To learn more about the other great books from Fox Chapel Publishing, or to find a retailer near you, call toll-free 800-457-9112 or visit us at *www.FoxChapelPublishing.com*.

Note to Authors: We are always looking for talented authors to write new books in our area of woodworking, design, and related crafts. Please send a brief letter describing your idea to Acquisition Editor, 1970 Broad Street, East Petersburg, PA 17520.

Printed in China
First printing: September 2010

Contents

What You Can Learn

Fabric, Tools, and Supplies, page 10

Choosing fabric will include considerations such as wear, sunlight, and use, but each fabric has something to recommend it.

Techniques for Custom Decorating, page 22

Details such as snap tapes and zippers are often taken for granted, but they give home furnishings the extra touches that mark the best work of custom decorators.

Curtains and Drapes, page 68

Gleaming glass in a bare window should be as exciting to the home decorator as an empty canvas is to a painter.

Slipcovers, page 96

From the very beginning, slipcovers have protected fine furniture, dressed it up for special occasions, and given new life to an old piece.

Bedrooms, page 128

Making bed coverings requires accurate measurements and careful estimates, but the effort is worth it to create the perfect bedroom.

Introduction

Common sense and some confidence in personal taste make decorating fun; some tricks of the trade from seasoned professionals make it easier. People who sew have a head start, for they already know how to deal with a major part of the problem—the part that involves fabrics. Curtains and draperies, window shades, slipcovers, and bedspreads often make the crucial difference in transforming a room from a tired cliché to a fresh and inviting environment. Fabrics help realize the dream by introducing new colors, textures, and designs. They can dramatize or disguise the lines of a piece of furniture, frame a lovely view, or erase a bleak one. They can cover upholstery that is worn or dull, and they can ensure a longer life to upholstery that is brand new.

There are excellent reasons for making these fabric furnishings at home, as opposed to buying them ready-made. Maximum advantage can be taken of a fantastic variety of fabrics, styles, and techniques. The results will look better because such projects can be made to fit exactly, using the same methods employed by the workrooms that serve high-priced decorators. Not least of the many benefits of home-sewed furnishings is economy; often they will cost no more than inferior ready-made products and about a third of the price of those made to order.

Few special skills are demanded in making fabric furnishings. Most of the sewing is done with straight seams on the sewing machine, and basic techniques are easy to master. But producing a perfect fit on a slipcover or a perfect drape on a curtain does take patience and care. With no paper patterns to serve as guides in cutting and sewing, measurements have to be meticulous, and mathematics must be accurate.

Chapter 1: Fabric, Tools, and Supplies

Photograph courtesy of Calico Corners—Calico Home

Fabric, Tools, and Supplies

1

A World of Fabrics for Furnishings

In 1760, not far from the royal compound of Versailles, in the French village of Jouy, an ambitious Bavarian businessman named Christophe-Philippe Oberkampf set up a factory for producing cotton prints. Soon he was delighting aristocratic customers with fabrics, printed in brick red or French blue, showing scenes from the life of the peasants and *petite bourgeoisie*.

Today, copies of Oberkampf's *toiles de Jouy* (Jouy cloth) are still much in demand, part of a remarkably diverse repertory of fabrics for home furnishings. Traditional and modern, printed and textured, designed to cope with every condition of use and every desired esthetic effect, the fabric available for draperies, curtains, and furniture coverings far exceeds in variety that for clothes.

Along with this greater selection go some unfamiliar concerns in determining which fabric to buy. Factors such as dye lot, durability, and ease of care matter as never before. So do stability of weave, fastness to sun, resistance to mildew, and even the interval at which the pattern is repeated.

A slipcover for a couch and two pairs of matching draperies can consume as much as 45 yards of 54-inch-wide fabric. And since that much material may have to be cut from more than one bolt, the color may not match unless both bolts carry the same dye-lot number—look for it on the hang tag. Yardage also makes the size of the pattern repeat an important consideration. The larger the repeat, the more fabric will be needed to make the pattern match across drapery panels, or fall in the center of slipcover cushions. Even the quantity itself can raise problems. Sometimes the only substitute for a large enough cutting board may be the floor.

Figuring in the fabric choice will be the kind of wear it gets—and the fact that slipcovers and draperies are cleaned less often than garments. Soil- and stain-resistant finishes like Zepel and Scotchgard prolong the freshness of fabric by holding soil on the surface, where it can easily be sponged away. When a fabric has been treated for soil resistance, this fact is generally noted on the selvage and on the bolt-end label.

Also on the bolt label or selvage is information useful in gauging a fabric's resistance to fading. If the label reads sunfast it means that the color will withstand a minimum of 60 hours of sunlight without fading; if it reads sun-resistant, it will withstand sun for at least 40 hours. But a curtain in a south window will surely get many more hours of sunlight than that, and will inevitably fade unless it is lined. One fabric that is especially vulnerable to sun is silk, whose fibers literally rot from the sun's ultraviolet rays, making blinds or shutters obligatory protection for silk draperies in sunny windows, even if they are lined.

Photograph courtesy of Calico Corners—*Calico Home*

Faux silk gives you the look of silk but not the price! Choose from embroidered, solids, stripes, and damasks in beautiful colors. All in crisp, you'll never guess it's polyester, faux silk.

Mildew attacks home furnishing fabrics made from natural fibers more quickly than synthetic ones. And humidity may also affect the stability of natural materials. Some linens expand and shrink so much with changes in moisture that, in one classic example, an irate customer complained that the linen curtains in her seaside home drooped when the tide was in and shrank when the tide went out.

Acclaimed designer Annie Selke has created a collection of distinctive fabrics and trims for the home. Her approachable elegance is realized in richly patterned fabrics in fresh colors that update any style room. Pattern fabrics, striped fabrics, and floral fabrics are reinvented once again.

Inspired by national magazines, indoor-outdoor fabrics celebrate how we live today — in colorful, casual comfort. Featuring vibrant colors and a young attitude, these designs are woven of high-performance acrylic Sunbrella® with smart fabric technology. These fabrics resist fading and ease of care is built in — spills cleanup with soap and water.

Obviously, the sturdiest fabrics are those that are most firmly woven. But sturdiness alone does not guarantee long life. The synthetics, for instance, are generally very tough. Yet, one expert maintains, they may not age gracefully. And when printed they may not hold their color well — especially when the printed surface must take the abrasion of human bodies. Indeed, one decorator who claims he "never uses anything but miracle fibers," identifies those fibers as "cotton, linen, wool, and silk."

Whether a miracle of nature or a miracle of chemistry, every home furnishings fabric has something to recommend it. The charts on pages 14–15 examine characteristics of the fibers and weaves with an eye to performance.

A check list for fiber qualities

Since fabrics for the home must last many years, how they will wear is the first question to ask. Such properties as ability to take abrasion, resistance to sunlight, and reaction to humidity are often determined by the fiber (or fibers) from which a fabric is made.

The three major categories of fibers are the natural animal and plant fibers; the cellulosics, which are made from plant fibers reduced to a chemical broth and then respun; and the noncellulosic synthetics, most of which are made from petroleum. The chart at right explains the advantages and disadvantages of fibers in each of these categories.

However, in blended or specially treated fabrics, the disadvantages of a fiber are often minimized or canceled out. Also, fibers do not always exhibit the same properties in clothing and furnishings: wool, for instance, wrinkles more when used for clothing than when used for draperies or slipcovers. The chart includes suggestions for adapting each fiber type to specific home furnishing uses, and information on the care of each. Many fibers are washable, but decorators often recommend dry cleaning since all fabrics shrink somewhat in laundering, and slipcovers and draperies often have trims and linings with different washing properties.

Fiber	Advantages
Acetate Lustrous cellulose fiber	Drapes well; resists mildew and moths; remains free of static electricity. Economical. Dyes easily, giving a good color range.
Acrylic Resilient synthetic fiber (Acrilan, Chemstrand, Orlon, Zefchrome)	Abrasion-resistant; resists mildew, moths, fading, and wrinkling; not damaged by sun; easily cared for. Holds color well. Feels soft.
Cotton Absorbent, versatile natural plant fiber	Strong and durable; abrasion-resistant; free of static electricity. Feels cool. Easily cared for. Dyes easily, giving excellent color range.
Linen Absorbent, lustrous natural plant fiber	Strong and durable. Excellent color range. Feels cool. Easy to care for.
Nylon Nonabsorbent, resilient synthetic fiber; exceptionally strong (Antron, Cadon, Caprolan, Enkalure, Qiana)	Durable, abrasion-resistant; resists moths, mildew, oil, and airborne dirt. Recovers shape if stretched and resists wrinkling. Dries rapidly. Usually easy to care for. Good color range.
Olefin Nonabsorbent synthetic fiber (Herculon, Marvess, Vectra)	Strong, abrasion-resistant; resists moths, mildew, stains, and wrinkling. Withstands weather and often recommended for use outdoors.
Polyester Nonabsorbent, resilient synthetic fiber (Ancron, Chemstrand, Dacron, Quintess, Trevira, Vycron)	Strong, durable; wrinkle- and abrasion-resistant. Not damaged by moths or mildew. Holds shape well and stays crisp. Resists sunlight. Dyes moderately well, giving reasonably good color range.
Rayon Absorbent, lustrous cellulose fiber	Drapes well; does not pill; is not affected by bleaches and household chemicals. Excellent color range. Relatively strong. Feels cool.
Silk Natural animal fiber, absorbent, resilient, lustrous, and luxurious	Particularly strong, permitting thin but durable fabrics. Resists mildew and wrinkles. Feels cool. Exceptional color range, on which all other fiber colors are based.
Wool Exceptionally absorbent and resilient, natural animal fiber	Strong; resilient; resists wrinkles; not damaged by sun. Abrasion-resistant in tightly woven fabrics. Excellent color range. Crease-resistant in home furnishing use.

Disadvantages	Suggestions for Use	Care
Injured by abrasion; weakened by sunlight; melts at low heat. Dissolved by perfumes and nail polish remover. Fades unless labeled "solution dyed."	For draperies, interline or line with sun-reflective fabric. For hard-wear covers, use blends containing a more abrasion-resistant fiber, such as a synthetic.	Dry-clean, unless otherwise labeled. Press with warm iron.
Accumulates static electricity; tends to pill.	Very good for curtains and draperies because it holds its shape. For covers, use blends containing nylon or polyester for firmness. Pile fabrics need special care.	Dry clean. If labeled washable, launder gently by hand or machine; tumble dry. Use fabric softener to control static electricity.
May wrinkle or shrink, if not treated. Weakened and faded by long exposure to strong sunlight, unless lined; attacked by mildew.	Excellent for all home furnishings. Look for fabric that is preshrunk and treated for crease resistance. Blends with synthetics also tend to crease less.	Dry-clean. If labeled colorfast and preshrunk, may be washed. Press with a medium-hot iron.
Wrinkles easily and shrinks unless treated; subject to mildew and may stretch and shrink in damp climates; may crack along creases. Colors tend to fade in sunlight.	Draperies should be lined if placed in direct sun. In damp climates, use a blend with a nonabsorbent synthetic fiber; for pleated curtains, use a blend with a more resilient fiber.	Launder gently if labeled colorfast and preshrunk; press while damp on both sides to restore luster. Excessive starching makes fiber break. Dry-clean if untreated.
Accumulates static electricity; pills; fades and tends to weaken in sunlight.	Line draperies; use reflective lining with medium and dark colors. For covers, choose a blend that includes an absorbent fiber to aid release of static electricity.	Dry-clean. If labeled washable, launder separately. Use fabric softener to control static electricity. Remove from dryer immediately; press with a warm iron.
Melts at low heat; accumulates static electricity. Retains heat from sun. Limited color range. Requires special care.	Excellent in blends with other synthetics for slipcovers that get heavy use or are exposed to weather.	Dry-clean. If labeled washable, launder gently and dry on low-heat setting; remove from dryer immediately. Use fabric softener to control static electricity. Pure olefin should never be ironed. Iron blends with a cool iron.
Pills; accumulates static electricity.	The major fiber for easy-care curtains, and the top priority fiber for all home furnishings. For covers, choose a blend with natural fiber for absorbency.	Dry clean. If labeled washable, launder gently with like colors. Remove from dryer immediately; press with warm iron. Use fabric softener to control static electricity.
Lacks resilience; injured by abrasion; damaged by sun; attacked by mildew. Wrinkles easily. Cannot be laundered	For draperies in direct sunlight, interline or use a reflective lining. For covers, choose a blend that contains a stronger fiber for better wear.	Dry-clean only, unless otherwise labeled. Press with a cool iron.
Weakens and fades in sunlight; damaged by abrasion; spotted by water. Delicate in weights and constructions generally used.	For draperies or curtains in sun, interline or line with reflecting fabric. Not recommended for slipcovers subject to heavy use.	Dry-clean only. Press with a warm iron.
Shrinks unless labeled shrinkproof; soft weaves may pill under heavy use. Damaged by moths and mildew. Feels warm; may be prickly.	Line and interline loosely woven draperies to retain shape. Use tightly woven fabrics for covers, and blends containing synthetics for added wear.	Dry-clean only. Press with warm iron or steam press.

A glossary of fabric usefulness

The characteristics of a fabric that determine its use in the home may depend less on the fibers from which it is woven *(preceding page)* than on the way these fibers are spun into yarn and woven into cloth—the same fiber can make a diaphanous voile, a rough homespun, or an elegant satin. Weight and weave control looks and practicality. Most pile fabrics and satins, for instance, are not recommended for slipcovers on furniture that gets a lot of wear. Sheers, loose weaves, and laces are primarily curtain materials, though when stabilized with lining a few are suitable for such applications as bedcovers or pillows, where a coordinated look is wanted.

In the glossary at right the most frequently encountered home furnishings fabrics are categorized according to their usefulness. The sturdiest weave, when closely woven, is the plain weave, in which lengthwise and crosswise yarns crisscross each other evenly, one for one. Less durable weaves are twill and satin weaves, in both of which the lengthwise yarns pass, or "float," over several crosswise yarns (or vice versa). In twill, this float yarn is staggered to create a diagonal effect; in satin, it jumps over as many as eight crosswise yarns, creating a luxuriously smooth surface—but one that "picks" very easily when subjected to any rough object, such as a jewelry clasp.

Multipurpose Fabrics

These fabrics can be used for curtains, draperies, or covers of all kinds. Most wear well and are easy to clean. None are difficult to sew.

Chambray: A durable, medium-weight plain weave traditionally made of cotton. The lengthwise yarn is a color while the crosswise yarn is usually white or off-white; when both yarns are colored, the variation is called iridescent.

Chintz: A crisp, glossy, tightly woven cotton plain weave that, when printed, is often in old-fashioned floral patterns. A coating is applied to give the smooth glazed finish. Also called polished cotton.

Corduroy: A sturdy, medium- to heavyweight plain weave, traditionally cotton, with pronounced pile ribs, called wales, of various widths, running lengthwise.

Denim: A heavier twill-weave version of chambray, usually cotton. It is characteristically made of light-colored crosswise yarns and darker lengthwise yarns.

Duck: A strong, medium-to-heavy plain weave made of evenly spun, closely woven yarns; traditionally cotton. Also called sailcloth and, in a heavier weight, canvas.

Gabardine: A durable, medium-weight cloth whose twill weave creates a noticeable diagonal cord or rib; traditionally cotton or wool. A heavier version is called whipcord.

Gingham: A light-to medium-weight plain weave in which lengthwise and crosswise stripes of colored yarn intersect to form a checked pattern; traditionally of cotton.

Herringbone: A medium- to heavyweight fabric whose twill weave alternates to create a distinctive zigzag pattern; traditionally cotton or wool.

Homespun: A fabric made from rough-textured yarn woven to reproduce a loosely woven hand-loomed look. Also called hop sacking, monk's cloth, and crash.

Muslin: A serviceable medium-weight plain woven fabric, traditionally made of cotton. Coarse muslin is often used as a basic covering for upholstered furniture. Fine muslin is used for sheeting and printed cloth.

Percale: A finer version of muslin made of fine-combed, closely woven yarn. Often used for quality sheets.

Poplin: A medium-weight plain weave, with a very slight crosswise rib produced by interweaving a heavier crosswise yarn with a finer lengthwise yarn; traditionally cotton; also called ribbed cotton. When it has a more pronounced rib, it is known as rep.

Sateen: very smooth, sleek medium-weight fabric whose weave creates a lustrous finish. Made in imitation of satin, but more durable and easier to sew; traditionally cotton.

Seersucker: A puckered, light to medium-weight plain weave with a distinctive pattern of striped or checked puckers; traditionally cotton. A very similar fabric is called plissé.

Ticking: A strong, medium-weight twill weave especially woven for bedding of all kinds; traditionally of cotton. Characteristically, it has a woven pattern of colored stripes of varying widths.

Tweed: A weave made by using rough-textured, randomly colored yarns. Best known in wool, it is now frequently made of cotton or linen.

Limited-Use Fabrics

Less durable than the preceding group, these fabrics are suitable for curtains, draperies, bedcovers and pillows, but they should not be used for slipcovers subject to heavy use. Most of these fabrics require care in sewing. Nap direction must be considered on the pile fabrics, and the slippery satin weaves require careful pinning and basting.

Bouclé: Any fabric made from a nubbly, or bouclé, yarn that gives it a spongy surface.

Brocade: A very formal, medium- to heavyweight satin weave—originally of silk or rayon—with a multicolored woven pattern similar in look to embroidery. When the pattern is raised, the cloth is called brocatel.

Chenille: Any fabric woven from the looped or fuzzy yarn called chenille, producing a textured or piled surface. Most often associated with bedspreads.

Damask: A reversible, medium- to heavyweight satin weave with a woven pattern created by a change in the direction of the long "float" yarns, from lengthwise to crosswise; traditionally cotton, linen, or silk.

Faille: A medium-weight plain weave similar to poplin or rep except for the glossy yarn of which it is made.

Moire: A light- to medium-weight faille impressed with a wavy pattern.

Pongee: A nubbly, medium-weight plain weave with an irregular rib produced by uneven crosswise yarns; traditionally made from wild silk in its natural beige color.

Satin: A lustrous fabric, available in many weights, whose lengthwise yarns "float" over many crosswise yarns (or vice versa). One variant, called antique satin, is a double-faced fabric whose textured surface results from a shantung backing.

Shantung: A plain weave with an uneven texture created by a nubbly yarn; traditionally made of a naturally slubbed silk yarn, it is now often reproduced by artificially texturing such yarns as cotton.

Taffeta: A crisp, rustling, tightly woven light- to medium-weight plain weave made from very fine yarn; traditionally made of silk.

Terry cloth: A soft, highly absorbent, medium- to heavyweight fabric with a looped pile; most often used for toweling; traditionally woven of cotton.

Velvet and velours: Smooth, fine-textured medium- to heavyweight fabrics traditionally made of such dissimilar fibers as silk, rayon, or linen. In crushed velvet the pile has been crushed by rollers to produce a randomly shadowed textured surface; in cut velvet, a design is created by selectively weaving some areas of the cloth without pile.

Velveteen: A pile fabric similar in appearance to velvet but with more body; usually made of cotton.

Curtain and Drapery Fabrics

These fabrics, mostly sheers and loose weaves, are best suited for curtains and draperies. But the function of eyelet or lace can occasionally be extended to coverings that receive little wear, provided that the covering is lined.

Burlap: A rough textured, medium-weight plain weave made of very coarse, loosely woven yarn, usually jute.

Dotted swiss: A crisp, lightweight sheer plain weave, traditionally cotton, characterized by a pattern of raised dots—woven into cotton, imprinted on synthetics.

Eyelet: An openwork embroidered design on fine-textured, lightweight plain weave; traditionally cotton.

Gauze: A soft, extremely lightweight fabric made of fine, loosely woven yarns; traditionally linen or cotton.

Lace: A fabric made by knotting and interweaving yarns to create designs on a netting background; traditionally linen. The designs are customarily floral in the same color as the net, though abstract designs are also available.

Leno: An open-mesh fabric produced by the special leno weave, which combines airiness with strength. In this weave, pairs of lengthwise yarns, often much thinner than the crosswise ones, intertwine each other over the crosswise yarns, forming figure 8s.

Marquisette: A very fine version of leno *(above)*, usually made of cotton or nylon.

Net: Any open-mesh material, from very fine to very coarse, made of yarns knotted or twisted together in the manner of fishing nets.

Ninon: A soft sheer plain weave made of fine yarns, usually nylon, in a very open mesh.

Organdy: A crisp, airy, almost transparent plain weave, which is made of very fine, closely woven yarn; it is traditionally cotton.

Voile: A soft, fluid plain weave made of fine yarns, closely woven; traditionally cotton. A less fine-textured version is known as scrim.

Lining, Interlining, and Stiffening Fabrics

These fabrics are used to give body and shape to draperies and coverings, and to add such characteristics as sunproofing, lightproofing, and extra warmth.

Buckram: A coarse, almost rigid woven fabric made of white cotton or brown jute and stiffened with heavy sizing. Available in various weights. For use in curtain and drapery headings.

Crinoline: A lighter-weight, finer-textured version of buckram; usually made of cotton or a blend, and usually available in white only. For use in curtain or drapery headings.

Flannelette: A soft, napped medium-weight plain weave, most often cotton or a blend. Used mostly for interlining lightweight draperies to give them body and shape.

Nonwoven stiffeners: Fabrics made of matted synthetics that look like a stiff lightweight felt. Available in neutral colors in a wide range of weights, under such brand names as Pellon, Interion, and Nonwoven Shapeflex.

Reflective lining: A medium-weight twill or satin-weave fabric coated on one side with a metallic or white finish that protects draperies by reflecting heat and sunlight.

Sateen lining: A less refined version of the sateen listed under Multipurpose Fabrics *(page 16)*, available in white or pale neutral shades for lining draperies and covers, and in black for use as a light-blocking interlining.

Tools to ease the task

The long yards of fabric used in home furnishings make the work different from dressmaking. Regular sewing tools — chalk, pins, a tape measure, a hem gauge—are handy and necessary but are best supplemented with equipment less often used for making clothes. For marking long lengths of cloth a yardstick is helpful, and a cutting board—with square and diagonal grids—allows you to cut large fabric sections accurately. A pencil gives a sharper line than chalk on firm, opaque fabric. And shears with extra-long blades shorten cutting time.

Several machine attachments are timesavers. Shown here *(left to right, at center):* a ruffler for gathers, a zipper foot for welting and zippers, a hemmer, and a binder for bias edgings. Especially useful for measuring windows is a springreturn metal tape. And when fitting fabric to a chair or sofa, broad-headed T pins will not get lost in the padding.

yardstick
rotary cutter
straight pins
hem gauge
shears
presser feet
thread puller

safety pins

thimble

zipper

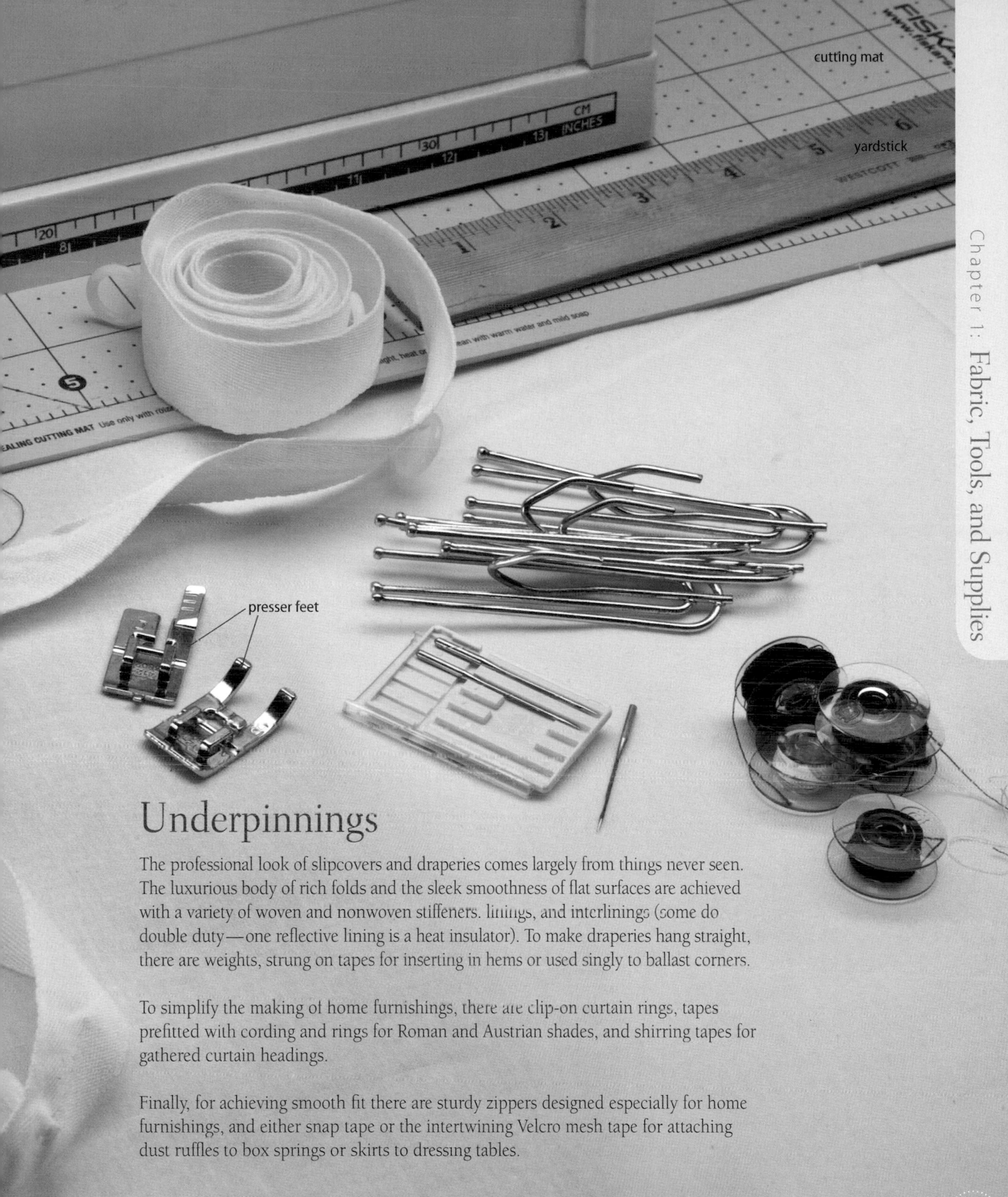

Underpinnings

The professional look of slipcovers and draperies comes largely from things never seen. The luxurious body of rich folds and the sleek smoothness of flat surfaces are achieved with a variety of woven and nonwoven stiffeners, linings, and interlinings (some do double duty—one reflective lining is a heat insulator). To make draperies hang straight, there are weights, strung on tapes for inserting in hems or used singly to ballast corners.

To simplify the making of home furnishings, there are clip-on curtain rings, tapes prefitted with cording and rings for Roman and Austrian shades, and shirring tapes for gathered curtain headings.

Finally, for achieving smooth fit there are sturdy zippers designed especially for home furnishings, and either snap tape or the intertwining Velcro mesh tape for attaching dust ruffles to box springs or skirts to dressing tables.

Chapter 2: Techniques for Custom Decorating

Photograph courtesy of Calico Corners—*Calico Home*

Techniques for Custom Decorating

2

Details that Make the Difference

Efficient fasteners such as hook-and-loop strips, heavy-duty zippers, and snap tapes are often taken for granted, but they make possible smooth fit and easy removal of fabric coverings for cleaning or even for seasonal changes. Such details and their proper application give home furnishings the extra touches that mark the best work of custom decorators.

Not all of the details of well-made home furnishings are hidden from sight. Some of them form the most visible part of the design while serving practical purposes of structure as well. Pleats and their softer counterparts, shirrings, are used to control the upper edges of curtains and draperies and cause them to fall in graceful folds.

Welting, too, serves a dual purpose. It outlines and defines the contours of cushions, sofas, chairs, and bedcovers. But it also serves to reinforce seams and guard against fraying.

Finally, there are details that simply give a finished look, the decorative touches that add character to a room. Dentil edges, for example, with their squared-off regularity, have an architectural and masculine look. Gracefully curving scallops, on the other hand, suggest femininity.

The making of home furnishings begins and ends with these details, visible or invisible, decorative or purely functional. Whether the project is a casual café curtain for a country breakfast room or draperies for a formal dining room, whether the material is gingham at a bargain $1.98 a yard or silk brocade at an extravagant $99.98, it is the care put into the making that separates the custom look from the ready-made.

Elegant silk curtains update and soften this look of the bay window.

Using Welting for Style and Practicality

Welting—whether plain or shirred (as on the pillow below)—is both a decorative and a practical addition to slipcovers, bedspreads, and valances. It delineates the shape like an artist's line. At the same time, it strengthens the seams and reduces wear on the edges of furnishings.

Plain welting is usually cut on the bias, and the tubular method *(page 25)* makes it easy to cut the long lengths needed for slipcovers and bedspreads. Shirred welting *(page 30)* is usually cut with the grain and is best made from light- or medium-weight cloth.

For a speedier finishing touch, ready-made trims are an alternative. Ribbon and braid trims are added to the fabric sections before any lining is attached. Fringe can be applied in the same way, but it is also frequently inserted in a seam, like welting.

Making Bias Strips for Small Amounts of Welting

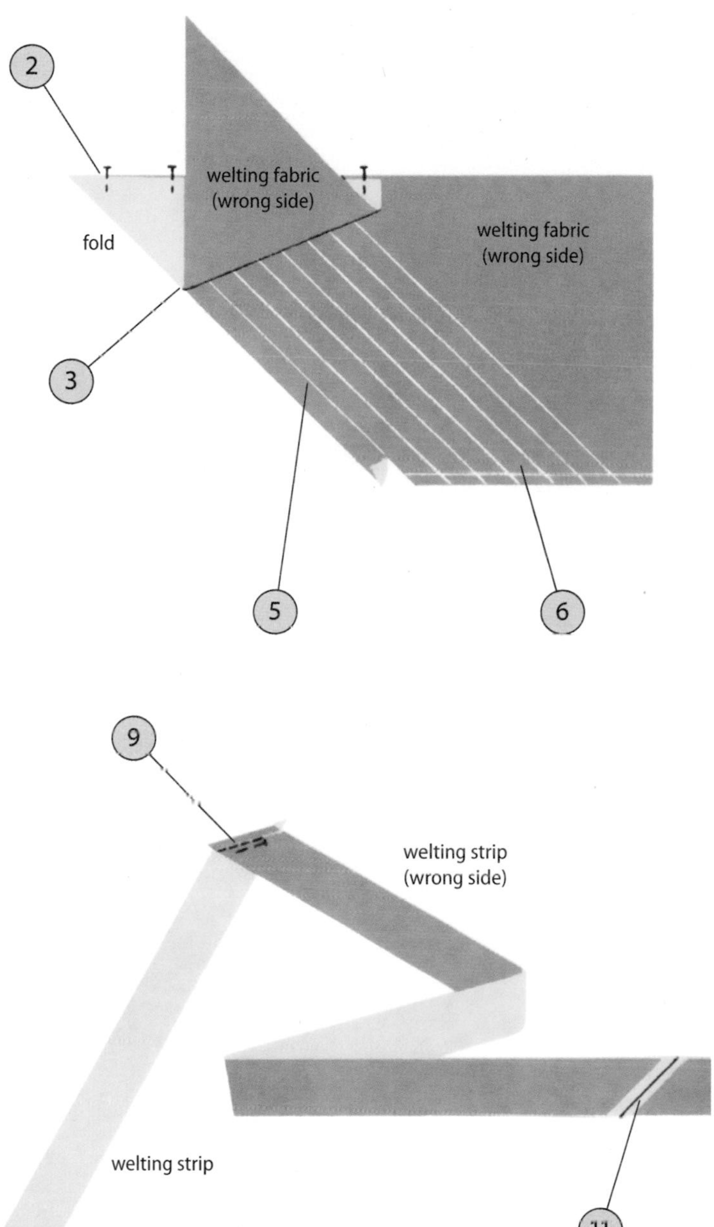

1. To determine the total length of the fabric strip needed, measure the seam into which the welting will be sewed. Then add about 12 inches.

2. Fold the fabric for the welting diagonally, wrong sides together. Make sure the fold is on the true bias. Pin the edges.

3. Cut along the diagonal fold. Remove the pins and the top piece of fabric, then trim off both selvages.

4. Measure the length of the diagonal edge and subtract ½ inch (to allow for seaming). Divide the result into the length calculated in Step 1 to get the number of strips needed.

5. Mark off the number of strips determined in Step 4 by drawing a series of chalk lines parallel to the diagonal edge. Make each strip wide enough to fit around the cord, with enough extra for double the seam allowance of the project.

6. Mark a ¼-inch seam allowance across the ends of all the strips.

7. Cut out the strips along the diagonal chalk lines.

8. Place two strips together, wrong sides out, and align the seam lines so that the strips form a V. Pin.

9. Machine stitch along the seam lines and remove the pins.

10. Repeat Steps 8 and 9 as many times as necessary to make one long strip of the length required.

11. Press open the seams and trim the extended points of the seam allowances.

Plain Welting

Making Bias Strips for Large Amounts of Welting

12. Prepare the fabric as shown in Steps 1–6, but mark off strips all the way to the bottom right corner of the fabric.

13. Trim off the unmarked triangular portion of the fabric along the last diagonal chalk line.

14. With the wrong sides out, pin together the shorter ends of the fabric piece along the seam lines. Match at the markings for each strip and be sure that one strip width extends beyond each edge.

15. Machine stitch along the seam lines and remove the pins.

16. Press open the seam.

17. Cut along the markings around the cylinder to form one long strip.

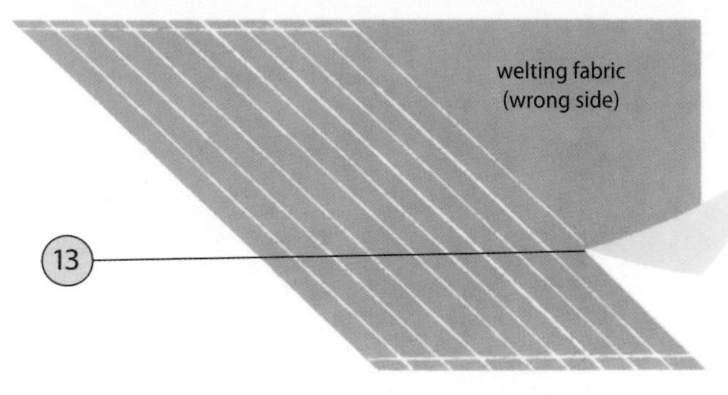

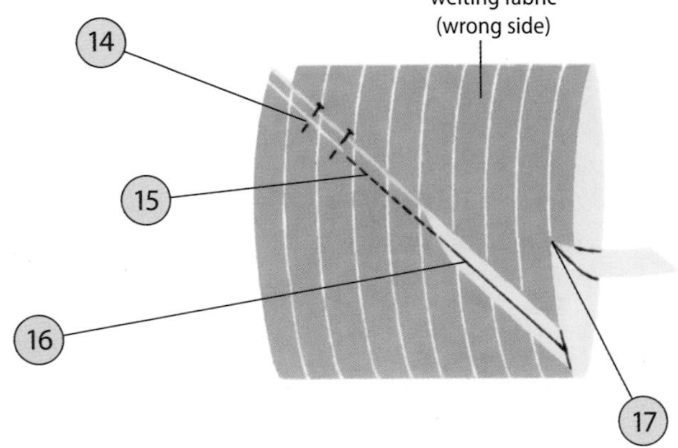

Making the Welting

18. Cut a piece of welting cord and a fabric strip the length needed *(Step 1)*.

19. Place the fabric strip wrong side up. Center the cord on the strip with the first end ⅜ inch from the end of the fabric. Then fold the end of the strip down ⅜ inch over the end of the cord.

20. Fold the fabric strip, wrong sides together, around the cord and align the edges. Pin at the end.

21. Using a zipper foot, machine baste at 6 to 8 stitches to the inch, close to the cord but not up against it, as shown for shirred welting *(Step 14, page 31)*. Hold the edges to keep them aligned as you stitch.

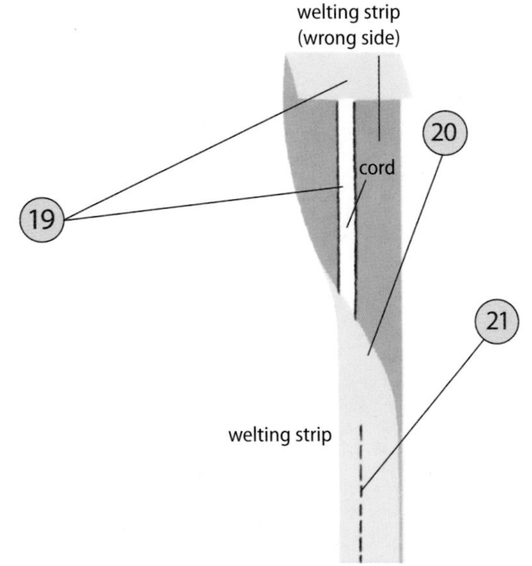

Plain Welting

Attaching the Welting

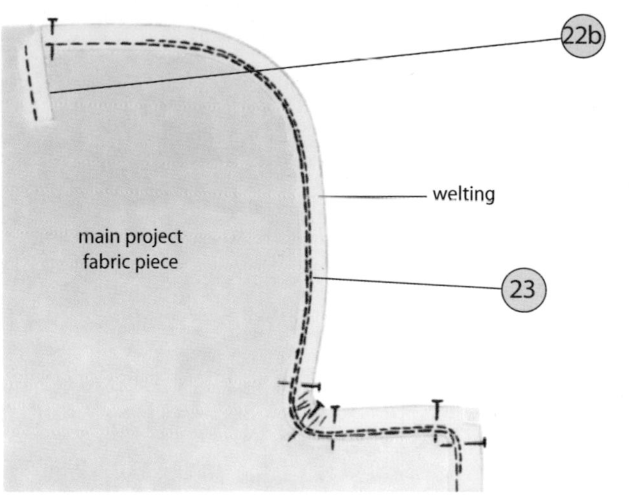

22a. If the welting will end at the edges of the fabric or at a hem or seam line, begin to attach it following the directions for shirred welting *(page 32, Steps 17a–19a)*.

22b. If the welting will be joined around a continuous edge, begin to attach it, as shown for shirred welting *(page 32, Steps 17b–19b)*, but leave several inches of welting extending beyond the joining point and insert the needle 2 inches from the joining point.

23. Stitch the welting to the main fabric piece as shown for shirred welting *(page 32, Steps 20–23)*.

Finishing the Welting at an Edge or a Hem

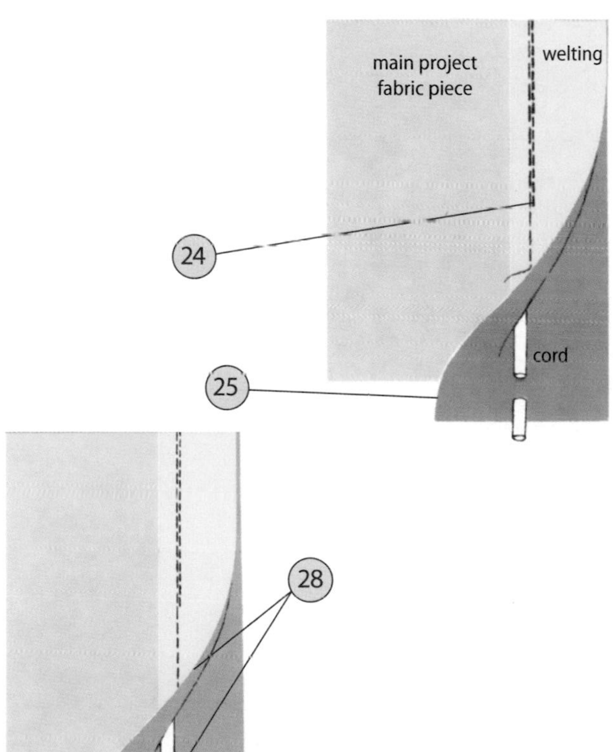

24. If the welting will be joined around a continuous edge, skip to Step. 31. To end the welting at a hem or seam line or a fabric edge, stop the machine 2 inches before that point, leaving the needle in the fabric.

25. Trim off the welting ⅜ inch beyond the desired ending point.

26. Remove the machine basting from the last inch of the welting and open out the welting.

27. Trim the cord at the desired ending point.

28. Fold the end of the welting strip fabric ⅜ inch over the end of the cord. Then refold the strip around the cord and align the cut edges. Pin at the end.

29. Machine stitch the remaining portion of the welting. Remove all pins.

30. To attach the second layer of fabric, follow the directions for shirred welting *(page 35)*.

Plain Welting

Finishing the Welting Around a Continuous Edge

31. To join the welting around a continuous edge, end the stitching about 2 inches from the joining point and remove the work from the machine.

32. Trim off the finishing end of the welting about 3 inches beyond the joining point.

33. Remove the last 4½ inches of machine basting from both ends of the welting. Open out the ends of the welting strips and fold the cord ends out of the way.

34. Fold up one unattached end of the welting strip diagonally. Press.

35. Fold down diagonally the other unattached end of the welting strip, so that the two diagonal folds meet. Press.

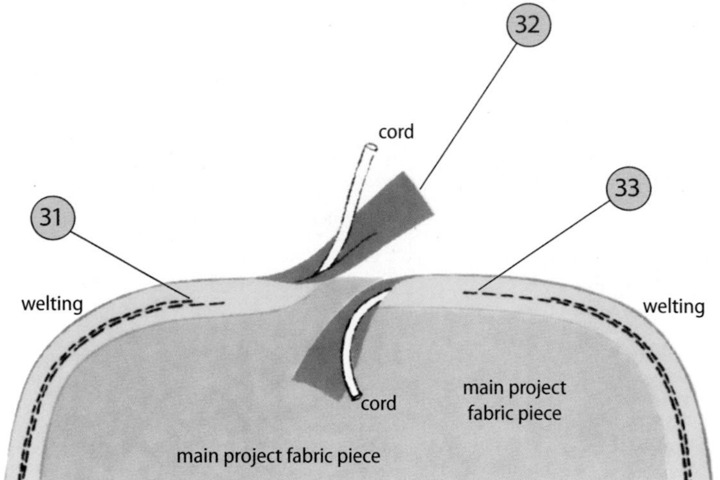

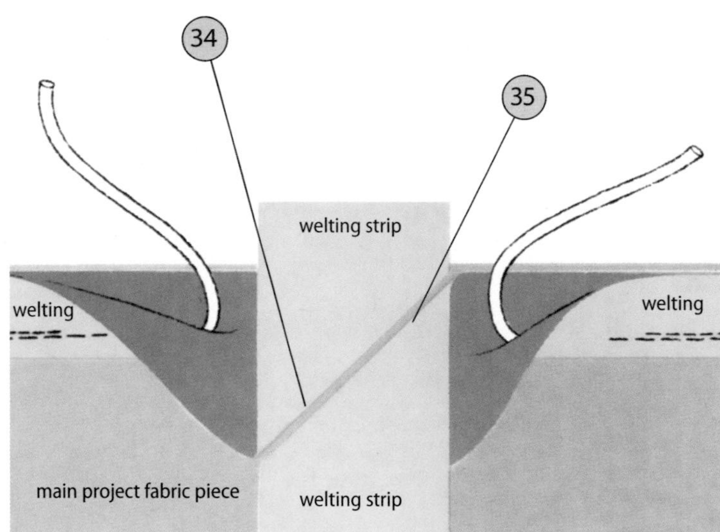

Plain Welting

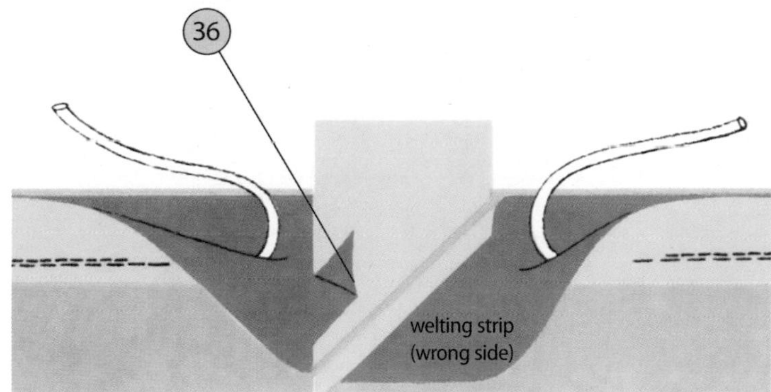

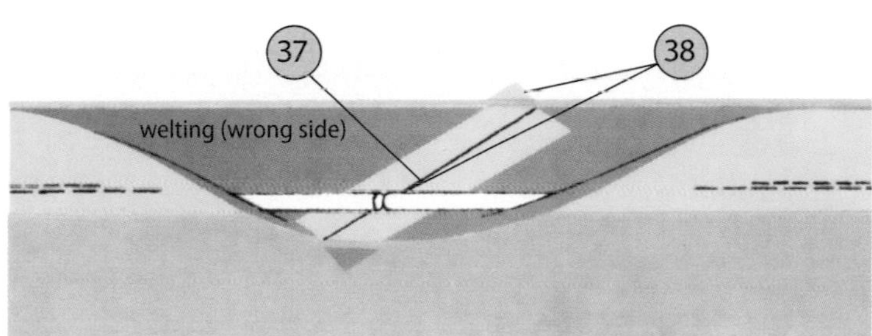

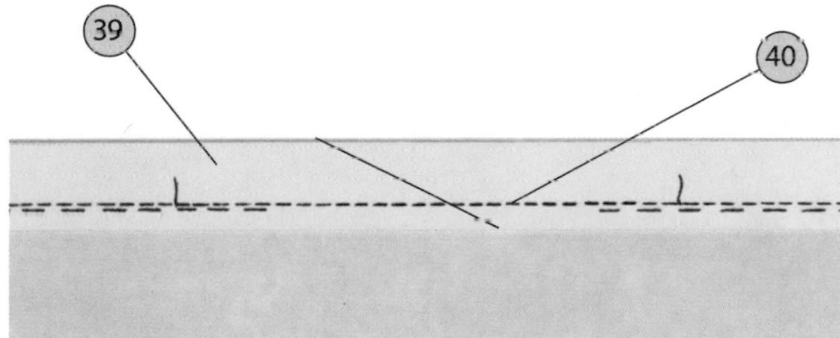

36. Trim each end ¼ inch outside the diagonal fold.

37. Fold the project fabric out of the way. Extend the two diagonal ends of the welting strip, wrong sides out, and align them along the fold lines made in Steps 34 and 35. Pin and machine stitch. Remove the pins.

38. Press open the diagonal seam of the welting, and trim off any extended points. Then trim the ends of the cord diagonally at the joining point so that they will butt together.

39. Refold the welting strip over the cord and align the cut edges with the project fabric edge.

40. Machine stitch the welting to the fabric in the unstitched area.

41. To attach the second layer of project fabric, follow the directions for shirred welting *(page 35, Step 45)*.

Shirred Welting

Cutting and Joining Welting Strips

1. Place the fabric wrong side up and trim off the selvages.

2. To determine the length of the fabric strip required, first measure the seam into which the welting will be sewed and add about 12 inches. Then, for heavy fabrics, double this figure; for lightweight fabrics, triple this figure.

3. Measure the length of the fabric and subtract ½ inch (to allow for seaming). Divide the result into the length calculated in Step 2 to get the number of strips needed.

4. Mark off the strips on the fabric by drawing a series of chalk lines parallel to the selvage edges. Make each strip wide enough to fit around the cord, with enough extra to double the seam allowance for the project.

5. Cut out the strips along the chalk lines.

6. Place two strips together, wrong sides out, and align the ends. Pin.

7. Machine stitch ¼ inch inside the ends and remove the pins.

8. Repeat Steps 6 and 7 as many times as necessary to make one long strip of the length required.

9. Press open the seams.

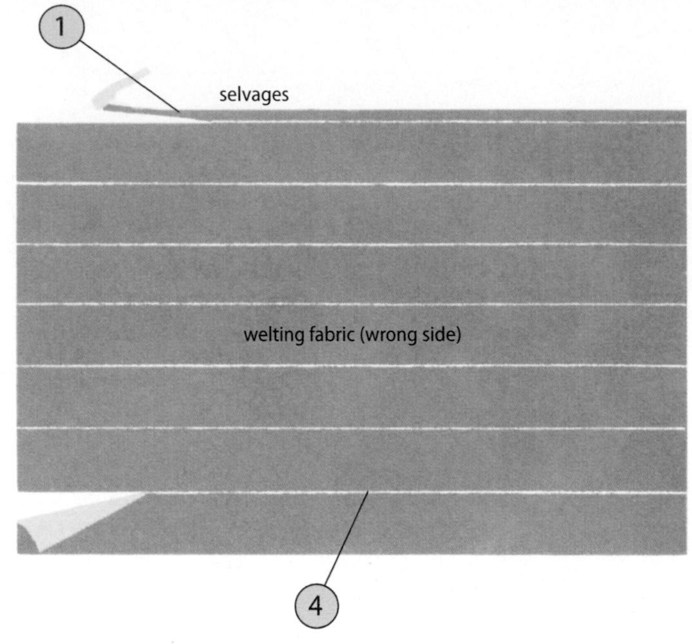

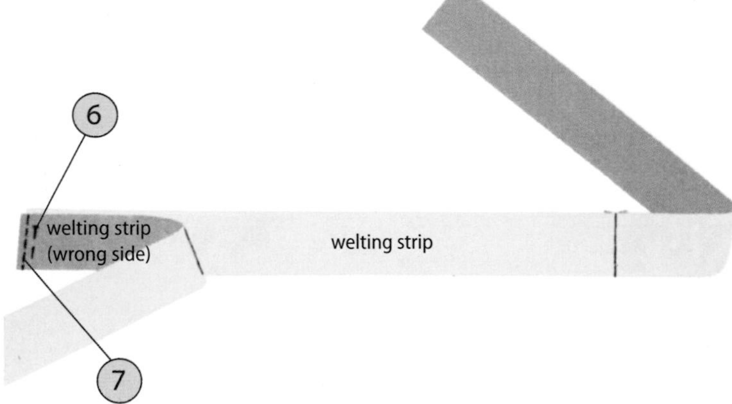

Making the Welting

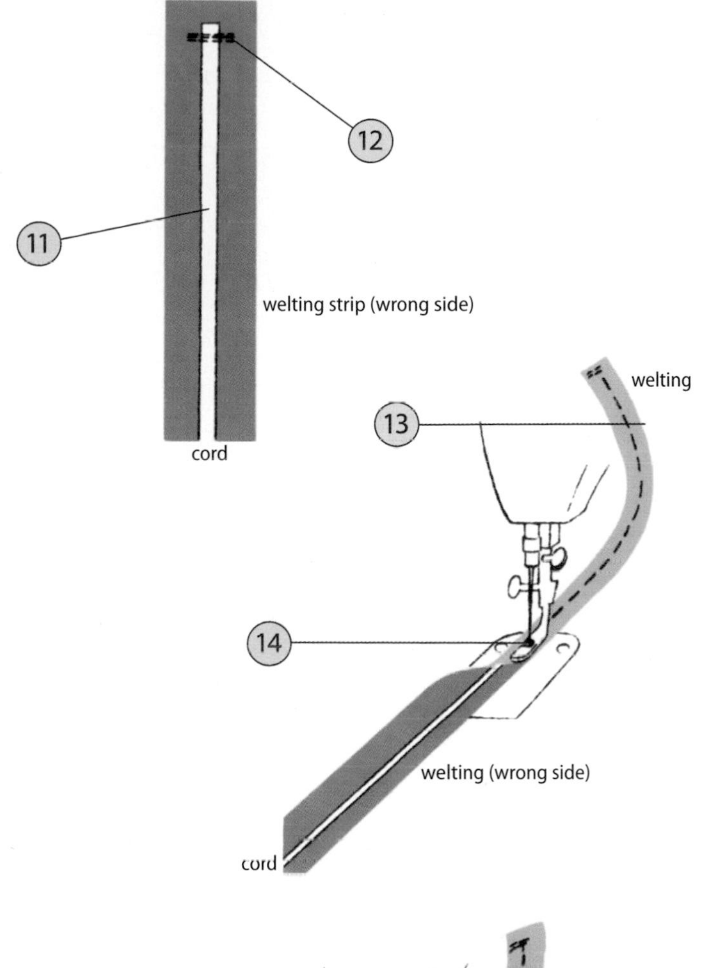

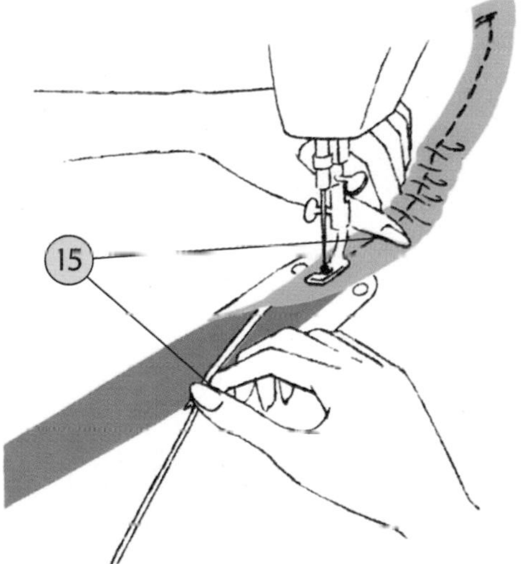

10. Cut a piece of cord the length of the seam into which the welting will be sewed, plus about 12 inches *(Step 2)*.

11. Place the welting strip wrong side up and center the cord on it. The beginning end of the cord should be ⅜ inch from the beginning end of the strip.

12. Holding the cord in place, machine stitch, at 12 to 15 stitches to the inch, across the cord ¼ inch from the end. Stitch forward, back and forward again.

13. Fold the end of the strip down over the stitched end of the cord. Then fold the strip, wrong sides together, lengthwise around the cord and align the edges.

14. Set your machine at 6 to 8 stitches to the inch. Using a zipper foot, machine baste close to the cord but not up against it. Keep the edges of the welting strip aligned as you stitch. When you have sewed about 6 inches, stop the machine, leaving the needle in the fabric.

15. Shirr the stitched portion of the welting. To do this, pull the cord forward gently with one hand. Hold the welting behind the presser foot with the other hand, pushing the fabric back toward the end until the entire stitched portion is tightly shirred. Then realign the edges of the strip along the unstitched portion.

16. Repeat Steps 14 and 15 as many times as necessary to complete the welting. At the finishing end, insert a pin through the strip and the cord.

Shirred Welting

Attaching the Welting to the Main Project Fabric

17a. If the welting will end at the edges of the fabric piece or at a hem or seam line, place the main project fabric wrong side down and lay the welting along the edge to be seamed. Align the cut edges of the welting with the project fabric edge and line up the beginning end of the welting against the hemline, seam line or the end of the fabric, as required. Pin at the end.

18a. Set the machine to the normal stitch length and attach a zipper foot.

19a. Place the fabric, wrong side down, in the machine and insert the needle at the end of the welting just outside the machine basting.

17b. If the welting will be joined around a continuous edge, place the main project fabric piece wrong side down and select an unobtrusive place for the joining, such as the center back on a cushion. Do not join at a corner. Place the beginning of the welting at the place selected for the joining and align the cut edges with the fabric edge. Pin at the end.

18b. Set the machine to the normal stitch length and attach a zipper foot.

19b. Place the fabric, wrong side down, in the machine and insert the needle 2 inches from the end of the welting just outside the machine basting.

20. Stitch the welting to the fabric just outside the machine basting. Hold the welting flat and keep the cut edges aligned with the fabric edge. If desired, use a large T pin to help push the shirred welting seam allowances under the presser foot.

21. Stretch the welting seam allowances around outside curves and ease them slightly around inside curves. Keep the cut edges aligned with the fabric edge.

22. To attach the welting around an inside corner, stop the machine 1 inch from the corner, leaving the needle in the fabric. Shape the welting with your hand, pinching the cord into a point at the corner. Pin. Sew straight to within a few stitches of the corner, then stitch in a sharp curve - pivoting several times.

23. To attach the welting around an outside corner, follow Step 22, but before shaping the welting with your hand, clip the welting seam allowances ½ inch from the corner — cutting up to but not into the machine basting.

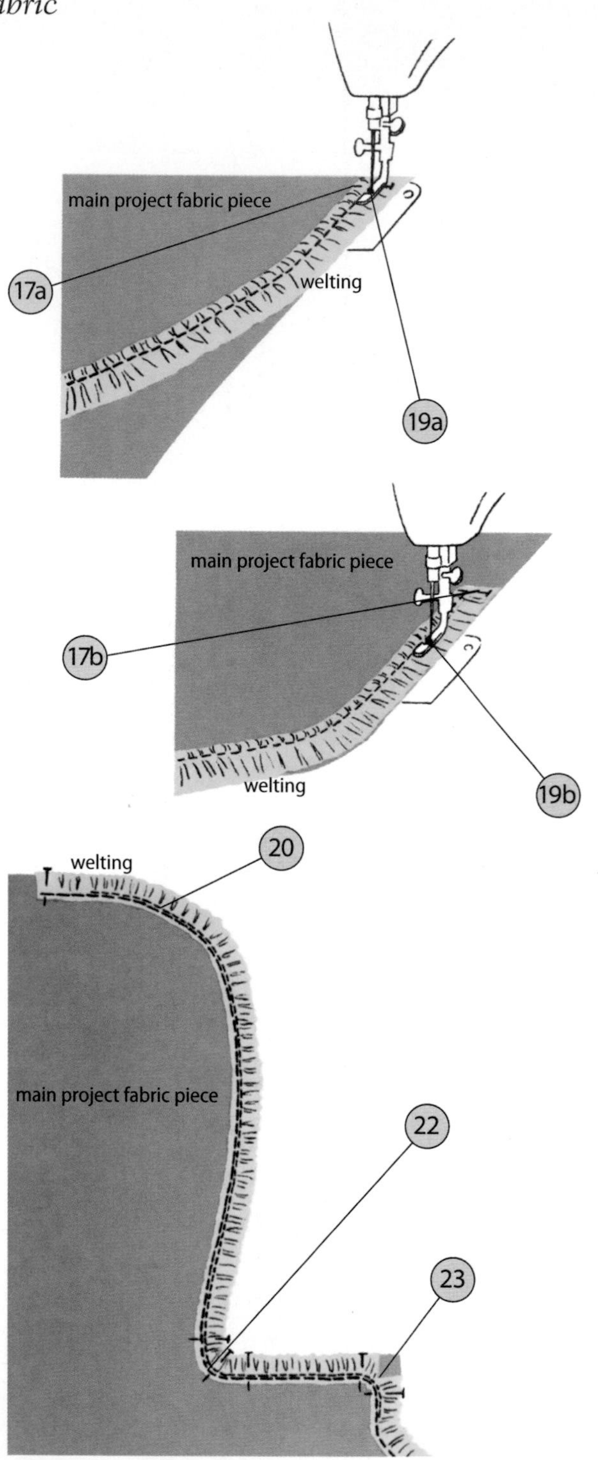

Shirred Welting

Ending the Welting at a Fabric Edge

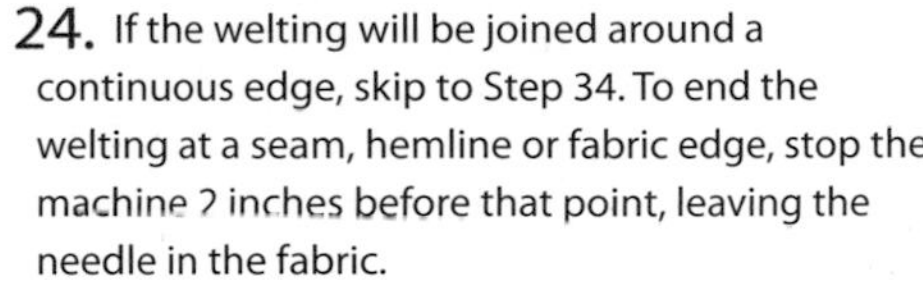

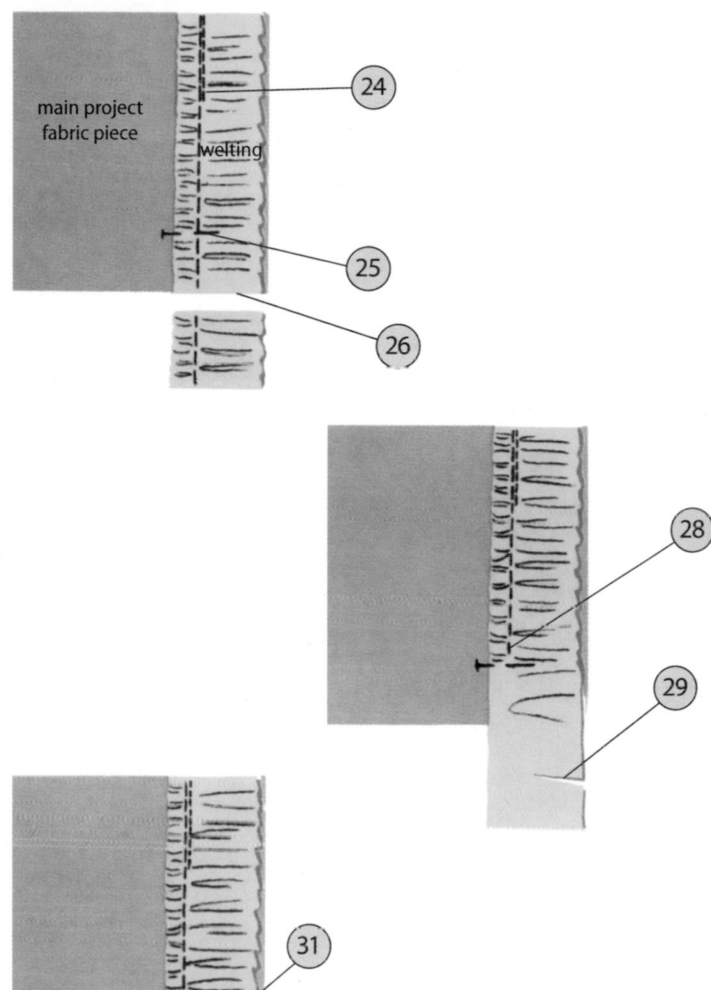

24. If the welting will be joined around a continuous edge, skip to Step 34. To end the welting at a seam, hemline or fabric edge, stop the machine 2 inches before that point, leaving the needle in the fabric.

25. Insert a pin into the welting strip fabric and through the cord about ½ inch from the desired ending point.

26. Trim off the welting at the desired ending point.

27. Pull out the welting strip fabric beyond the pin, eliminating the shirring.

28. Remove the machine basting on the welting up to the pin.

29. Trim the welting strip fabric ⅜ inch beyond the desired ending point.

30. Open out the welting strip and fold the end over the end of the cord. Then refold the strip around the cord and align the cut edges.

31. Insert a pin into the welting strip and through the cord near the folded end. Then remove the pin inserted in Step 25.

32. Adjust the shirring so that it continues to the end of the welting.

33. Machine stitch the remaining portion of the welting. Remove all pins. Skip to Step 45.

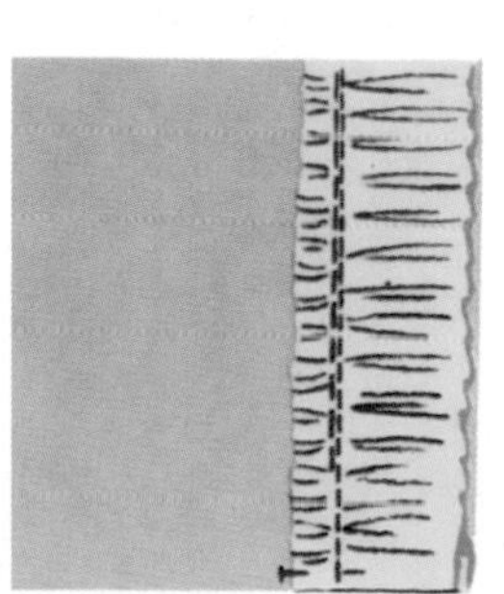

Shirred Welting

Joining the Welting around a Continuous Edge

34. Stop the machine 2 inches before reaching the joining point, leaving the needle in the fabric.

35. Insert a pin into the welting strip fabric and through the cord about ¼ inch before the point where the two ends of the welting will be joined.

36. Trim off the finished end of the welting ¾ inch beyond the joining point.

37. Pull out the welting strip fabric beyond the pin, eliminating the shirring.

38. Remove the machine basting on the welting from the pin to the cut end.

39. Open out the end of the welting strip.

40. Trim the end of the cord so that it will butt against the beginning end of the welting when the two are joined.

41. Trim the finishing end of the welting strip fabric ¾ inch beyond the joining point.

42. Fold under the cut end of the welting strip fabric ¼ inch.

43. Lap the folded finishing end of the welting around the beginning end. Pin.

44. Machine stitch the open portion of the welting and remove the pins.

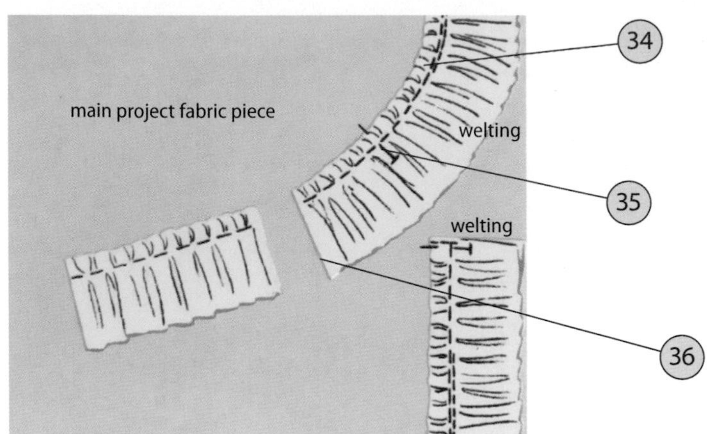

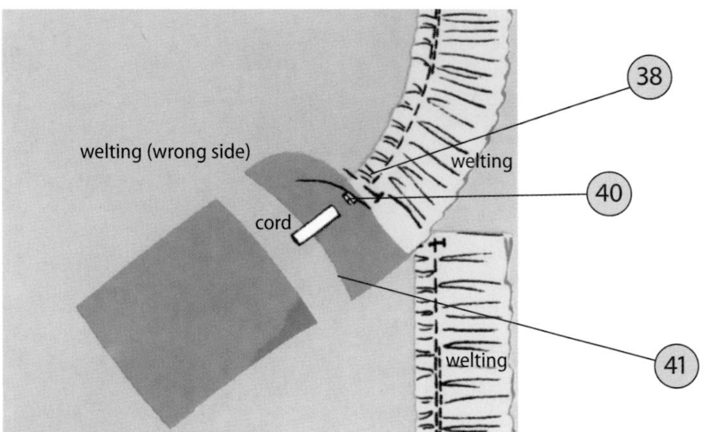

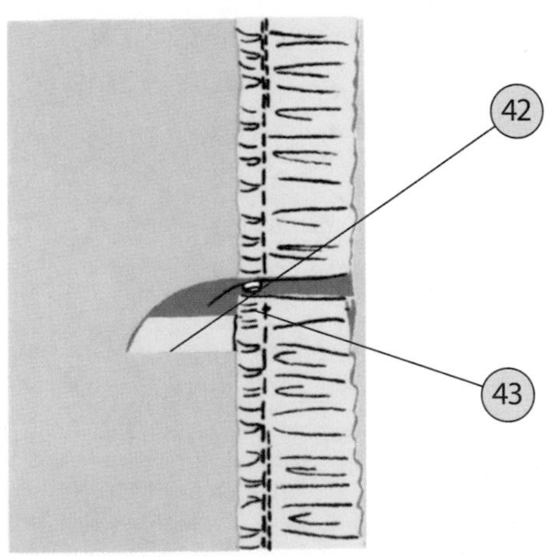

Shirred Welting

Attaching the Second Layer of Project Fabric

45. Place the welted fabric piece wrong side down and lay the second project fabric piece, wrong side up, on it. Align the edges to be seamed.

46. Pin along these edges. Insert the pins so they enter and emerge from the fabric on either side of the ridge formed by the corded part of the welting. Pins should not catch the first, or bottom, layer of fabric.

47. Turn the project so that the first, or welted, fabric piece faces up.

48. Machine stitch, using a zipper foot. Sew just inside the original line of machine stitching, crowding the corded part of the welting underneath. Remove the pins.

49. Clip the seam allowances around inside curves and notch around outside curves, cutting up to, but not through, the outer line of machine stitching.

50. Clip inside corners diagonally and trim the seam allowances of outside corners diagonally.

51. Turn the project right side out and push out the corners.

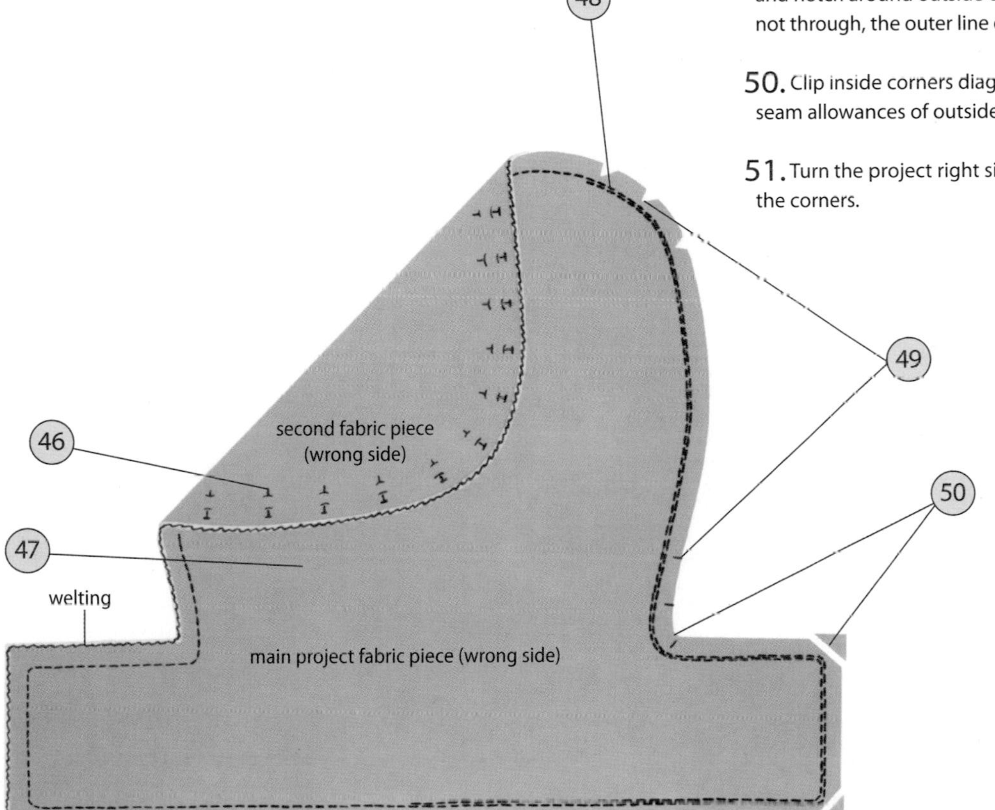

Attaching Flat Trims

1. Decide how far from the edges of the project the trim is to be placed.

2. With the project fabric wrong side down, turn up the edge at the distance determined in Step 1, using a ruler as a guide. Press a crease into the fold, but make sure not to press beyond the points where the trim will end. Repeat along other edges. Open out the folds.

3. Lay the trim on the fabric, wrong side down, lining up the outer edge of the trim against the crease. If the trim will be attached around a continuous edge, as shown, align one end with the creases at a corner. For a trim that will not be joined around a continuous edge, align one end with the edge of the fabric. Pin.

4. To miter the trim at a corner, pin along the first side to within several inches of the corner. Fold up the unpinned portion of the trim so that the fold is flush with the creased marking for the second side of the corner. Then fold the unattached portion of trim down diagonally so that its outer edge lines up against the second crease. Press the diagonal fold.

5. Fold the project fabric out of the way near the corner.

6. Fold up the trim, wrong side out, and pin through both layers near the diagonal crease line.

7. Machine stitch through both layers of the trim along the diagonal crease. Remove the pin.

8. Open out the trim at the corner and press open the triangular seam allowance of the miter.

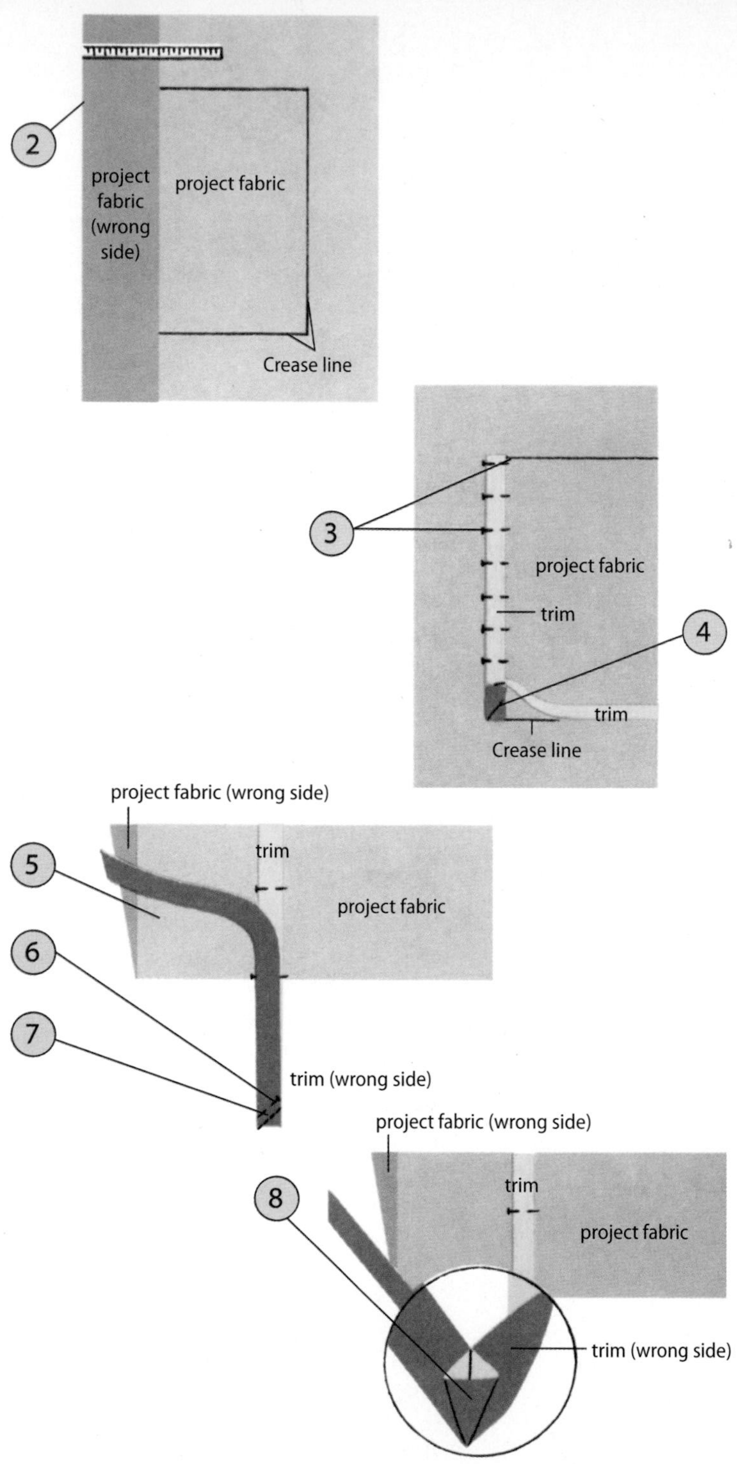

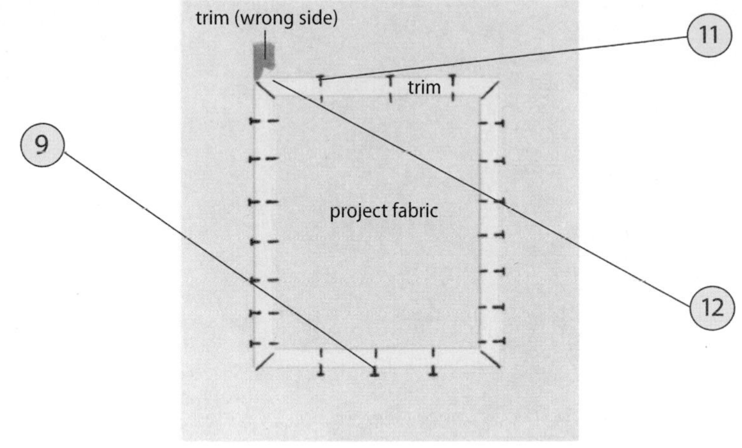

9. Open out the project fabric and turn the trim right side up. Pin the trim to the project fabric along the second side, aligning the outer edge with the creased guide line.

10. Repeat Steps 4–9 to miter the trim around additional corners.

11. If the trim will end at a fabric edge, pin to that edge and cut off the excess. To join the trim around a continuous edge, as shown in this example, pin to within about 6 inches of the last corner.

12. At the last corner, lap the finishing end of the trim over the beginning end. Then fold the finishing end under diagonally. Press the crease. Cut off the excess trim flush with the outer edge.

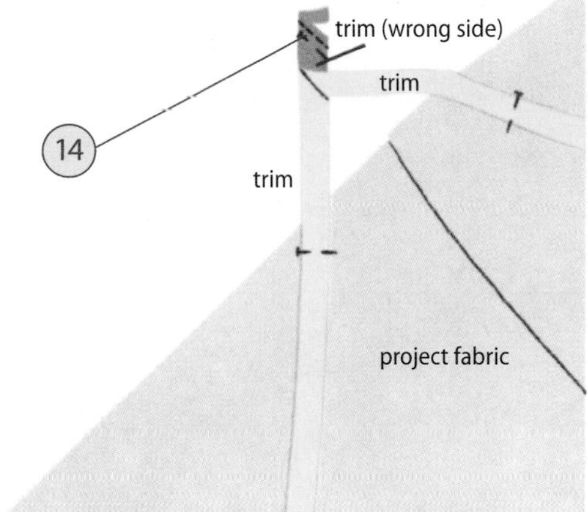

13. Fold the project fabric out of the way near the corner.

14. Align the ends of the trim, wrong sides out. Pin near the diagonal crease and machine stitch along the crease.

15. Trim the seam allowances ¼ inch outside the machine stitching. Press open.

16. Open out the project fabric. Turn the trim right side up and repin.

17. Machine stitch close to the inner and outer edges of the trim. Be sure to stitch both edges of the trim in the same direction. (For an invisible finish, attach the trim with slip stitches instead of machine topstitching.) Remove the pins. Press.

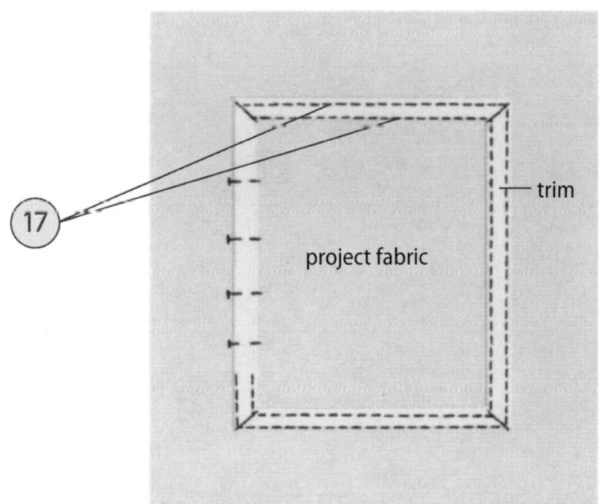

Fringed Trim

Enclosing Fringed Trim in a Seam

1. Decide how much of the fringed trim heading you wish to be visible and subtract from the total width of the heading to determine how far from the edge of the project fabric to place the edge of the fringe heading.

2. Place the project wrong side down. Place the trim, wrong side up, on the project, with the heading edge of the trim closest to the fabric edge. Align the edge of the heading at the distance from the fabric edge determined in Step 1. Pin.

3. At corners, pinch the heading into a point. Stretch the heading slightly around outside curves, and ease it slightly around inside curves.

4. Machine baste the trim to the fabric at 6 to 8 stitches to the inch. Sew ⅜ inch or ½ inch inside the fabric edge, depending on the width of the seam allowance of the project.

5. Place the facing or lining for the project wrong side down and place the trimmed fabric on top of it, wrong side up. Pin the edges.

6. Machine stitch at the normal stitch length just inside the line of machine basting made in Step 4. At corners, pivot and take several stitches across the point. Remove the pins.

7. Trim the seam allowances diagonally at corners, clip them around inside curves, and notch them around outside curves.

8. Turn the project right side out and push out the corners. Press.

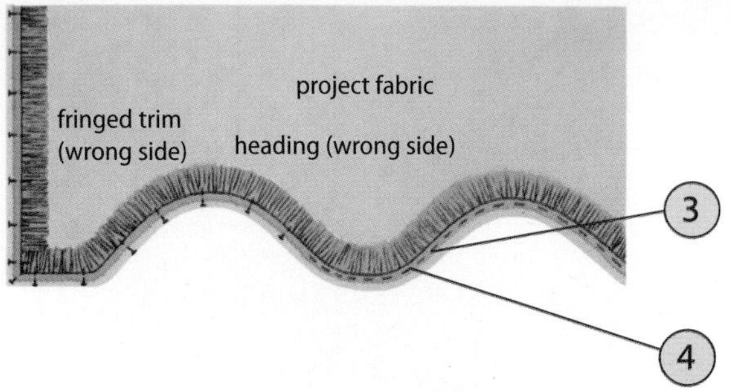

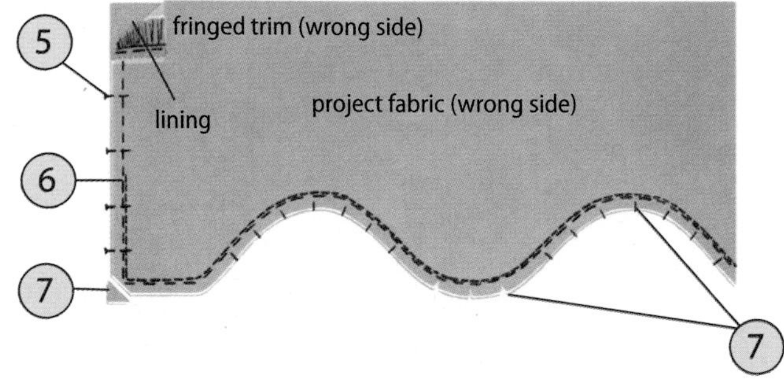

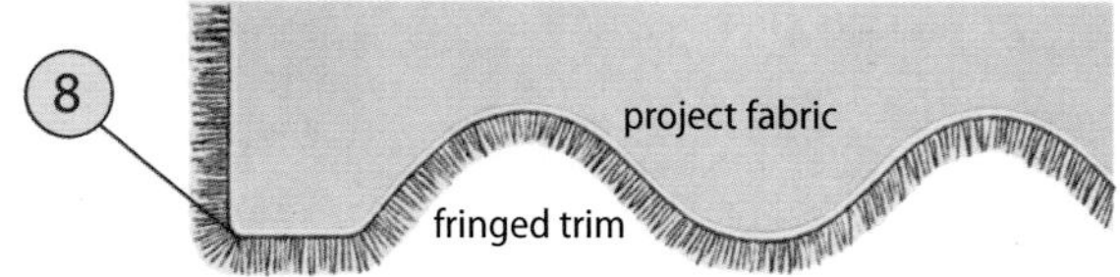

Adding Fringed Trim to the outside of the Project

9. If the fringed trim will be attached by hand with slip stitches, attach the facing or lining to the project before adding the trim. Otherwise, sew it in place before attaching the facing or lining.

10. Place the lined or unlined project wrong side down and lay the trim on it, wrong side down, with the fringed portion outward. Pin.

11. Attach the trim by hand with slip stitches or with machine topstitching. Remove the pins.

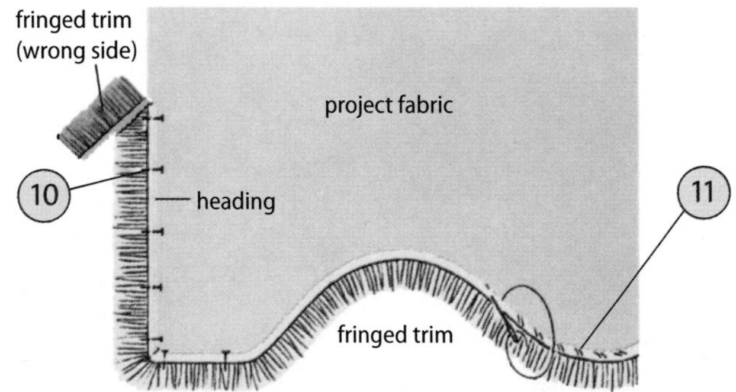

The Ruffle with a Heading

Preparing the Ruffle Fabric

1. To calculate the width of fabric needed for a ruffle with a heading, decide how high the ruffle and heading will be and add a total of ½ inch for the top and bottom double hems.

2. Multiply the desired finished length by two and a half if the fabric is lightweight, by three if the fabric is sheer. Then add a total of 2 inches for double hems at both sides if the ends of the ruffle will be finished or 1 inch for seam allowances if the ends will be inserted into seams.

3. To determine the number of strips you will need for the ruffle, divide the length calculated in Step 2 by the width of the fabric if it has a design, or by the length of the fabric if it does not. Allow ½ inch for seam allowances on each strip.

4. Straighten the grain of the fabric *(page 73)* and trim off the selvages.

5. Fold the fabric in half lengthwise if it has a design and crosswise if it does not. Pin edges.

6. Mark off the strips by drawing a series of parallel chalk lines at right angles to the fold and cut along lines. Remove pins.

7. Join the strips with ⅛-inch French seams or with narrow hemmed seams. To make the hemmed seams, use a narrow-hemmer foot. Place two strips, right sides together, with the end of the bottom strip extending ⅛ inch beyond the end of the top strip. Press the seams.

Hemming the Ruffle Strip

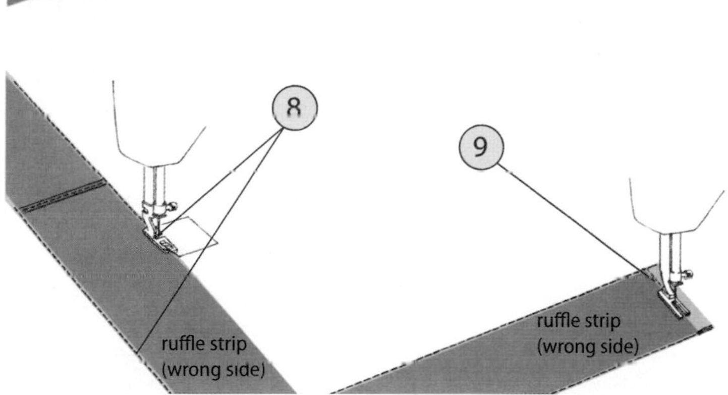

8. Finish the top and bottom edges of the ruffle strip with a narrow double hem, using the narrow-hemmer foot. Press the hems.

9. If the ends of the ruffle will stand by themselves, fold both ends into ½-inch-deep double hems, pinning 1 inch from the ends. Machine stitch across the inside edge of both hems. Press.

The Ruffle with a Heading

Gathering and Attaching the Ruffle Strip

10a. To gather the ruffle strip with a ruffler attachment, place the strip wrong side down and stitch across the top edge at a distance equal to the desired depth of the ruffle heading.

10b. To gather the ruffle by hand, machine baste at 6 stitches to the inch with nylon thread. Stitch across the top edge at a distance equal to the desired depth of the ruffle heading, then pull the bobbin thread to create the desired fullness.

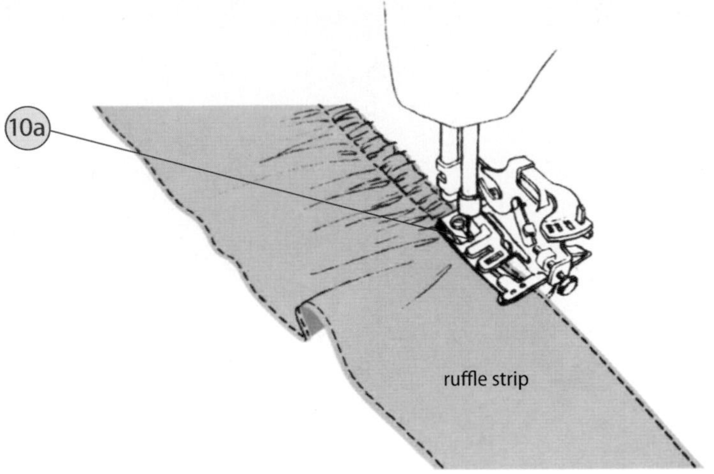

11. If the ends of the ruffle will be inserted into seams, reduce their bulkiness by pulling out ½ inch of the ruffling at each end. If the ends will become part of the hems of the project, pull out enough ruffling to equal the depth of the hems.

12. Using the narrow-hemmer foot, make a narrow double hem on the right side of the project fabric along the edge to which the ruffle will be attached. Press the hem.

13. Place the project wrong side down and place the ruffle on top of it, also wrong side down. Align the gathering stitches on the ruffle with the inside edge of the hem. Pin.

14. Machine stitch just outside the gathering stitches on the ruffle. Ease in extra fullness around curves and corners, pivoting at the corners. Remove the pins.

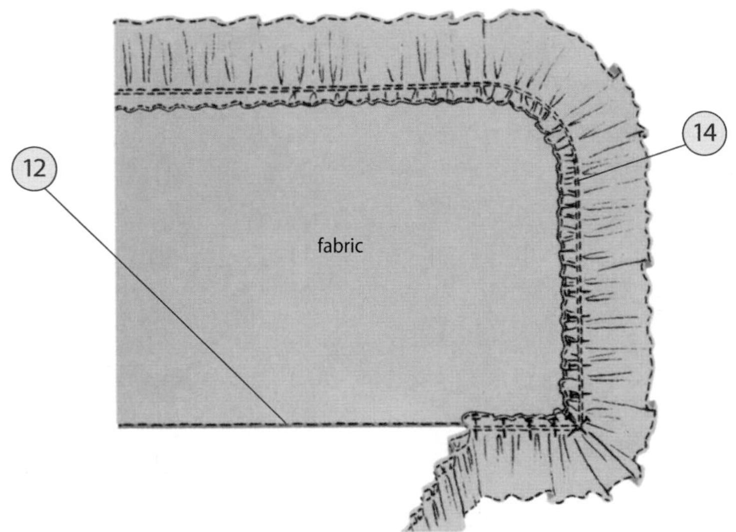

Shaping for hemlines

Although a well-made hemline for a fabric furnishing usually goes unnoticed, it can be made an eyecatching focus by curving the edge with scallops or indenting it with the toothlike pattern called dentils. The crisp dentil edge is especially attractive on valances, Roman shades, and fitted bedcovers. The graceful curves of a scalloped edge are more often used for such unfitted furnishings as coverlets.

Whether scalloped or squared, shaped hemlines require careful planning. If using dentils or scallops, they must fit evenly along the bottom of a valance or covering. Wherever there is a corner, one dentil or scallop must wrap around the turn. In fact, corner dentils and scallops should always be slightly wider to compensate for the foreshortening that occurs when they are seen on two planes at once.

The Dentil Edge

Blocking out the Pattern

1. To plan a dentil edge for a project such as a valance or a bedcover, measure the width of the edge where the gap-toothed pattern of dentils will be used and divide it by two. If the project fabric must go around corners, measure only the center section, not the sides.

2. On a piece of graph paper—using a scale of one square to equal 1 inch—measure off the distance determined in Step 1 and trim the graph paper to this width. The graph represents half the completed edge.

3. If the project fabric does not turn a corner, the left-hand end of the graph represents the side of the project. If the project fabric must go around corners, the left-hand end represents the point at which a corner turns.

4. The right-hand end of the graph represents the center point because the completed pattern will be flipped over in order to mark the second half of the edge identically.

5. Decide approximately how wide you wish the projections to be. Then determine how wide and how deep you wish to make the cutout spaces.

6. Place a piece of tracing paper over the graph paper. Starting at the center point, sketch half the width of a projection, following a horizontal line on the graph. Then sketch a full-width space and a full-width projection.

7. Continue marking full-width projections and spaces until you reach the left-hand end of the paper. The design must end with at least a half-width projection, not a space.

8. If the design does not end in a projection, reposition the tracing paper sketch over the graph, and place half a space at the center point.

9. Check the left-hand end of the sketch to be sure you will have half—or more—the width of a full projection.

10. Draw the design on the graph paper, measuring the squares carefully and using a ruler to guide the pencil.

11. Adjust the width of the projections or spaces and the depth of the spaces, until you are satisfied with the results.

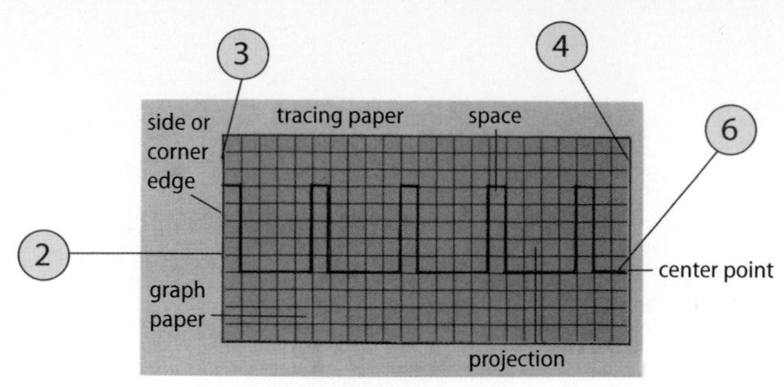

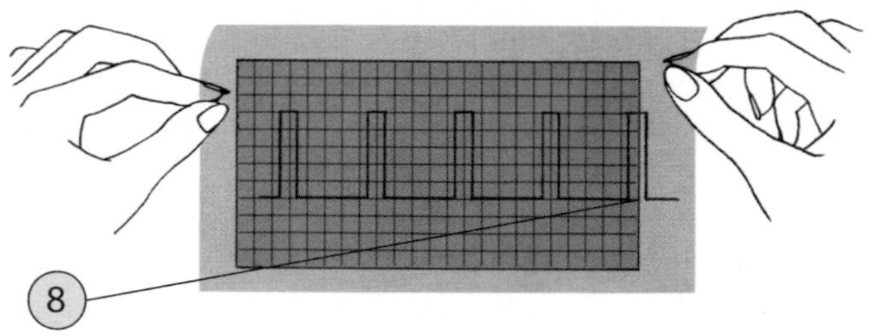

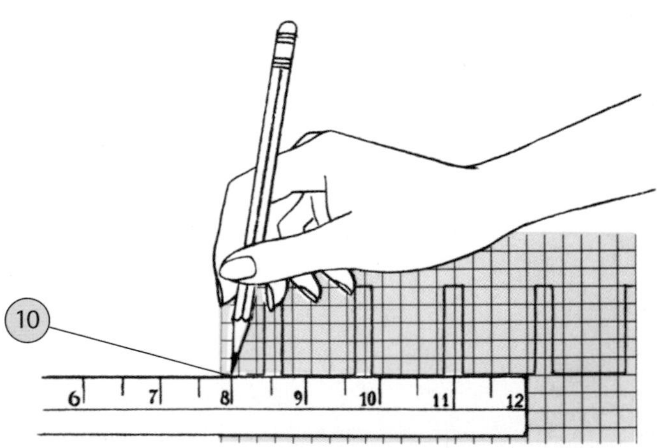

The Dentil Edge

Making the Pattern

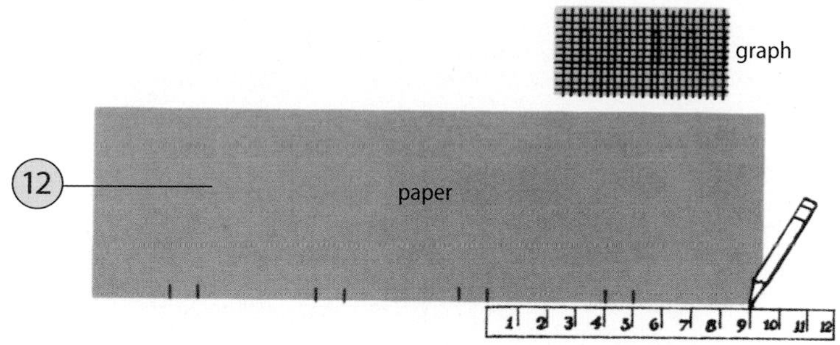

12. Cut out a piece of heavy paper equal in width to the measurement determined in Step 1 and several inches deeper than the spaces between the projections.

13. Indicate along the bottom edge of the paper the points where the spaces should be. At each mark, draw lines at right angles to the bottom edge of the paper. Remember to begin with half the width of a space or projection at the center point. Connect the lines with a horizontal line across the top.

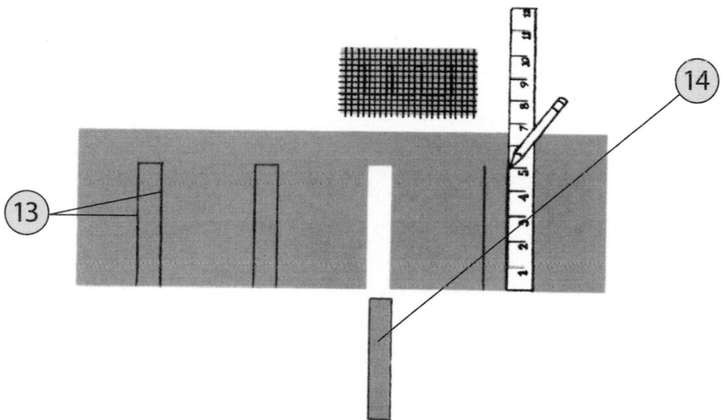

14. Cut out the spaces along the lines to form the design. This pattern will be used to mark the stitching lines. It represents the finished edge, rather than the cutting line, because no seam allowances are included.

15. If you are using striped or patterned fabric, place the completed pattern over the fabric to determine where you want the design to be positioned and whether it can be accommodated to the fabric design.

Preparing the Fabric

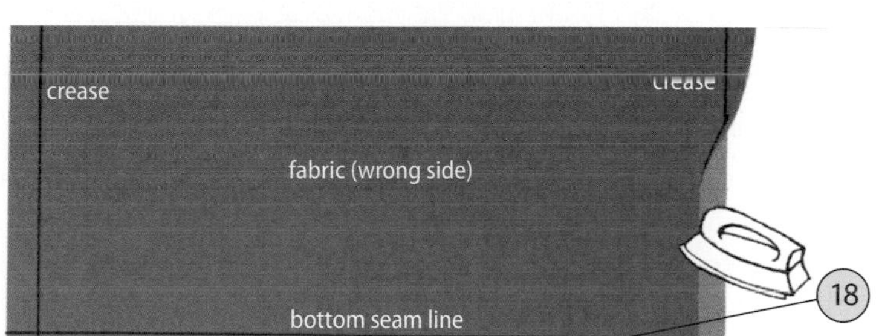

16. Measure your project fabric, adding ½ inch for a bottom seam allowance. If the project is wider than a fabric width, or goes around corners, add a ½-inch allowance for each seam.

17. Cut out the fabric, using your pattern to gauge the placement of the fabric design—if any. If necessary, pin and then stitch the fabric widths or corner sections together. Press the seams open.

18. Press in creases to indicate the side hemlines and mark the bottom seam line on the wrong side.

The Dentil Edge

19. Cut out a strip of facing from the project fabric that measures the same width as the project minus the side hemline allowances. The strip should measure about 2 inches deeper than the cutout spaces on the pattern, plus 1 inch for top and bottom seam allowances.

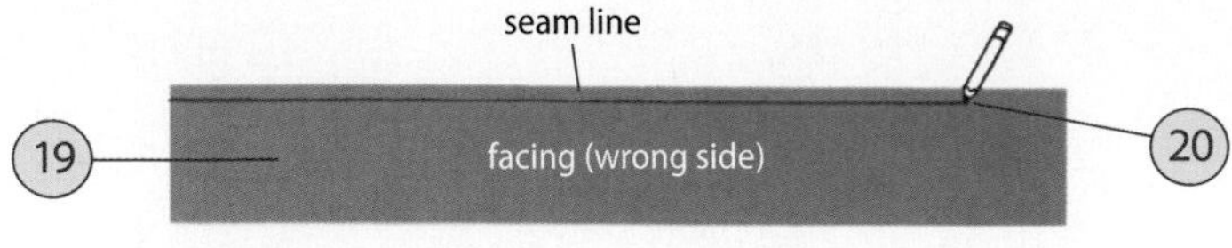

20. Mark a seam line ½ inch from the top to indicate where the facing will be attached to the lining.

21. Cut the lining to the width of the facing and the same length as the fabric.

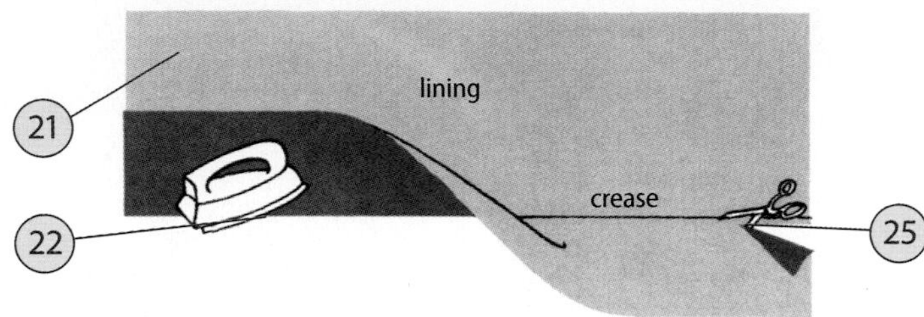

22. Press a crease on the lining to mark a seam line the same distance from the bottom as the facing seam line.

23. If you are making a project that requires stiffening, and therefore does not need to be lined all the way to the bottom, leave a ½-inch seam allowance below the crease made in the previous step, and trim off the rest of the lining, as shown.

Attaching the Facing to the Lining

24a. If you are working with a full length of lining, place the lining wrong side down and cover it with the facing, wrong side up. Position the facing with the bottom extending away from the bottom of the lining. Match the seam line on the facing to the crease on the lining.

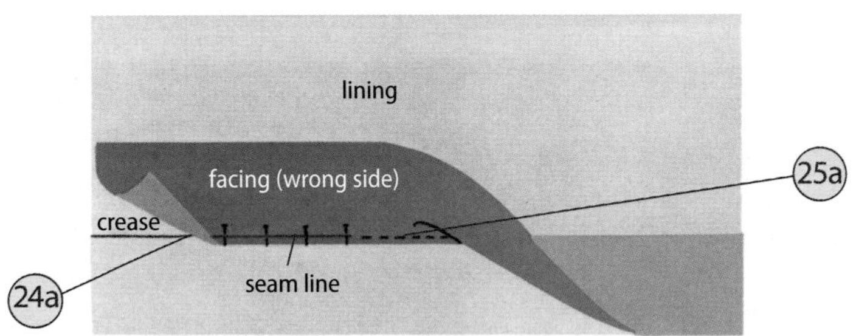

25a. Pin the pieces together, then machine stitch on the seam line, removing the pins as you go.

26a. Turn the facing down toward the bottom of the lining so that both pieces are wrong sides down. Press along the seam.

24b. If you are working with lining that has been trimmed, place the facing, wrong side up, over the lining, wrong side down. Match the seam line on the facing to the crease on the lining.

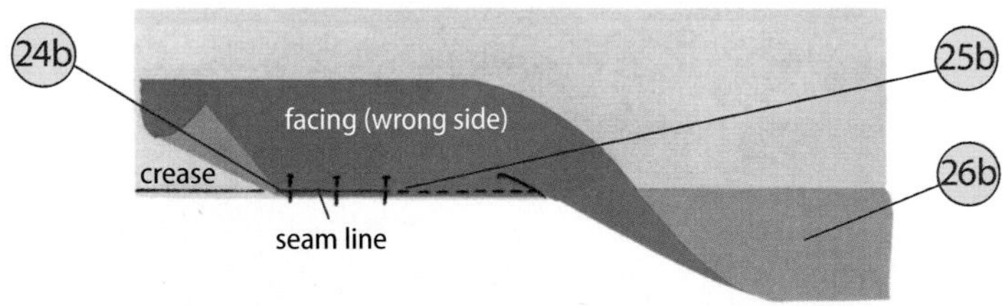

25b. Pin the pieces together, then machine stitch on the seam line.

26b. Turn the facing so that it extends away from the lining. Press the seam open on the wrong side.

The Dentil Edge

Marking a Flat Edge

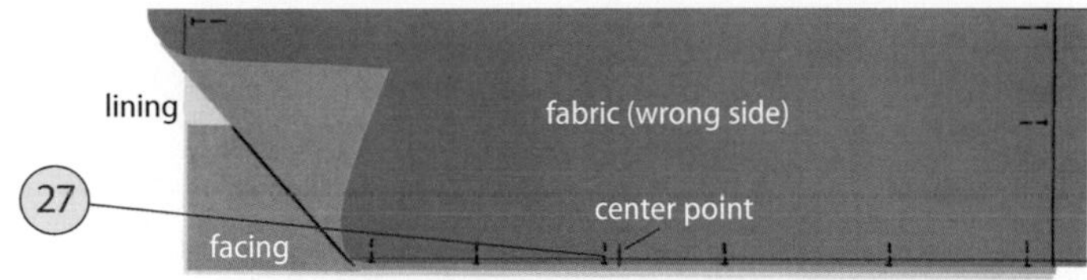

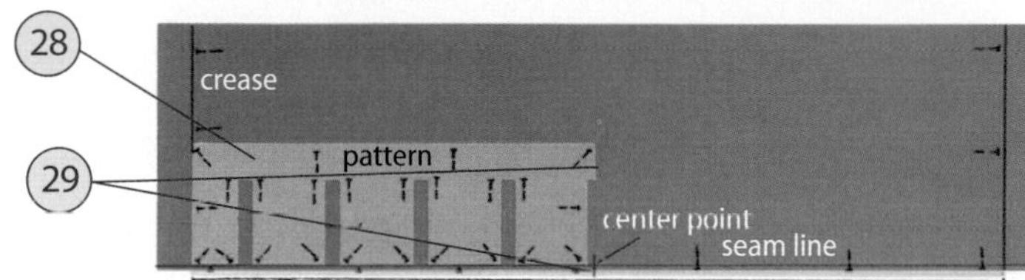

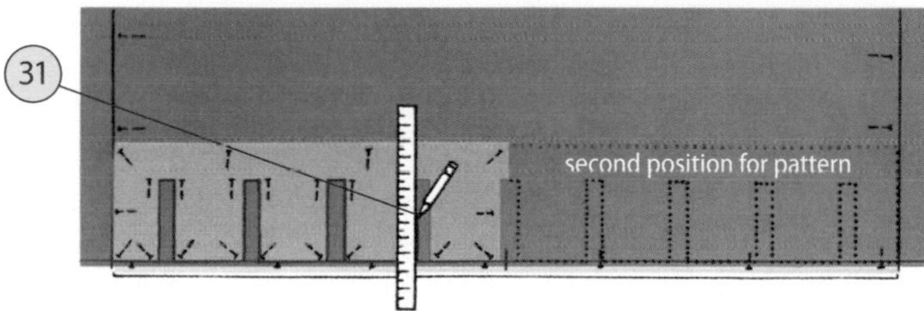

27. Place the facing and lining wrong sides down, and lay the fabric over them, wrong side up. Pin the pieces together. Mark the center point.

28. Place the pattern on the fabric. Match the bottom edge of the pattern to the bottom seam line.

29. Align the center of the pattern to the center point marking on the fabric. The other end of the pattern should align with the side hemline crease.

30. Pin the pattern securely to the fabric.

31. Mark around the three sides of the cutout spaces. Use a pencil to mark heavy fabrics, chalk on lightweight or sheer fabrics. Guide your marker with the edge of a ruler.

32. When all the spaces are marked, remove the pattern, then flip it over at the center point. Repeat Steps 28–31 to mark the other half, as indicated by the dotted lines. Remove the pattern. Skip to Step 40.

Marking an Edge with Corners

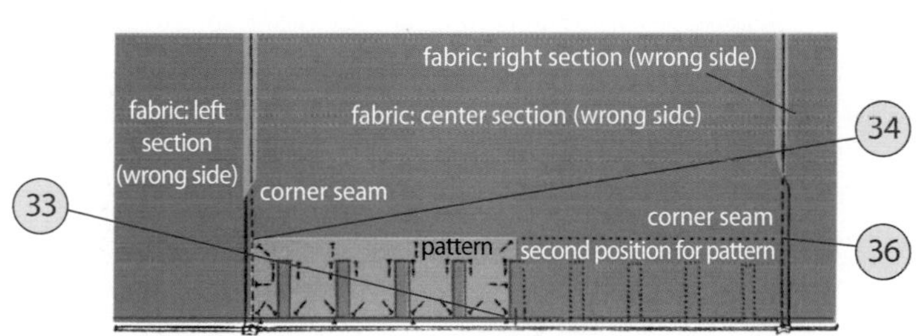

33. Place the facing and lining wrong sides down, and lay the project fabric over them wrong side up. Pin the pieces together. Mark the center point of the center section of fabric.

34. Working on the center section only, fold back the seam allowance at the left-hand corner as shown. Align the left-hand end of your pattern to the machine stitching.

35. Repeat Steps 28-32 — folding back the right-hand seam allowance in the opposite direction — to mark the outlines of the spaces across the entire center section.

36. To go around the corner, fold back the seam allowances toward the center section as shown. Flip the pattern over once more and align the side edge to the machine stitching of this corner seam.

The Dentil Edge

37. Repeat Steps 28–32 once more to begin marking the right section of the fabric. When you have drawn the last space *(arrow)*, slide the pattern along the edge, without flipping it over, and match the first space to the last space you drew in the previous step. Draw in the spaces.

38. As you approach the crease for the side hemline, estimate how many more spaces you can accommodate without having a space or less than half a full projection at the hem. Continue the line for the last projection to the hemline crease, marking over the bottom seam line. On the finished article, it will not be easily visible.

39. Repeat Steps 36–38 on the left section of the fabric, working in the opposite direction.

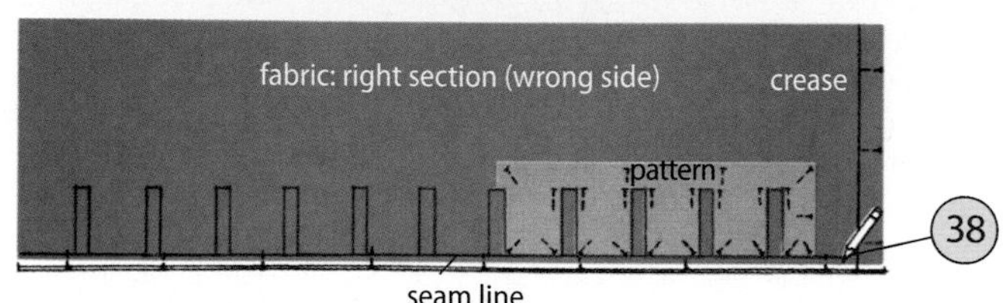

Finishing the Edge

40. Insert more pins, if necessary, to secure the fabric layers. Then machine stitch around the entire edge. Sew along the bottom seam line to form the bottom edge of the projections, then continue up, over and down the sides of the spaces. Pivot the fabric with the needle inserted at all bottom points of the projections and all top corners of the spaces.

41. Trim the seam allowances of all layers to ¼ inch beyond the machine stitching.

42. Trim the bottom points of the projections diagonally, and clip into the top corners of the spaces, cutting up to — but not through — the machine stitching.

43. Turn the fabric right side out. The right side of the facing will be visible on the underside. Using a ruler, push out the bottom points and smooth out the top corners. Press the finished edge on the underside.

44. Finish the side edges or the end hems as instructed for your project.

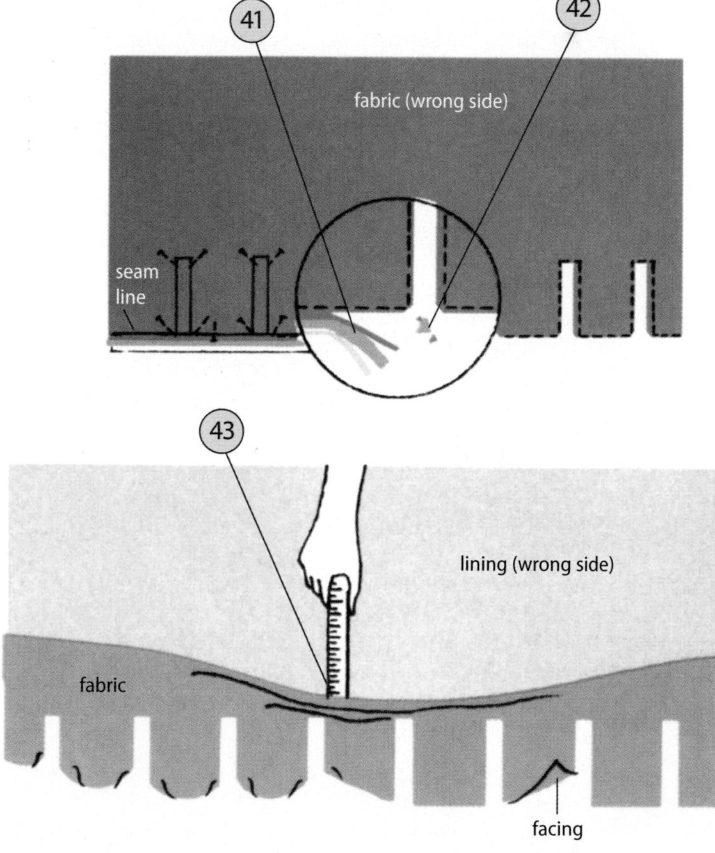

The Scalloped Edge with Loosely Rounded Corners

Blocking Out the Pattern

4

graph paper

1. To scallop around the bottom edge of a cover with loosely draped corners — for a bed or a studio couch — first measure the edge that will be most prominent when the cover is made, such as the foot of a bed or the front side of a studio couch.

2. Measure the distance — called the overhang, or drop — from the top surface to the level at which you want the finished edge.

3. Divide the edge measurement in half and add the overhang.

4. On a sheet of graph paper — using a scale of one small division of graph marking to 1 inch of measurement — draw a square with each side equal to the sum determined in Step 3. Trim the graph paper along the lines of the square. This graph represents half the pattern which will be used to mark the scallops.

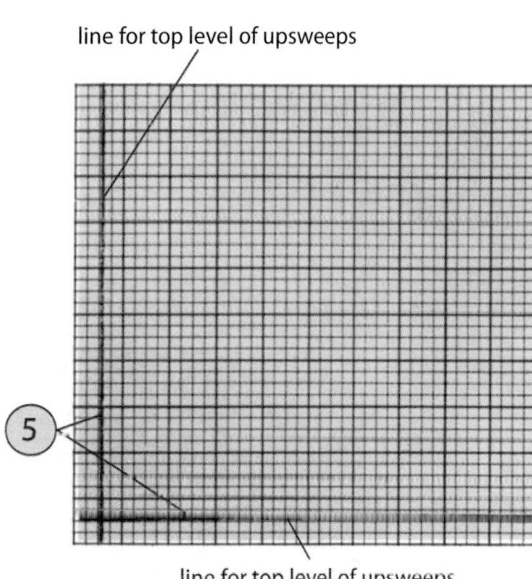

5. Decide how high you wish to make the upsweeps between scallops. Measure in this distance (to scale) from the bottom edge of the trimmed graph and draw a horizontal line parallel to the trimmed edge. Make a similar line parallel to the left-hand edge of the graph.

6. Starting at the bottom left-hand corner of the paper, measure a distance to scale equal to the overhang *(Step 2)* along the bottom and then along the left edge of the paper. Make marks at these points.

7. From each mark draw a line at right angles to the edge of the paper. The point at which these lines intersect indicates the top corner of the overhang on the cover.

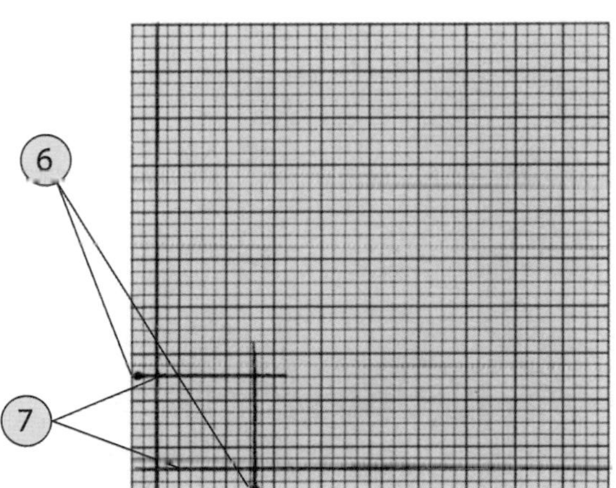

The Scalloped Edge with Loosely Rounded Corners

8. Place the point of a compass at the intersection of the lines drawn in Step 7 and adjust the compass to touch the marks made in Step 6.

9. Draw the corner scallop by making an arc broad enough to intersect the two lines that indicate the top level for the upsweeps of the scallops.

10. Measure to scale from one end of the graph to the point where the corner scallop intersects a line that marks the top of the upsweeps. Double this measurement to determine how much space you have for other, smaller, scallops along the prominent edge of the cover.

11. Decide approximately how wide you wish the smaller scallops to be — usually about half the width of the corner scallop will look right.

12. Divide the measurement determined in Step 10 by the approximate width of the scallops determined in Step 11. The result is the total number of scallops you can have along the edge. Since the division will probably not come out even, repeat it with slightly different width figures until you do get a whole result, with no fractional remainder.

13. Sketch in the scallops on the graph. If in Step 12 you found you needed an even number of small scallops, begin at the right hand of the graph at the top level line, and sketch in full scallops until you reach the upsweep for the corner scallop. For an uneven number, start at the right-hand bottom end of the graph, draw half a scallop, then full scallops. Because the graph represents half the total width, you will be drawing half the total number of small scallops.

14. Repeat Step 13 on the left-hand side of the graph.

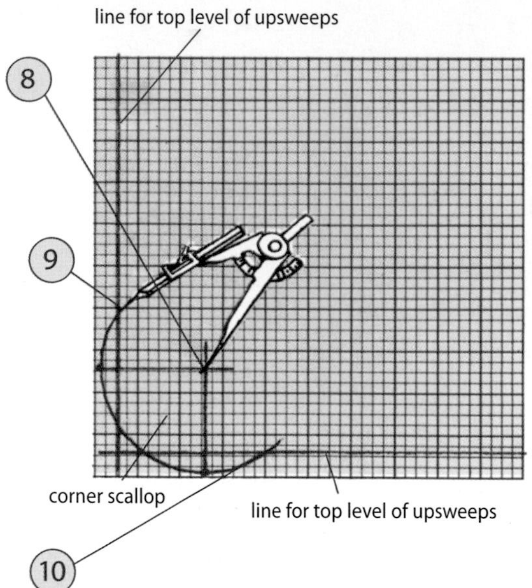

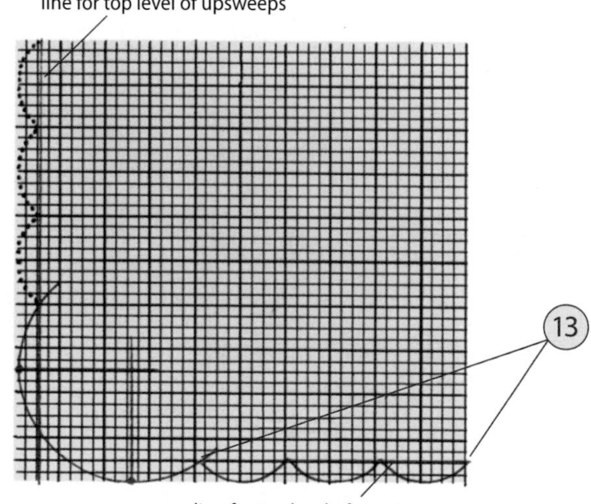

Making the Actual-Size Pattern

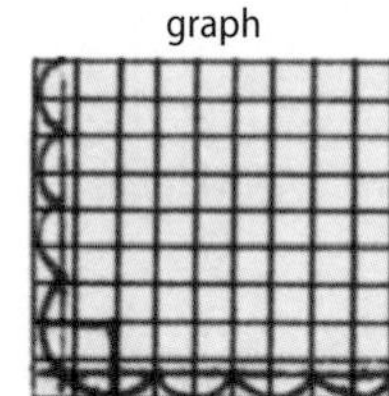

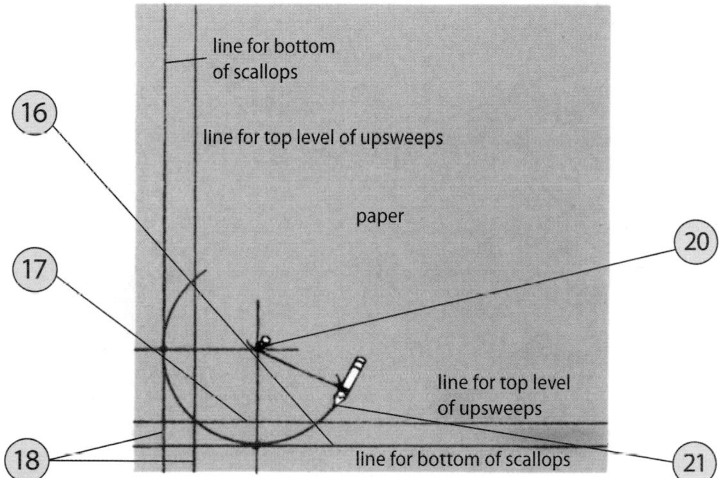

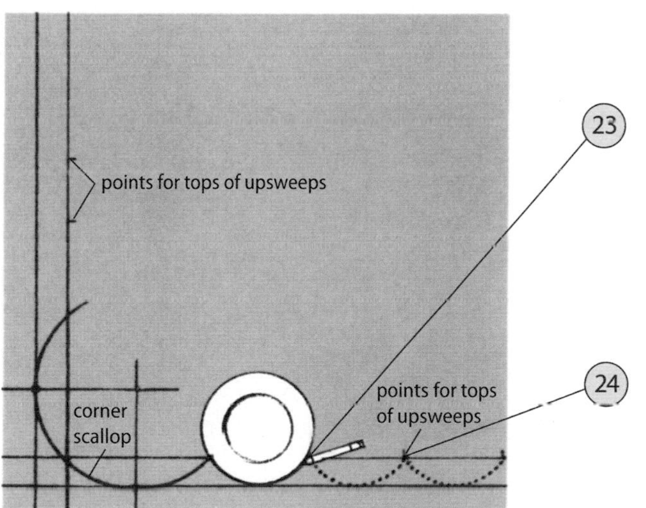

15. Cut out of heavy paper a square with each side an inch longer than the measurement in Step 3.

16. Draw a horizontal line 1 inch — actual measurement, not scaled down — above the bottom edge of the paper to indicate where the bottom of the scallops will fall.

17. Draw a second line above the first one at a distance equal to the height of the upsweeps determined in Step 5.

18. Repeat Steps 16 and 17 on the left-hand side of the paper, drawing two vertical lines to indicate the bottoms of the scallops and the tops of the upsweeps along this edge.

19. Using the actual measurements, not scaled-down ones, repeat Steps 6 and 7 to mark the length of the overhang on the bottom and left-hand sides of the pattern, and to draw the intersecting lines that mark the top corner overhang, this time working along the outside lines indicating the bottoms of the scallops.

20. Tie one end of a piece of string to a thumbtack and insert it in the intersection point made in Step 19. Tie the other end to a pencil, adjusting the length of the string so that when taut it brings the pencil point to the overhang-length marks made in Step 19.

21. Holding the string taut, draw the corner scallop, making sure the ends of the arc cross the upsweep lines at both sides of the paper.

22. Taking scale measurements from your graph and converting them to full size, use a ruler to mark the points where the tops of the smaller scallops will cross the upsweep lines on the full-size pattern.

23. Sketch in the first curve freehand, starting at one edge of the corner scallop and continuing to the first upsweep mark. Find a plate with a similarly shaped curve, and use the rim of the plate to smooth the freehand curve.

The Scalloped Edge with Loosely Rounded Corners

24. Using the plate, draw in the rest of the scallops along this edge, beginning and ending at the upsweep marks made in Step 22.

25. Repeat Steps 23 and 24 to draw the scallops on the left-hand side of the paper.

26. Cut out around the scallops to form a full-scale paper pattern. Then trim the paper to within several inches of the upsweep line so that it will be easier to handle. The bottom edge of this pattern represents half the prominent edge of the article — measured in Step 1—and will be flipped over at the center to mark the other half. The side edge will guide the marking of the remaining edges of the cover.

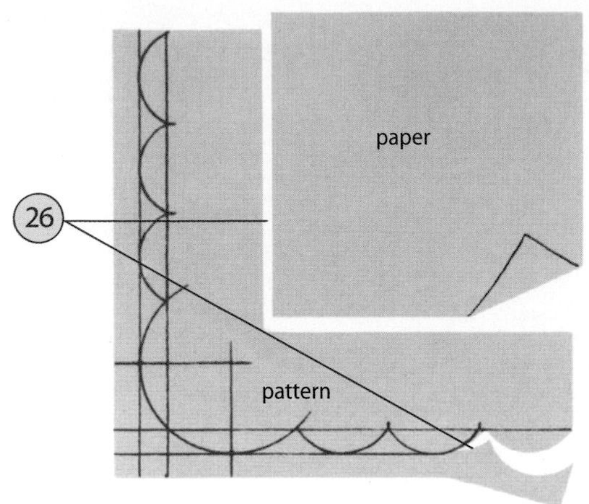

Marking the Fabric

27. Cut fabric and lining — leaving 1-inch seam allowances around the edges — to fit the object being covered. At the fabric edges press in creases to mark the seam lines.

28. To face the lining, cut out three 5-inch-wide sections of project fabric. Make two sections equal to the length of the lining plus ½ inch; make one section equal to the width plus 1 inch. Fold under the inside edge of the facing strip ½ inch and press.

29. Place the lining wrong side down and lay the facing strip over it, matching the raw outside edges. Pin the facing to the lining, then machine stitch, sewing just inside the fold.

30. Place the facing and lining wrong sides down and lay the fabric over them, wrong side up. Pin the pieces together.

31. Place the pattern on the fabric so that the bottom edge of the pattern is at the most prominent edge of the cover. Align the bottom curves with the creases marking the seam lines at the edges of the fabric.

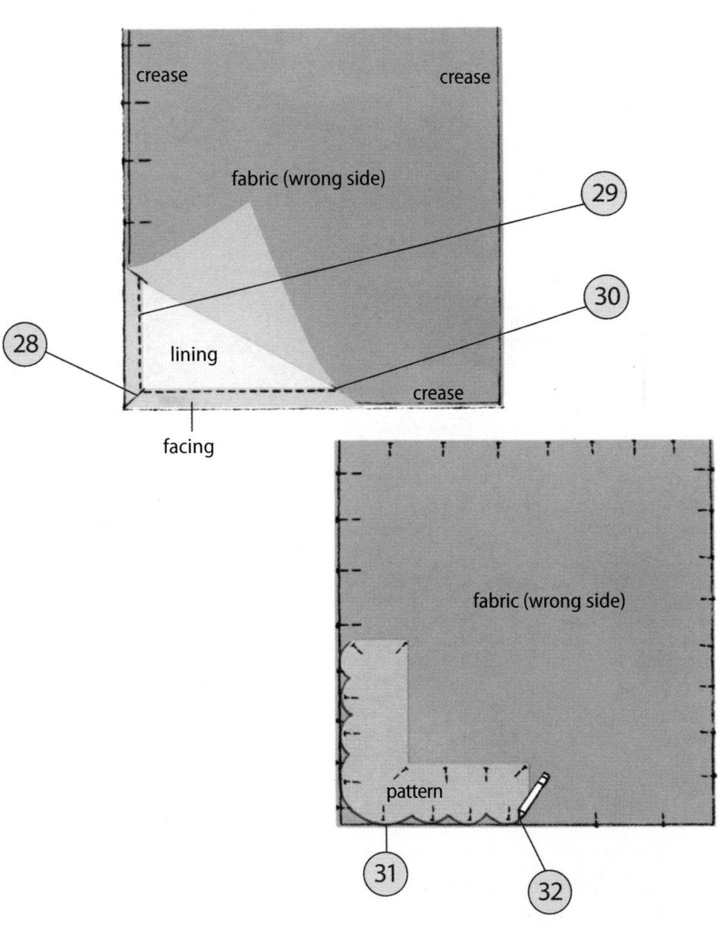

The Scalloped Edge with Loosely Rounded Corners

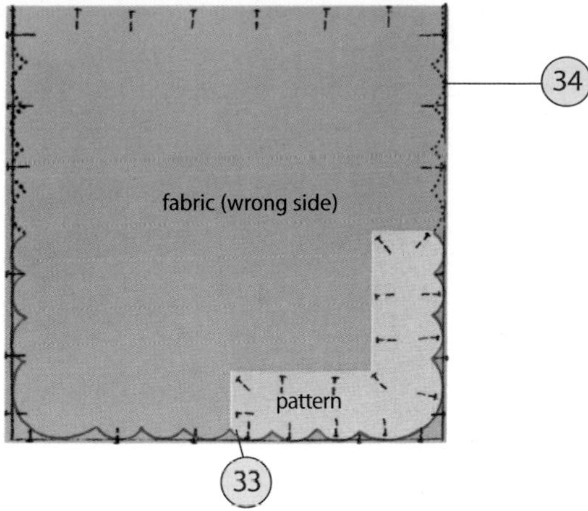

32. Pin the pattern to the fabric and draw around the scallops, using pencil to mark heavy fabrics and chalk to mark lightweight or sheer fabrics.

33. Remove the pattern, then flip it over at the center, aligning it to the seam lines and marking the scallops on this side of the fabric as in Steps 31 and 32.

34. To mark the remaining scallops, as indicated by the dotted lines, repeat Steps 37–39 for the dentil edge *(page 46)*. Use only the small scallops on the pattern as your guide for marking, as you slide the pattern along the fabric. As you go, be sure to match the curves and upsweeps of the last scallop you drew to the first scallop on the pattern so that all the scallops are correctly positioned.

35. As you reach the corners of the edge to be left unscalloped, continue the last scallop on each side to the corner with a straight line, if necessary, to make sure there is not an upsweep at or near the corner. Remove the pattern.

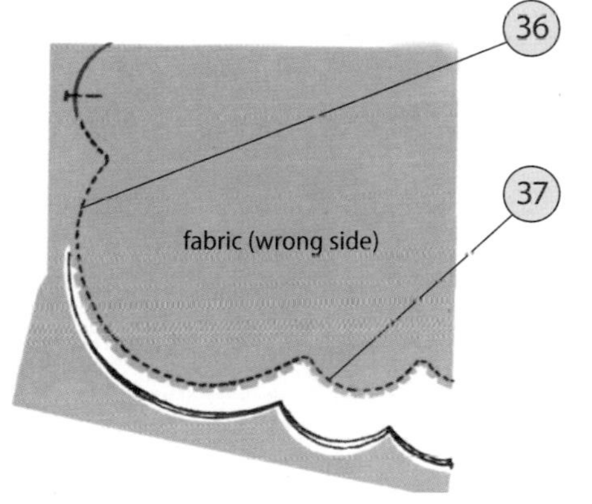

Finishing the Edge

36. Machine stitch around the scallops, squaring off the stitches at the tops of the upsweeps by making two horizontal stitches.

37. Trim the seam allowances of all layers of fabric to ½ inch all around the stitching.

38. Clip into the seam allowances at the upsweeps, cutting right up to, but not through, the stitching. Notch the curves around the bottom of the scallops.

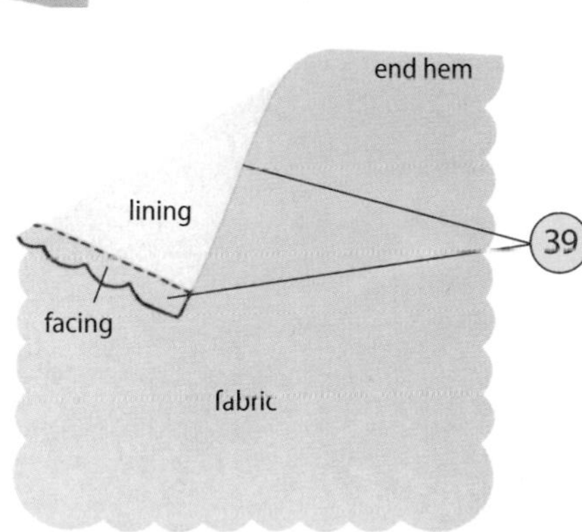

39. Turn the fabric right side out through the opening at the unscalloped and unstitched edge of the cover. The right side of the facing will be visible on the underside. Smooth out the curves, then press the finished edge on the underside.

40. Finish the unstitched edge—the end hem —following the procedure for hemming the bedcover *(page 136)*.

Inconspicuous closures

The neat fit of a carefully crafted slipcover is secured by the zipper that holds the cover in place. But to create this illusion of a second skin—one that can be removed quickly and easily for cleaning—the closure should be as inconspicuous as possible. Not only must the zipper itself be hidden by overlapping fabric but zipper and opening should be located strategically out of view—centered on the back of a box cushion *(right)*, or inserted in the welted seam of a knife-edge cushion or slipcover *(page 56)*.

For short closures not subjected to stress, color-matched metal dress zippers can be used, and on pillows even nylon zippers will do. But if the closure is large, and it must hold tight large expanses of heavy fabric, then only a heavy-duty upholstery zipper is suitable.

The Centered Zipper for Boxed Cushions

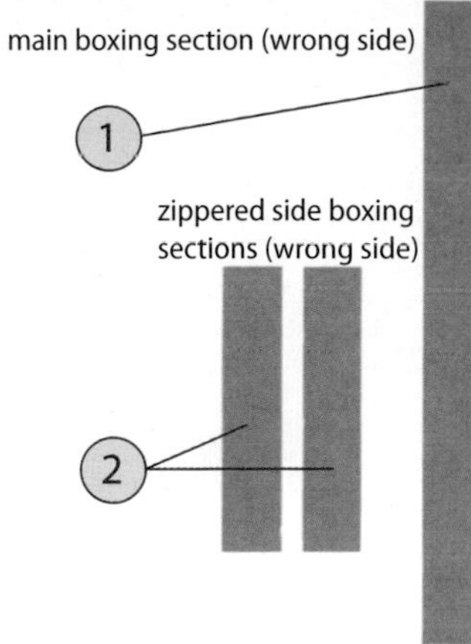

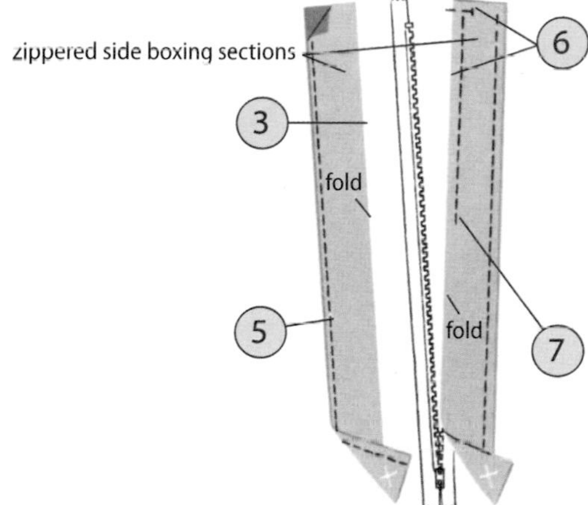

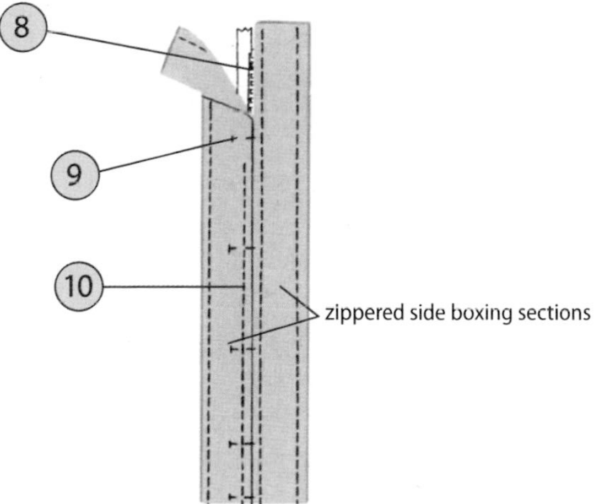

1. Cut fabric for the main section of the boxing that will fit around three sides of the cushion, following the project directions. Make sure the fabric is wide enough to include ¾ inch for seam allowances. To allow for the seams and the zipper flap, add 2½ inches to the desired finished length of the fabric for a small pillow and 3½ inches for a large cushion.

2. Cut two pieces of fabric for the zippered side of the boxing. Each should be the length of the zipper tape and the same width as the main section.

3. Fold each section of the zippered side of the boxing in half lengthwise, wrong sides together. Press the folds.

4. Chalk an X on one half of each section to identify it as the wrong side of the boxing.

5. If the fabric is light- or medium-weight, machine stitch together the long cut edges of each section of the zippered side of the boxing. Sew ¼ inch from the edges. For heavyweight fabrics, pin the long cut edges together, but do not machine stitch.

6. Open the zipper and place it face up. With the X-marked side of the fabric down, place one of the sections of the zippered side of the boxing over one side of the zipper. Align the folded edge of the fabric with the edge of the zipper teeth, and the top and bottom edges with the top and bottom edges of the zipper tape. Pin at the top and bottom of the zipper tape.

7. Using a zipper foot, machine stitch ¼ inch from the folded edge of the fabric. Sew from the top edge to the bottom and hold the fabric to keep the folded edge aligned with the edge of the zipper teeth. Remove the pins.

8. Close the zipper.

9. Position the second section of the zippered side of the boxing, X-marked side down, on the zipper so that the folded edge butts against the folded edge of the first section. Align the top and bottom edges of the two sections of the boxing fabric. Pin.

The Centered Zipper for Boxed Cushions

10. Machine stitch ¼ inch from the folded edge of the second section. Sew from the bottom edge to the top. Remove the pins.

11. Turn the zippered boxing pieces so that the X-marked portions face up.

12. Machine stitch across the top and bottom of the zipper tapes ¼ inch from the ends.

13. If the fabric is light- or medium-weight and the long cut edges were stitched together in Step 5, skip to Step 14. For quilted or other heavy fabrics, remove the pins from the long cut edges and trim off each X-marked layer of fabric ¼ inch outside the edge of the zipper tape. Do not cut through both layers of fabric.

14. Place the main section of the boxing wrong side down and lay the zippered side section on it with the wrong, or X-marked, sides up. Align the ends of the zippered side section with the ends of the main section. Pin.

15. Machine stitch along the ends ½ inch from the edges. Remove the pins.

16. Turn the boxing right side out.

17. At the tab end of the closed zipper, fold the main fabric section over onto the zippered side section. On small pillows this folded overlap should extend ¾ inch beyond the seam line made in Step 15; on large cushions the overlap should extend 1¼ inches beyond the seam. Pin the fold to the zippered section.

18. Machine stitch, sewing ¾ inch from the fold on small pillows and 1¼ inches from the fold on large cushions. Remove the pins and press.

19. Attach the completed boxing to the main fabric sections of the project following the project instructions.

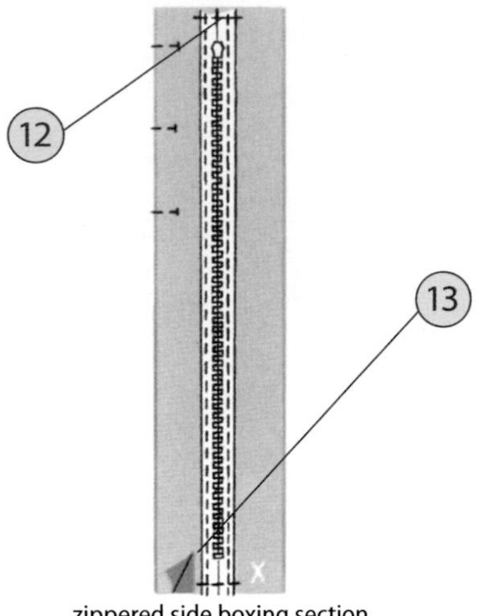

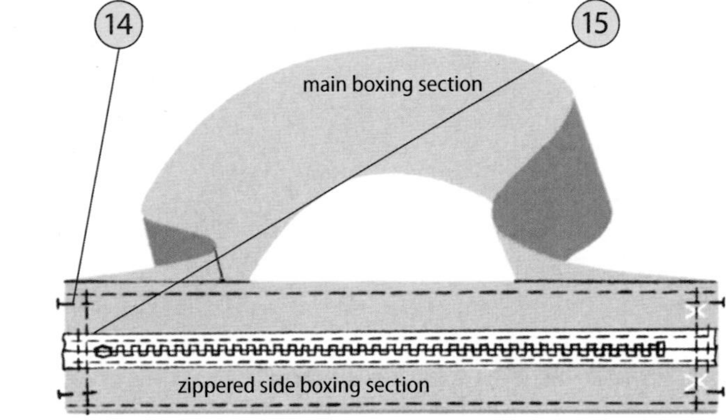

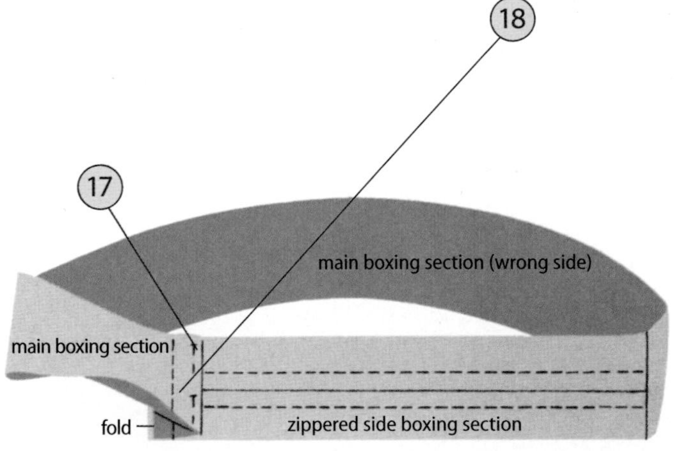

The Lapped Zipper for Slipcovers

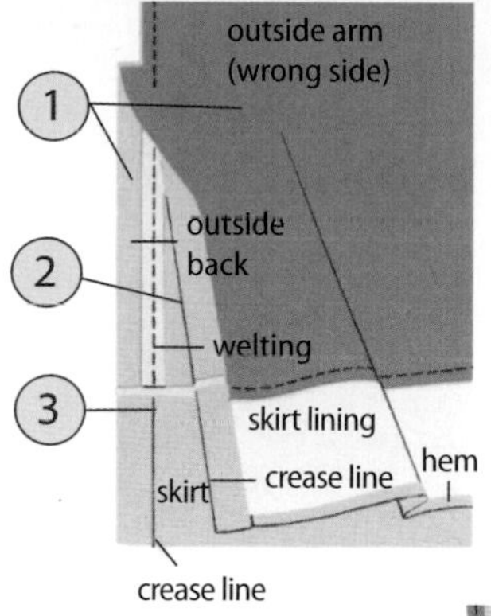

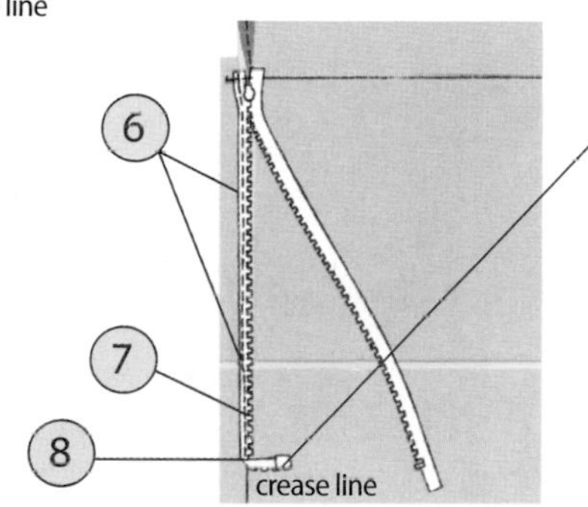

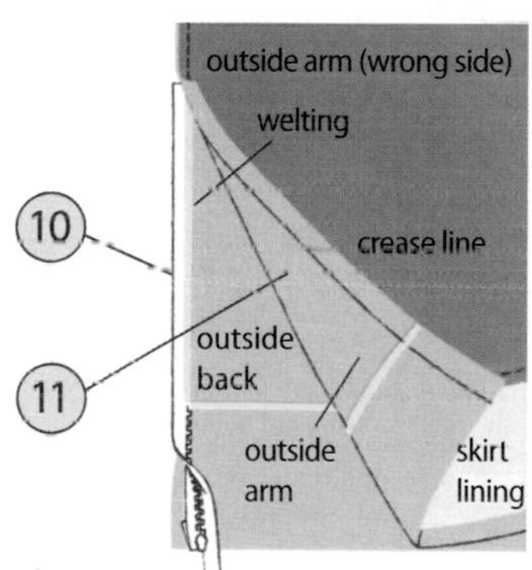

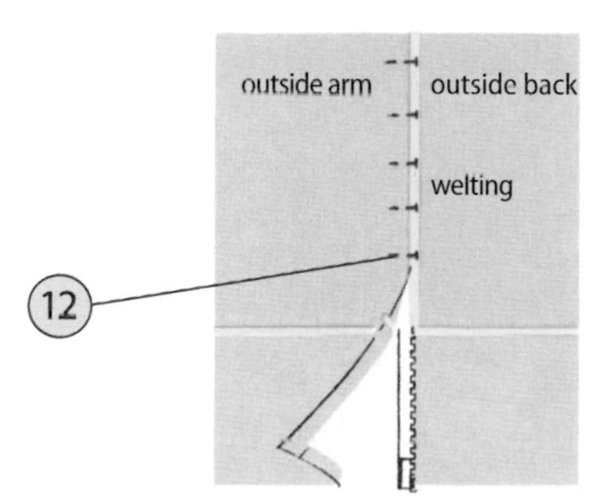

1. Place the slipcover, wrong side out, so that the outside back section is underneath and the outside arm section is on top.

2. To mark a guide for positioning the zipper, turn under the 1-inch seam allowance on the unstitched outside arm of the zipper seam. Press a crease.

3. Turn under the 1-inch seam allowance on the nonwelted bottom portion of the outside back section. Press a crease.

4. Open the zipper and place it face down on the welted seam of the back section, with the bottom zipper stop at the top. Pin.

5. Align the zipper teeth along the middle of the corded part of the welting.

6. Holding the zipper in place, using a zipper foot, machine stitch partway along the left-hand strip of zipper tape ¼ inch from the teeth. Stop stitching at the skirt seam line.

7. Reposition the zipper extending beyond the skirt seam line so that the teeth fall just inside the creased seam-line marking made in Step 3.

8. Sew at an angle to bring the stitches ¼ inch from the zipper teeth in their new position. Then continue stitching close to the teeth to about 1½ inches from the hem; stop the machine.

9. Lift up the zipper and fold under the end of the tape so that it clears the zipper teeth. Reposition the zipper and continue stitching, making sure to stitch through both layers of the folded zipper tape. Remove the pin.

10. Close the zipper and fold under the seam allowance of the outside back section to turn the zipper face up.

11. Fold down the outside arm section so that it is wrong side up on top of the outside back section.

12. Lap the folded edge of the outside arm section over the zipper teeth, covering them completely. Pin, making sure to catch the unstitched strip of the zipper tape underneath. At the hem edge, fold up the end of the zipper tape to clear the teeth. Pin.

13. Open the zipper. Using a zipper foot, machine stitch the unattached fabric sections to the unattached side of the zipper. Sew from the finished side of the fabric ½ inch from the fold. Begin the stitching 1 inch above the open portion of the seam. Remove the pins and press.

The Lapped Zipper for Welted Knife-Edged Pillows

1. Cut the fabric pieces for the pillow or cushion following the directions for the project. Make sure to leave a 1-inch seam allowance on both the front and back sections along the entire length of the side where the zipper will be inserted.

2. On each fabric section, fold the seam allowance toward the wrong side along the edge where the zipper will be attached. Press to crease in guide lines for the placement of the welting and the zipper.

3. Attach the welting to the front fabric section, aligning the machine basting on the welting with the creased guide line on the zipper edge and following the instructions for shirred welting *(pages 30–35)* or plain welting *(pages 25–29)*. Then stitch together the front and back sections, wrong sides out, for ½ inch along each end of the seam line into which the zipper will be inserted.

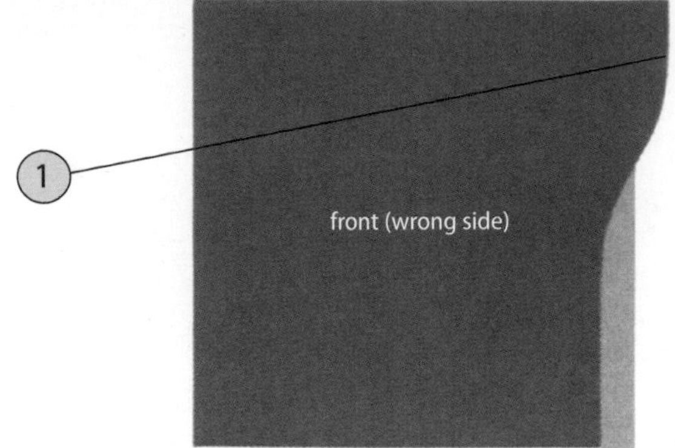

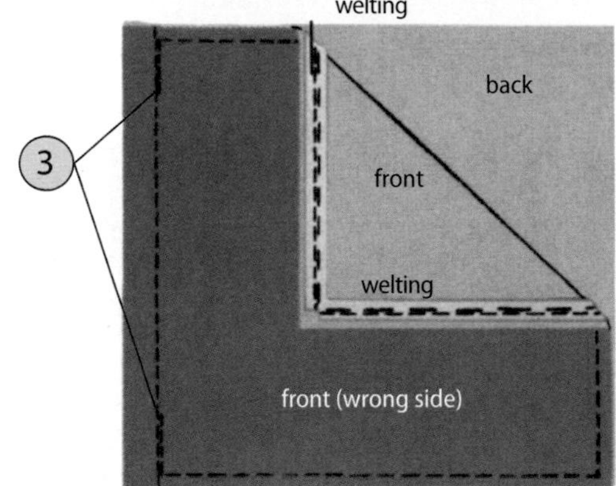

The Lapped Zipper for Welted Knife-Edged Pillows

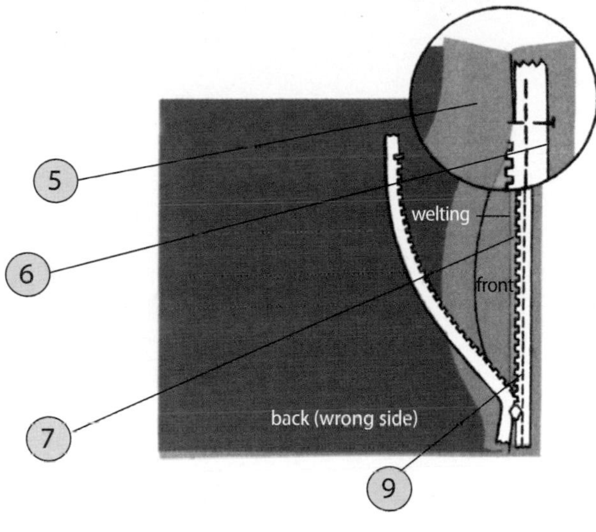

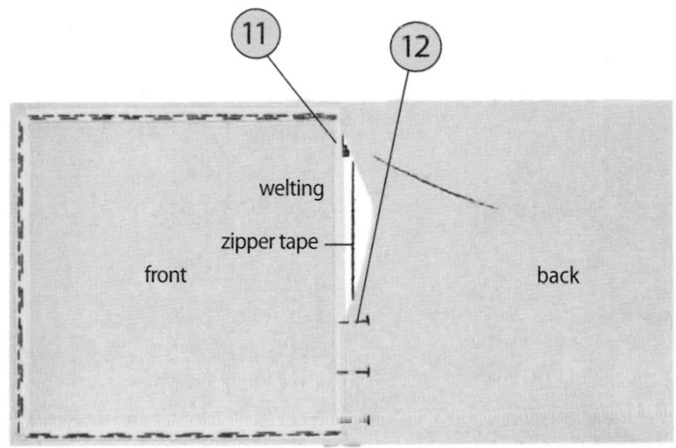

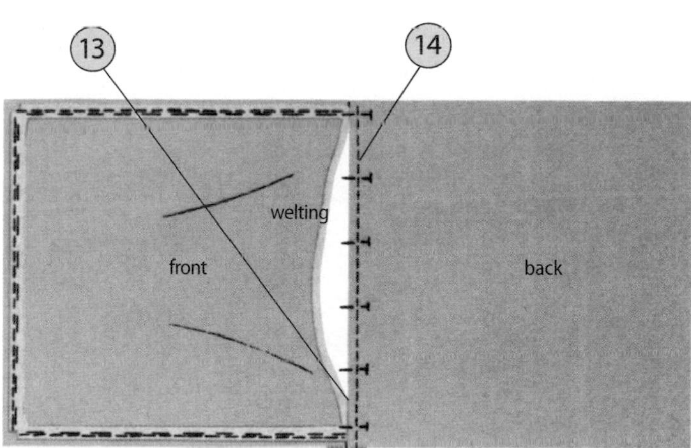

4. Place the fabric sections, wrong sides out, so that the front section is underneath.

5. Push the top layer of fabric out of the way along the seam where the zipper will be inserted.

6. Open the zipper and place one side of it face down on the welted seam with the outer edge of the zipper tape toward the fabric edge.

7. Align the top stop of the zipper just below the stitched portion of the seam and midway on the corded part of the welting. Insert a pin at the top end of the tape. Align the zipper teeth along the middle of the corded part of the welting.

8. Attach a zipper foot to the machine.

9. Machine stitch ¼ inch from the zipper teeth. Stitch from the top edge of the zipper tape to the bottom edge, holding the zipper in place with your hand to keep the teeth lined up along the middle of the corded part of the welting. Remove the pin.

10. Open out the fabric so that both the front and back sections are wrong side down.

11. Close the zipper and fold under the seam allowance of the front section to turn the zipper face up.

12. Lap the unattached folded edge of the back section of the pillow over the zipper teeth, covering them completely. Pin, making sure to catch the zipper tape underneath.

13. Open the zipper.

14. Using a zipper foot, machine stitch the zipper to the back section of the pillow. Sew from the finished side of the fabric ½ inch from the fold. Remove the pins. Press.

Pleats for elegant folds

Pleats have a happy faculty of adding surface interest and dimensional depth to fabrics; sometimes they do both at once. They anchor graceful folds in full draperies and give a decorative finish to slipcovers. The rollback pleat at left releases maximum fullness, while the cartridge pleat economizes on fabric and the box pleat has a full but tailored look.

How pleats are made depends partly on their use. Slipcover pleats are folded, then anchored with a line of stitching across the top; drapery pleats begin with a short vertical seam through the heading to secure the material for the pleat allowance, then are folded and tacked in place.

Sewing the Pleat Allowance Seam

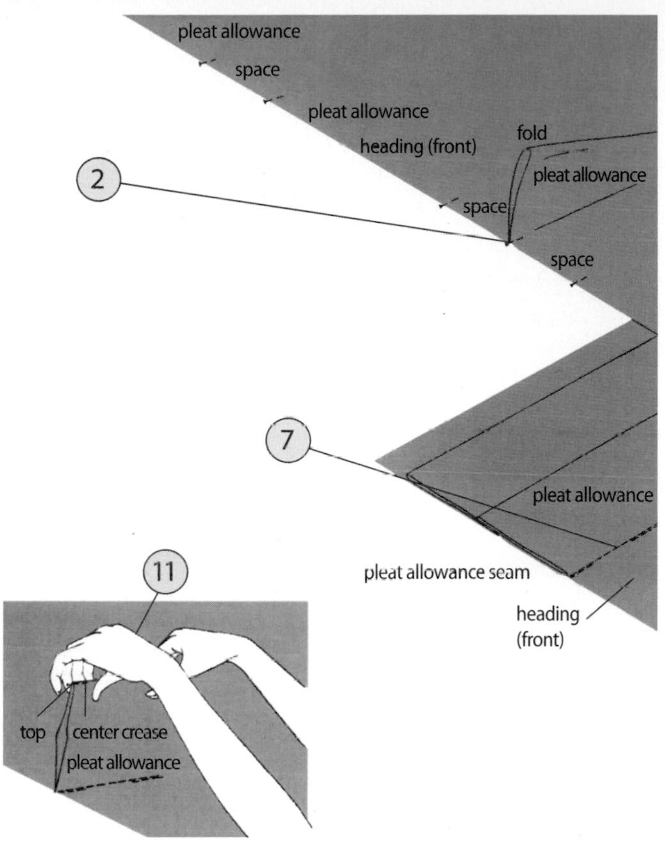

1. Plot and mark off the pleats with pins, then match the pins that designate one pleat, folding the pleat allowance in half.

2. Secure the pleat allowance by eliminating one pin and inserting the other through both layers of heading.

3. Repeat Steps 1 and 2 on each of the remaining pleat allowances.

4. When all of the pleat allowances have been folded and pinned, measure the width of the heading to make sure it is the exact size you intended. Adjust the size of some or all of the pleats, if necessary.

5. Measure the distance from one pleat allowance fold to the pin holding the allowance in place.

6. Measure off an equal distance at the base of the heading and insert a second pin directly below the first.

7. Machine stitch between the pins from about ¼ inch above the base of the heading to the top of the drapery, backstitching at both ends.

8. Repeat Steps 5–7 on each of the remaining pleat allowances.

Folding the Pleat

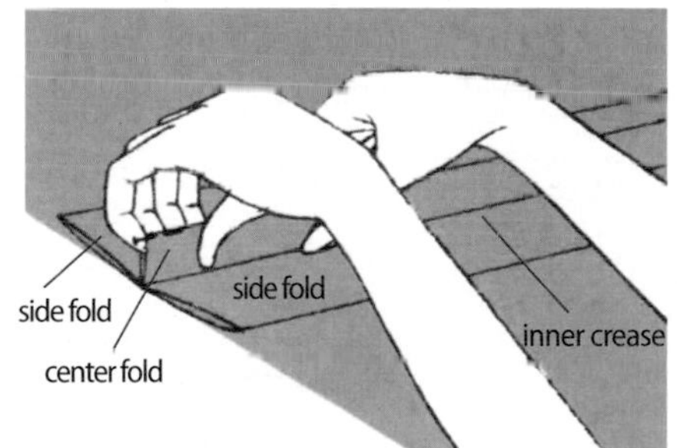

9. Thread a needle with a double strand of heavy-duty thread, and make a knot at the end.

10. Form a crease lengthwise along the fold of one pleat allowance by pressing with your fingers. Mark the top of the crease with a pin.

11. Grasp the pleat allowance with both hands approximately one fifth of the way down from the center crease.

12. Push down on the pleat allowance to form three folds. Each side fold should be twice as deep as the center fold. Be sure the inner creases align with the pleat allowance seam.

13. Pinch the folds together at their outer creases to be certain the side folds are equal. Then remove the marking pin and press in all the creases.

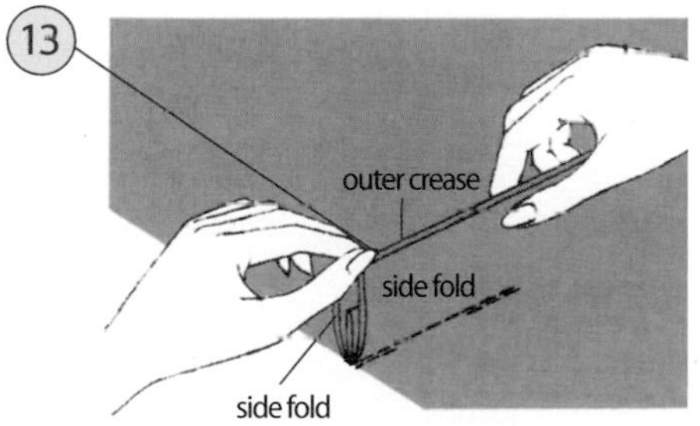

The Rollback Pleat

Tacking the Bottom of the Pleat

14. With your left hand, grasp the pleat ½ inch above its base and insert the threaded needle through all three folds ½ inch above their bases, making sure to catch the smaller center fold.

15. Make several tacking stitches through all three folds.

16. Insert the needle through the first fold at the tack, and then bring the needle back out at the pleat allowance seam.

17. Insert the needle ¼ inch below the outer crease of the first fold directly above the tack. Bring the needle out at the crease.

18. Pull the thread to roll the base of the first fold back so that its outer crease aligns with the pleat allowance seam.

19. Make several fastening stitches, attaching the crease to the pleat allowance seam.

20. Insert the needle through the pleat allowance seam, and repeat Steps 17–19 on the other side fold.

21. Push the needle to the back of the heading, and finish the thread with a fastening stitch over the pleat allowance seam.

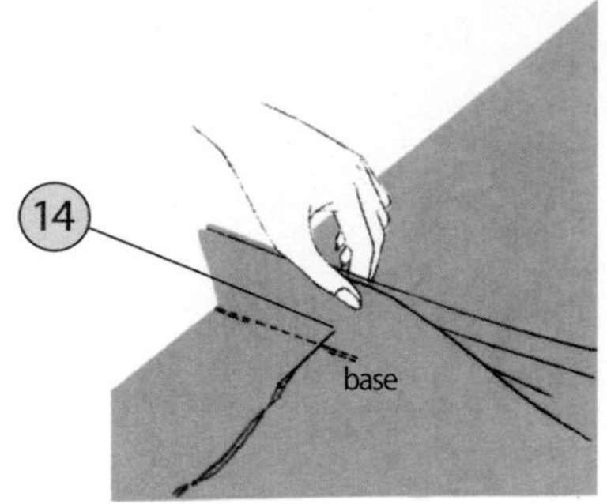

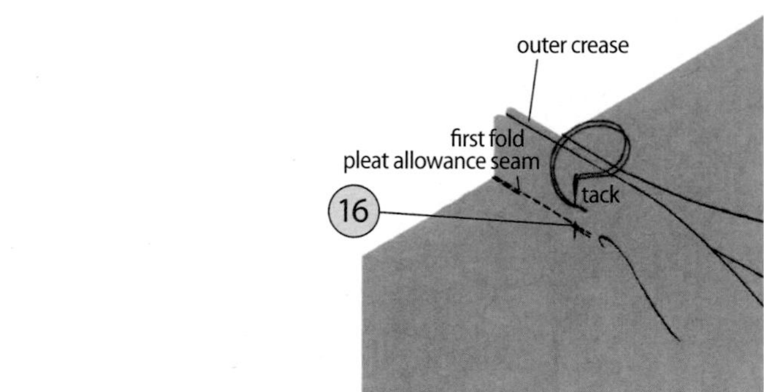

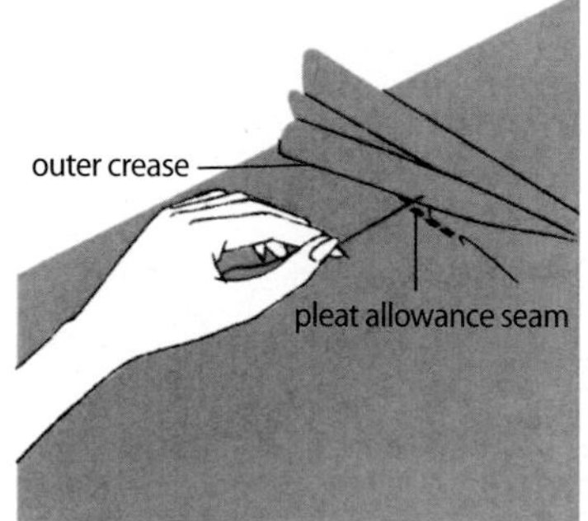

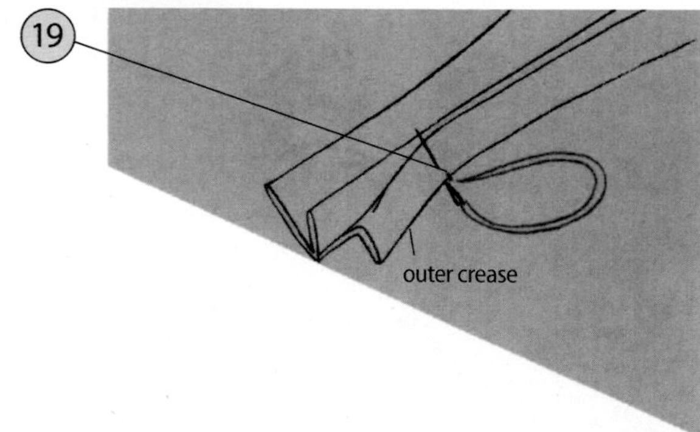

The Rollback Pleat

Tacking the Top of the Pleat

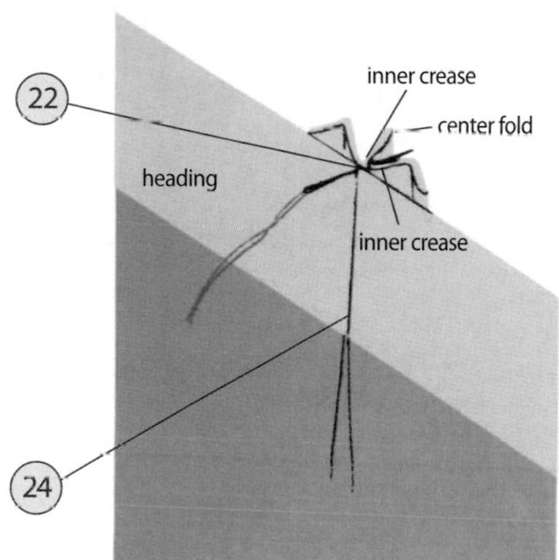

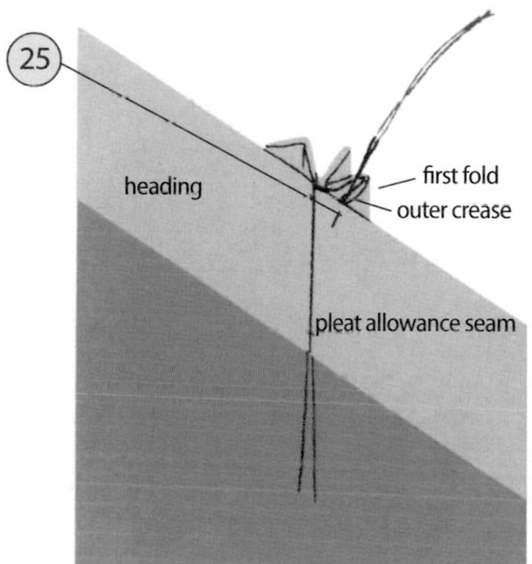

22. Knot the thread again. Insert the needle through the back of the pleat allowance seam 1⁄16 inch below the top of the heading. Catch the inner crease between the center fold and one of the side folds.

23. Make several tacking stitches, allowing a 1⁄4-inch shank between the crease and the pleat allowance seam. Then repeat on the other inner crease.

24. Finish the thread with a fastening stitch over the back of the pleat allowance seam.

25. Knot the thread again. Insert the needle from inside the outer crease of the first fold 1⁄16 inch below the top edge of the heading.

26. Attach the outer crease to the heading 1⁄2 inch from the pleat allowance seam by making several tacking stitches over the top edge of the heading.

27. Make a fastening stitch on the back of the heading to finish the thread.

28. Repeat Steps 25–27 on the other side fold.

29. Repeat Steps 9–28 on each of the remaining pleat allowances.

The Three-Fold Pinch Pleat

Folding the Pleat

1. Plot and mark off the pleats with pins and stitch the pleat allowance seams according to the instructions in Steps 1–8 of the rollback pleat.

2. Thread a needle with a double strand of heavy-duty thread, and make a knot at the end.

3. Form a crease lengthwise along one pleat allowance and mark the top of the crease with a pin.

4. Grasp the pleat allowance with both hands approximately one third of the way down from the center crease.

5. Push down on the pleat allowance to form three folds. Be sure the inner creases align with the pleat allowance seam.

6. Pinch the folds together at their outer creases to be certain they are equal. Then remove the marking pin and press in the creases with your fingers.

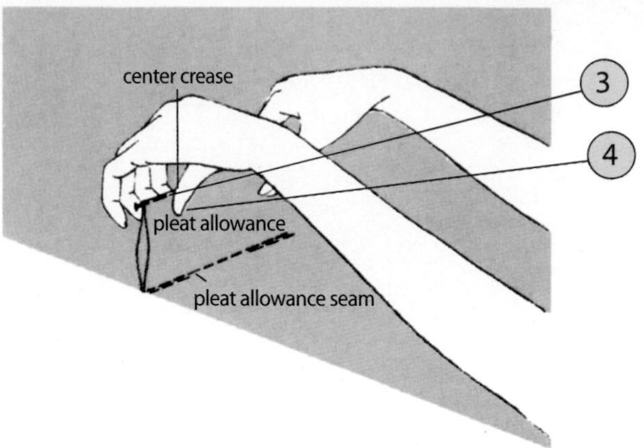

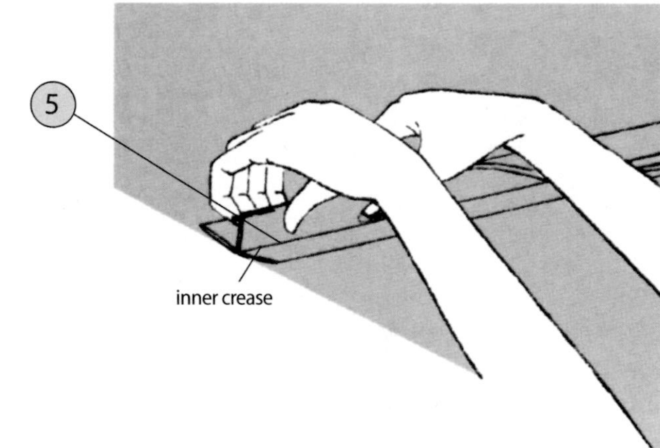

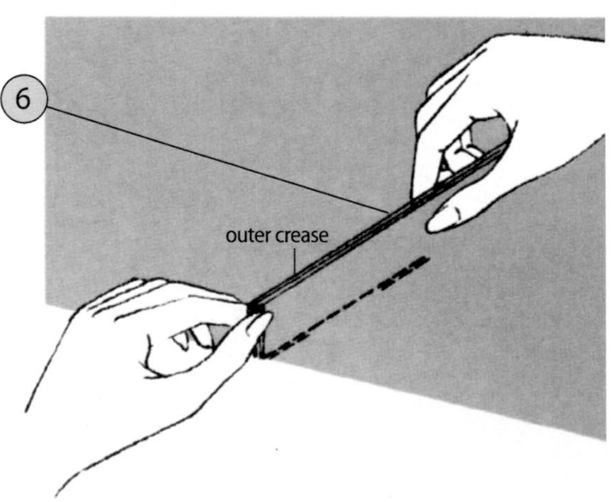

The Three-Fold Pinch Pleat

Tacking the Pleat

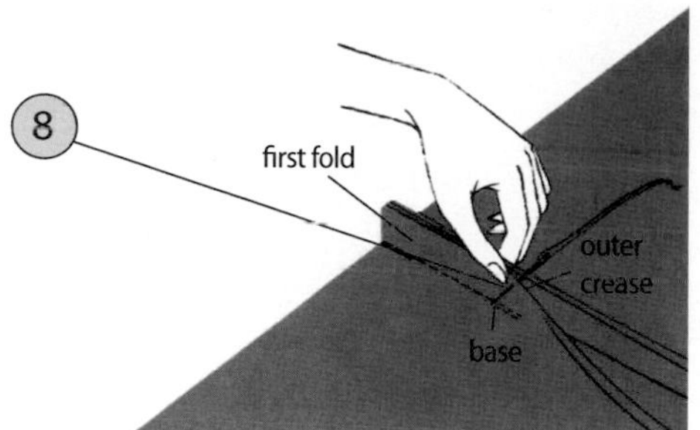

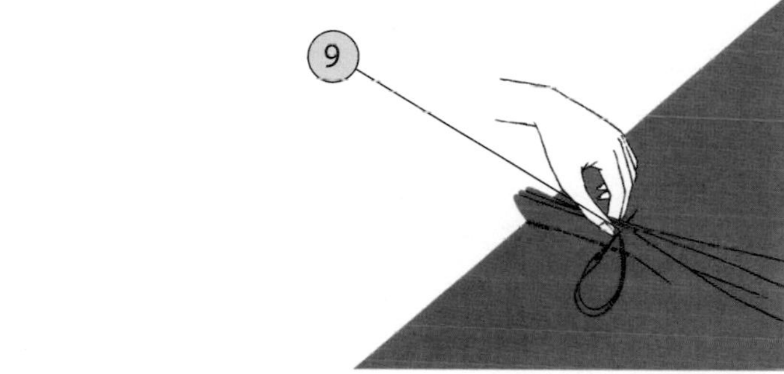

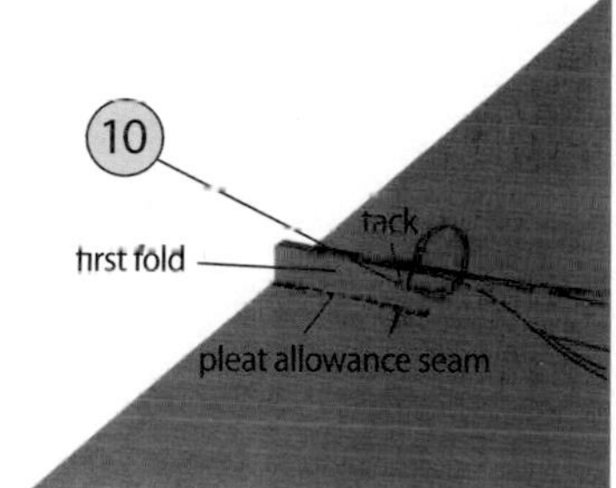

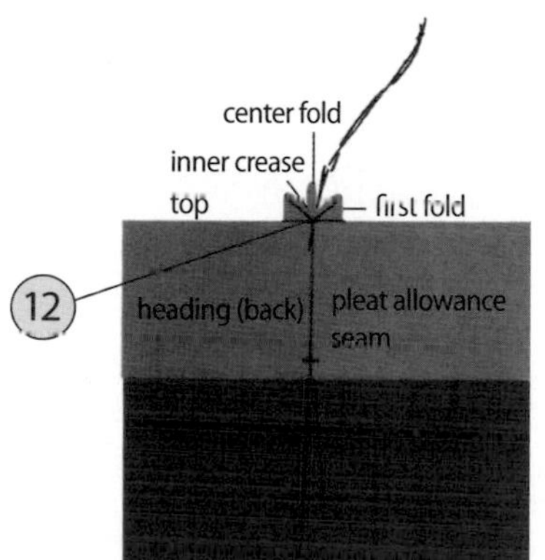

7. With your left hand, grasp the pleat ½ inch above its base.

8. Insert the threaded needle from the inside of the pleat through the first fold ¼ inch below its outer crease.

9. Make several tacking stitches through all three folds.

10. Insert the needle into the first fold at the tack and bring the needle out at the pleat allowance seam. Then tack again at the seam, catching both inner creases.

11. Push the needle to the back of the heading; finish with a fastening stitch over the pleat allowance seam.

12. Knot the thread again. With the back of the pleat facing you, insert the needle into the inner crease between the first and center folds 1/16 inch below the top of the heading. Bring the needle out at the seam.

13. Attach the crease to the seam with tacking stitches.

14. Tack the other inner crease in the same manner.

15. To finish the thread, make a fastening stitch over the seam at the back of the pleat.

16. Repeat Steps 2–15 on each of the remaining pleat allowances.

The Four-Fold Pinch Pleat

1. Plot and mark off the pleats with pins *(pages 62–63)* and stitch the pleat allowance seams according to the instructions in Steps 1–8 of the rollback pleat.

2. Thread a needle with a double strand of heavy-duty thread, and make a knot at the end.

3. Form a crease lengthwise along the center of one pleat allowance, and mark it with a pin.

4. Flatten the pleat so that the pin inserted in Step 3 aligns with the pleat allowance seam.

5. Mark the creases formed at the sides with pins.

6. Form two pleats on each side of the center pin by aligning each of the side pins with the center one. Be sure the inner creases align with the pleat allowance seam.

7. Finish the pleat by following the procedure in Steps 6–15 of the three-fold pinch pleat.

8. Repeat Steps 2–7 on each of the remaining pleat allowances.

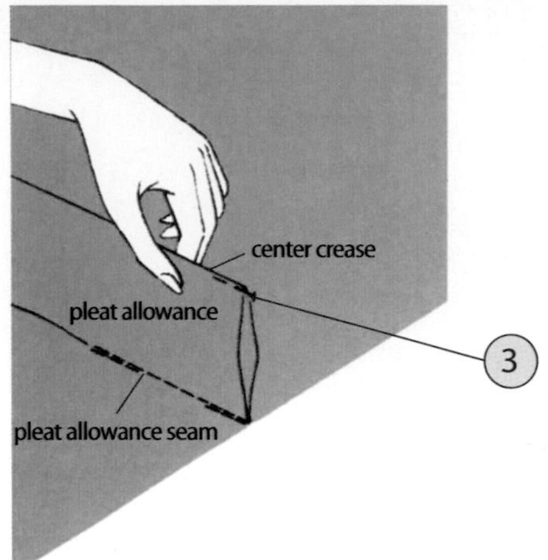

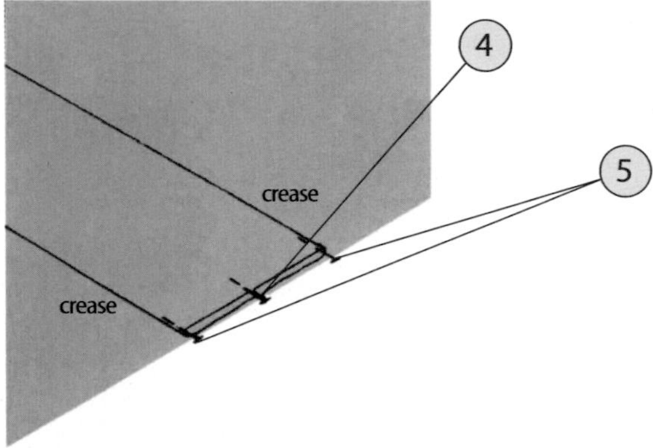

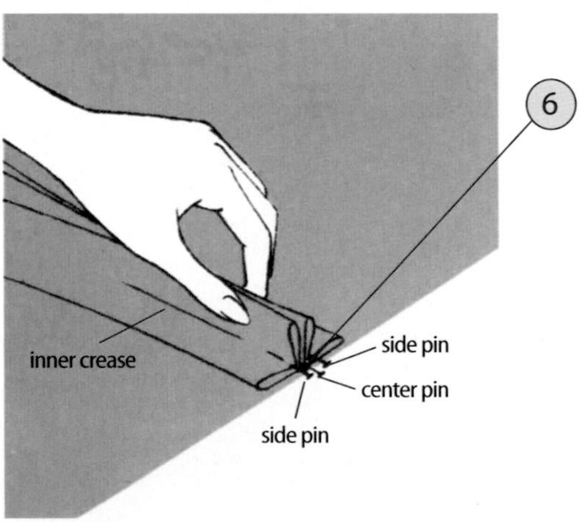

The Box Pleat for Draperies

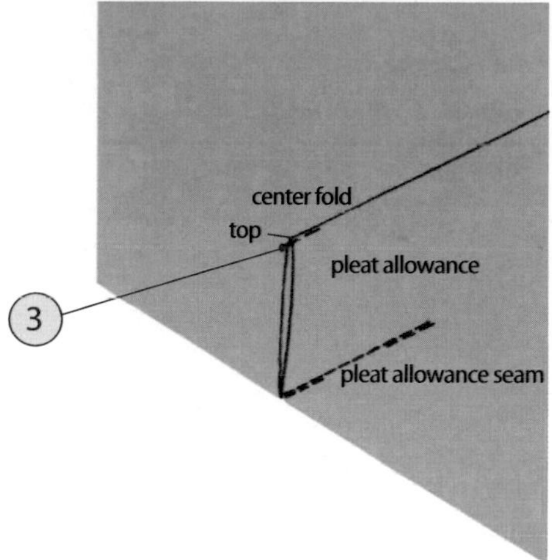

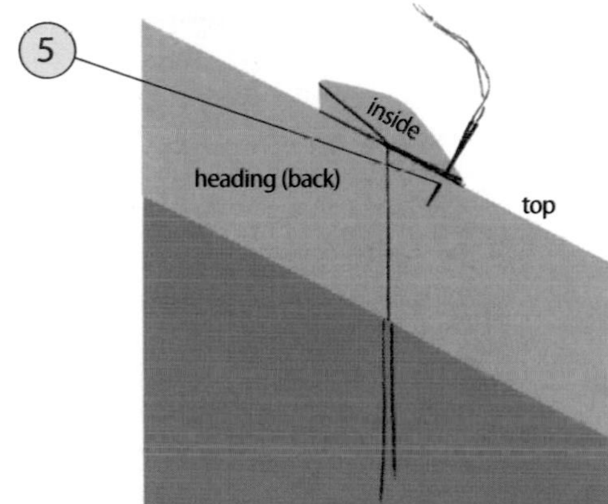

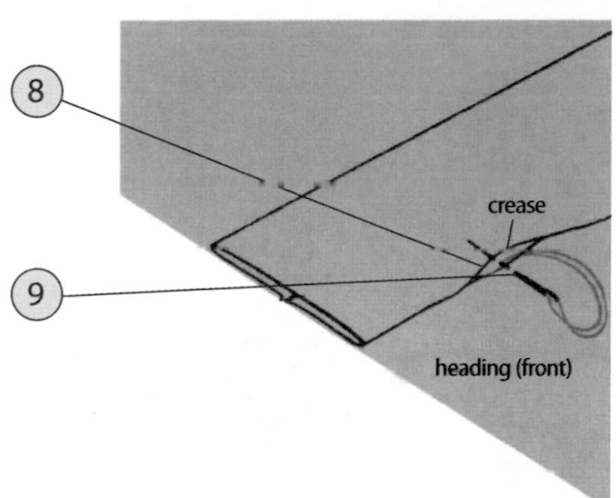

1. Plot and mark off the pleats with pins *(pages 62–63)* and stitch the pleat allowance seams according to the instructions in Steps 1–8 of the rollback pleat.

2. Thread a needle with a double strand of heavy-duty thread, and make a knot at the end.

3. Mark the top of one folded pleat allowance with a pin.

4. Flatten the pleat so that the pin aligns with the pleat allowance seam. Then, with your fingers, press in the creases formed at the sides. Remove the marking pin.

5. With the back of the heading facing you, insert the needle through the inside of the pleat about 1/16 inch below the top edge and 1/4 inch from one of the side creases. Bring the needle out at the back.

6. Make several tacking stitches about 1/16 inch below the top of the heading, then finish the thread on the back of the heading with several fastening stitches.

7. Knot the thread again and repeat Steps 5 and 6 on the other side of the pleat.

8. If you want the pleat to lie flatter, fold back the side crease near the base of the heading.

9. Make several fastening stitches through the back and inner layers of the pleat 1/4 inch above the base of the heading and 1/4 inch from the side crease. Then repeat on the other side.

10. Repeat Steps 2–9 on each of the remaining pleat allowances.

The Double Box Pleat

1. Plot and mark off the pleats with pins *(pages 62–63)* and stitch the pleat allowance seams according to the instructions in Steps 1–8 of the rollback pleat.

2. Mark the top of one folded pleat allowance with a pin. Measure from this pin to the pleat allowance seam. Then divide that figure in half and add ¼ inch.

3. Measure off the distance figured in Step 2 from the seam toward the top of the fold and insert a pin at this point.

4. Machine stitch the same length as the pleat allowance seam and parallel to it at the distance marked off in Step 3. Remove the pin.

5. Thread a needle with a double strand of heavy-duty thread, and make a knot at the end.

6. Push down on the pleat allowance to form three folds, aligning the seam made in Step 4 with the pleat allowance seam. With your fingers, press the creases of the two side folds.

7. Flatten the remainder of the pleat allowance so that the pin inserted in Step 2 aligns with the seam made in Step 4. Again, press in creases with your fingers.

8. Tack the top of the pleats, following the procedure in Steps 5–7 of the box pleat for draperies, but tacking through both pleats at once.

9. Tack the bottom of the pleats as shown in Steps 8 and 9 of the box pleat for draperies, again tacking through both pleats at once.

10. Repeat Steps 2–9 on each of the remaining pleat allowances.

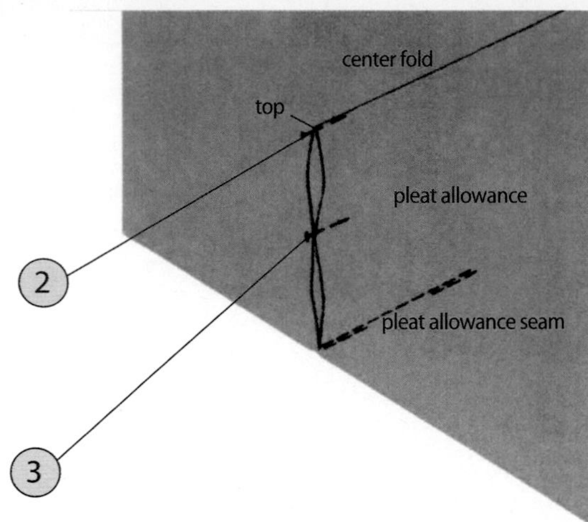

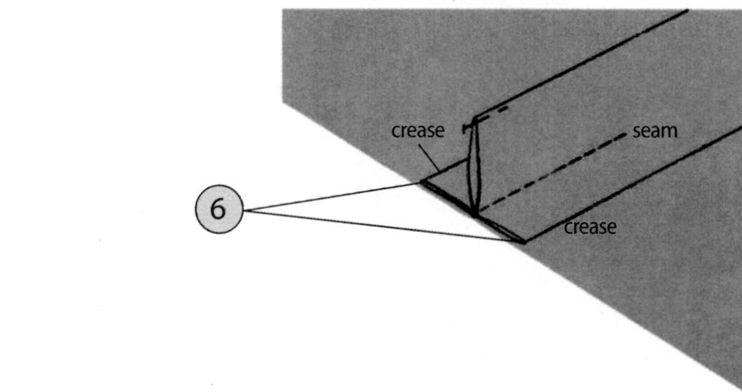

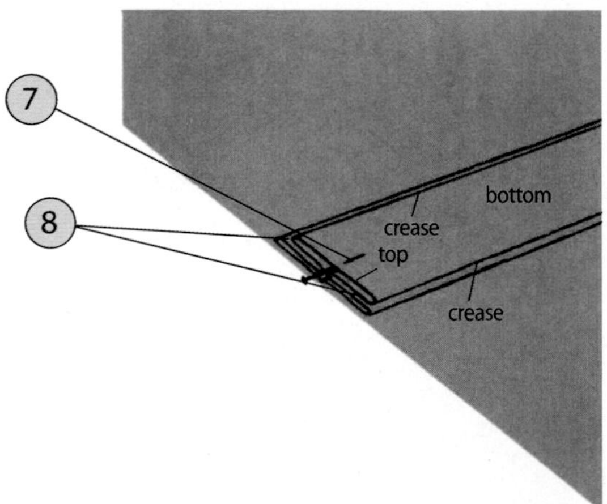

The Box Pleat for Furniture Skirts

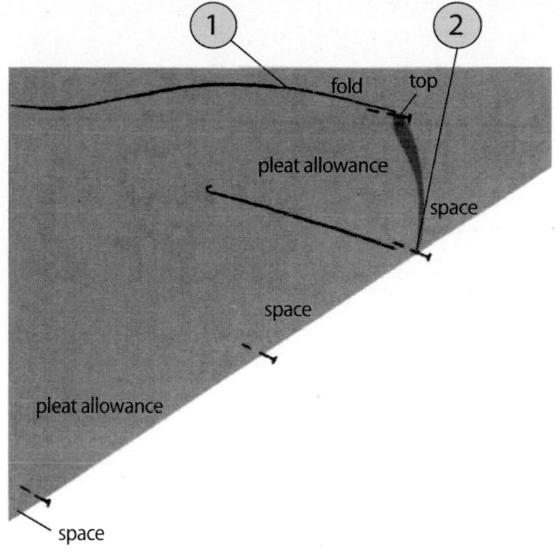

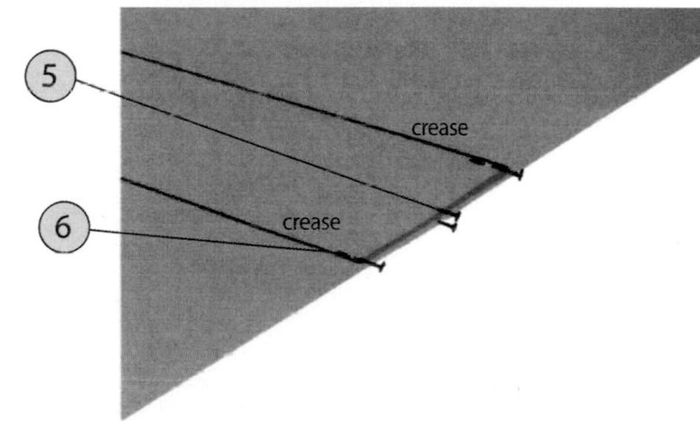

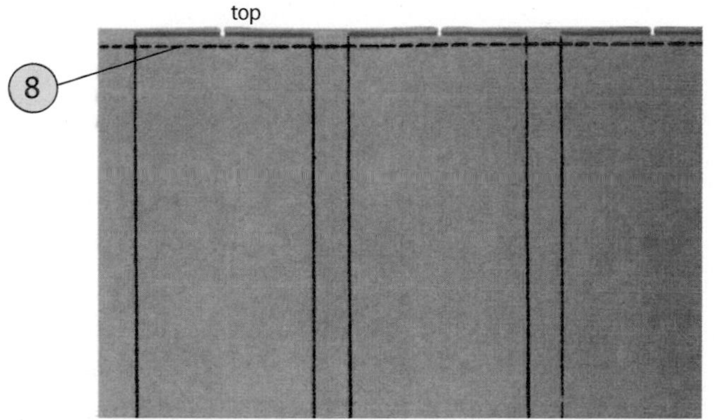

1. Plot and mark off the pleats with pins *(pages 62–63)*. Then match the pins that designate one pleat, folding the pleat allowance in half.

2. Secure the pleat allowance by eliminating one pin and inserting the other through both layers of the pleat.

3. Repeat Steps 1 and 2 on each of the remaining pleat allowances. When all of the pleat allowances have been folded and pinned, measure the width of the top edge of the fabric to make sure it is the exact size you intended. Adjust the size of some or all of the pleats, if necessary, to achieve the desired width.

4. Insert a pin at the top of one folded pleat allowance.

5. Flatten the pleat so that the two pins align with one another.

6. With your fingers, press in the creases formed at the sides. Then pin the creases flat against the fabric behind the pleat.

7. Repeat Steps 4–6 on each of the remaining pleat allowances.

8. Machine stitch ⅜ inch from the top edge of the fabric, removing the pins as you go.

Photograph courtesy of Calico Corners—*Calico Home*

Curtains and Drapes

3

More than Window Dressing

Gleaming glass in a bare window should be as exciting to the home decorator as an empty canvas is to a painter. Imaginative window treatments can set the crowning touch of elegance or informality to a room and make it a lasting pleasure.

Draperies and curtains are particularly suited to home sewing. Long lines of straight machine stitching make the work go fast, and the detailing described in this chapter and throughout the book ensures the custom finish that store-bought draperies lack. In addition, the home seamstress can make exact allowances for the inconsistencies in the size of individual windows; even the pile on the carpet will make a difference in the final length.

As well as decorating a room, window treatments have to perform specific functions that may be contradictory. Windows let in light that can sometimes be too much of a good thing; they look out upon a view that can either delight or depress; and at night they turn into black holes through which the outside world can look in. To cope with these contradictories, a variety of window coverings have been invented. Draperies, curtains, blinds, and shades regulate light in varying degrees and can be combined to satisfy fluctuating needs for privacy. For a living-room window with a spectacular view, simple draperies alone may suffice. But if the window faces south, the midday sun may have to be diffused with an additional curtain of transparent material, or blocked with a shade or blind.

Draperies are classic window treatments that work with any decorating style. Whatever you choose—drapery panels in slubby linen with banding, striped silk draperies with a tab top, pinch pleated draperies in a bold print fabric, or grommet draperies in a trendy new sheer—custom draperies are an elegant solution.

In a bedroom, where privacy is apt to be a major concern, transparent curtains and opaque draperies are frequently combined. An alternative to this arrangement are café curtains made of an opaque fabric; when made in tiers, they permit the top to be opened for light while the bottom remains closed for privacy. And the daytime darkness required by people who want to sleep late calls for draperies that are lined or interlined with black fabric—a substitute for blackout curtains.

Although lining takes extra work, it adds durability, reduces fading and makes the draperies hang better. It helps to insulate a room against cold, especially at night, and its extra folds will soak up a lot of sound—a boon for city dwellers. When draperies in different rooms are lined with the same fabric, the exterior view of the house is unified.

Inside the house, a drapery or curtain can help the home seamstress to disguise an ill-proportioned room, or the ungainly shape of windows that are too narrow or short. The vertical line of a floor-length drapery can make a low-ceilinged room look more spacious, while draperies that are carried across adjacent windows can make the two windows read as one and unify a wall.

Photograph courtesy of Calico Corners—*Calico Home*

Window shades are often the simplest solution for window treatments and include roman shades, balloon shades, London shades, and more.

Finally, there is the role that a window treatment plays in helping to establish the character and style of a room. Café curtains are informal; full-length curtains are formal. The soft fullness of a shirred heading complements period furnishings, while the crisp line of a box-pleat heading is ideal for a room furnished in contemporary style. Austrian shades are inherently feminine in feeling; Roman shades are tailored and masculine. Furthermore, the fabrics in which these window treatments are executed will also affect the overall look of a room.

Calculations for draperies and curtains

Whatever type of window you are curtaining—casement, double-hung sash, sliding or fixed; single or multiple; flush with a wall or set in a dormer or bay—first mount the rod that you plan to use. Then make the window measurements as described below, and, with these measurements, estimate the total yardage for the materials you will need by the formulas given in the chart at right.

Separate formulas are given for drapery and curtain fabric, lining, and stiffening. Insert the measurements that are called for, as identified by the letters, and then perform in sequence the necessary mathematical operations that are indicated by the standard symbols.

If you are using fabric that has a pattern, you will also need the repeat measurement. To determine this dimension, measure lengthwise from the center of one prominent design detail in the fabric to the center of the next identical design detail.

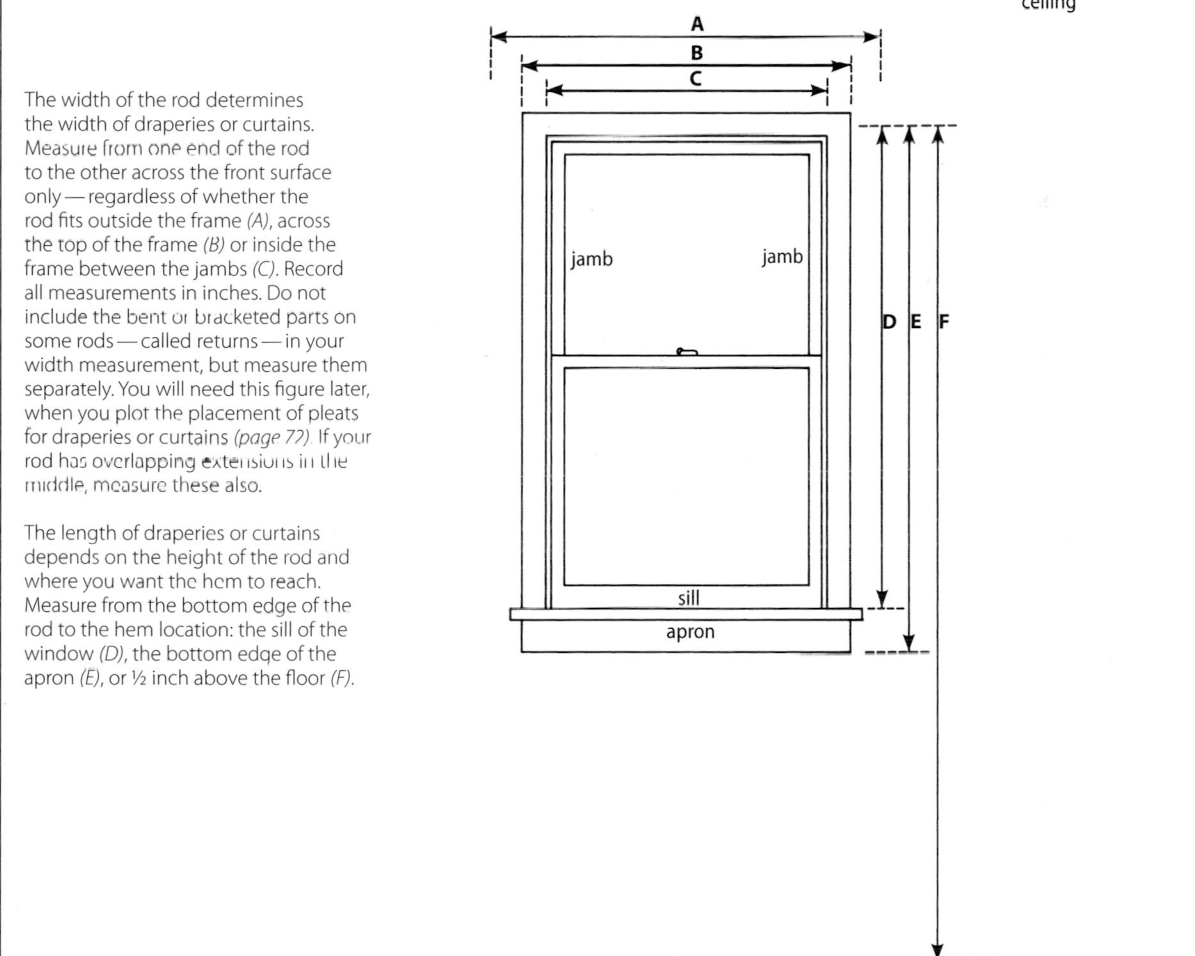

The width of the rod determines the width of draperies or curtains. Measure from one end of the rod to the other across the front surface only — regardless of whether the rod fits outside the frame *(A)*, across the top of the frame *(B)* or inside the frame between the jambs *(C)*. Record all measurements in inches. Do not include the bent or bracketed parts on some rods — called returns — in your width measurement, but measure them separately. You will need this figure later, when you plot the placement of pleats for draperies or curtains *(page 72)*. If your rod has overlapping extensions in the middle, measure these also.

The length of draperies or curtains depends on the height of the rod and where you want the hem to reach. Measure from the bottom edge of the rod to the hem location: the sill of the window *(D)*, the bottom edge of the apron *(E)*, or ½ inch above the floor *(F)*.

Estimating Materials

Drapery and Curtain Fabric

Width	For pleats 7 inches wide or less	Number of fabric widths required for a pair of panels = **A, B, or C × 2½ ÷ Fabric Width in Inches***
	For pleats more than 7 inches wide	Number of fabric widths required for a pair of panels = **A, B, or C × 3 ÷ Fabric Width in Inches***
	For very light or sheer fabric	Number of fabric widths required for a pair of panels = **A, B, or C × 3 ÷ Fabric Width in Inches***
Length	For fabrics that do not require matching a pattern	Length of each panel in inches = **D, E, or F + 18**
	For fabrics that require matching a pattern	Length of each panel in inches = **D, E, or F + 18 + Length of Pattern Repeat in Inches**
Yardage	Total yardage required = **Number of Widths × Length of Each Panel in Inches ÷ 36**	

Lining Fabric

Width	For pleats 7 inches wide or less	Number of fabric widths required for a pair of panels = **A, B, or C × 2½ ÷ Fabric Width in Inches***
	For pleats of more than 7 inches	Number of fabric widths required for a pair of panels = **A, B, or C × 2½ ÷ Fabric Width in Inches***
Length	For all lining fabrics	Length of each panel in inches = **D, E, or F + 4**
Yardage	Total yardage required = **Number of Fabric Widths × Length of Each Panel in Inches ÷ 36**	

Stiffening for Heading

Width	For pleats 7 inches wide or less	Total length required in inches = **A, B, or C × 2½ + 3****
	For pleats more than 7 inches wide	Total length required in inches = **A, B, or C × 3 + 3****
	For very light or sheer fabric	Total length required in inches = **A, B, or C × 3 + 3****
Depth	For D or E length draperies and curtains	Total depth required equals 3 inches.
	For F length draperies and curtains	Total depth required equals 4 inches.

*Round off fractions to the nearest full width.

**Round off fractions to the next highest inch.

Cutting and Preparing the Fabric

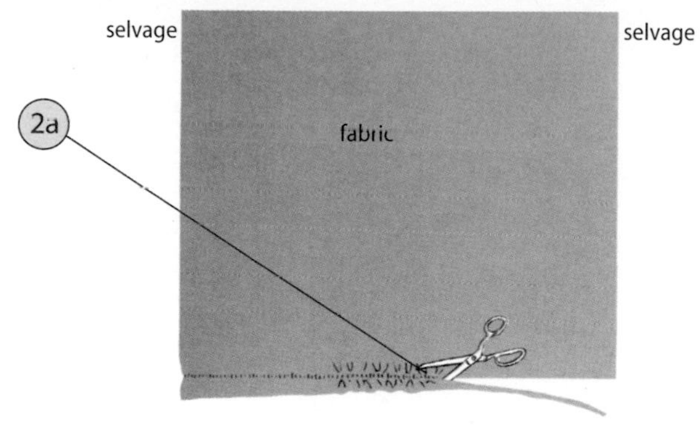

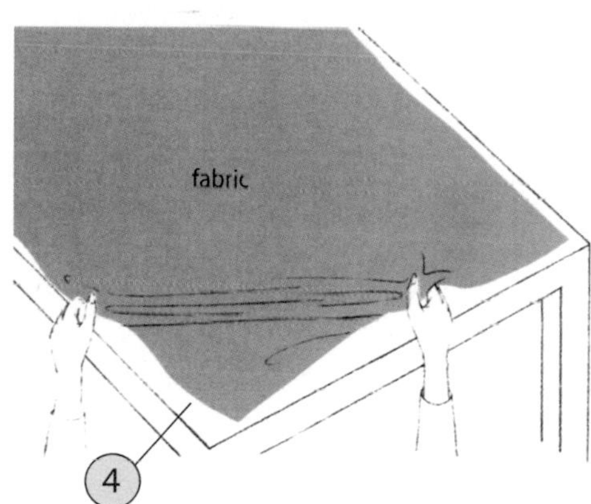

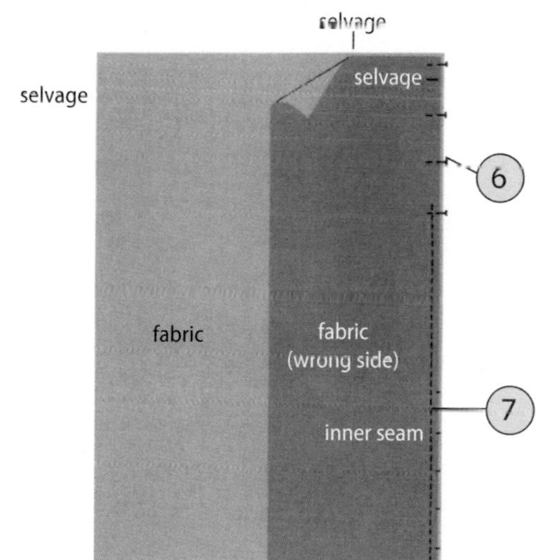

1. Place the fabric, wrong side down, on a large table.

2a. For fabrics that are not glazed or permanently finished, straighten one edge by drawing a crosswise thread. Cut along the thread.

2b. For glazed or permanently finished fabrics, draw a chalk line at right angles to the selvages and cut along the chalk line.

3a. For fabric that does not require matching a pattern, use the panel length measurement determined by the formula on page 72 to mark and cut off as many sections as you need. Make all cuts along crosswise threads or chalk lines.

3b. For fabric with a pronounced pattern, cut off a section equal to the panel length as determined by the formula on page 72. Examine fabric and window to decide where pattern repeats should fall, then trim the section on crosswise threads or chalk lines.

4. Align two adjacent sides of a section to a right-angled corner of a table. If the edges do not align properly, gently pull on the true bias of the fabric until its sides are at right angles, then steam-press. Repeat on the other sections.

5. If you need to divide one fabric section into two half widths, fold the section lengthwise down the center and cut it along the fold.

6. To make a panel out of more than one section of fabric, place one piece on top of the other wrong sides out if the fabric is opaque, but wrong sides together if the fabric is sheer. Match the pattern at the selvage, if necessary, then pin. Repeat for each additional section of fabric required.

7. Machine stitch along the inner edge of the selvages. Make a plain seam for lined draperies, an interlocking fell seam for unlined draperies and opaque curtains, a French seam for sheer curtains. Clip into untrimmed selvages at regular intervals to prevent the seams from puckering.

8. Join the second panel of the pair similarly.

Making Draperies and Curtains

Pressing Hem and Heading Creases

9. Place one drapery or curtain panel wrong side up, and press any inner seam. (If it is a plain seam, press it open.)

10. To form a double bottom hem, first turn up the bottom edge 4 inches if the draperies or curtains are floor length, 3 inches if they are sill or apron length. Crease along the fold by hand. Then turn the creased hem up another 3 or 4 inches and crease again. Baste along the top fold. (The hem will be finished after the panel is hung.)

11. Turn the side hem 1 inch, then press. Turn the fold another 1 inch to form a double hem, then press again.

12. Turn the center hem 1½ inches, then press. Turn the center hem another 1½ inches and press.

13. To crease the top edge of the panel, measure the length for the finished drapery or curtain *(page 86)* from the lower edge of the bottom hem, and mark this distance by inserting a pin on both sides of the panel.

14. If your drapery or curtain will hang below the rod, turn down the top edge at the pin marking, then press. If your drapery or curtain will hang in front of the rod to hide it, turn down the top edge the depth of your rod plus ¼ inch above the pin marking, then press. Remove the pins.

15. Repeat Steps 9–14 on the second panel of the pair. If you are making lined draperies, skip to Step 27.

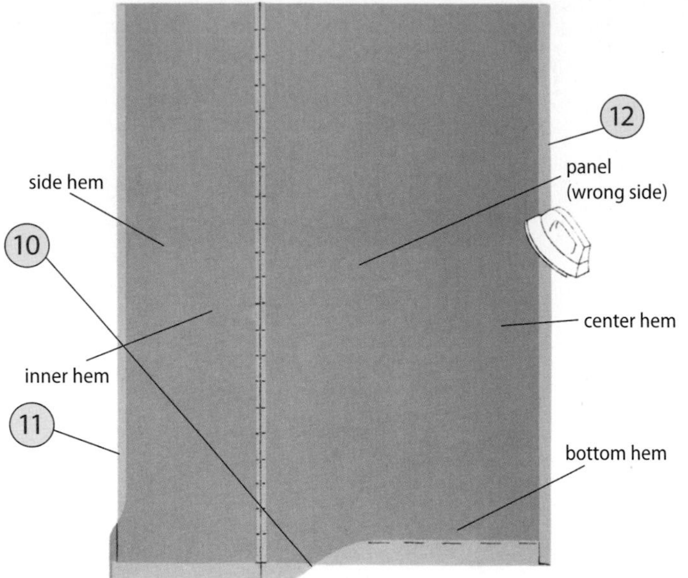

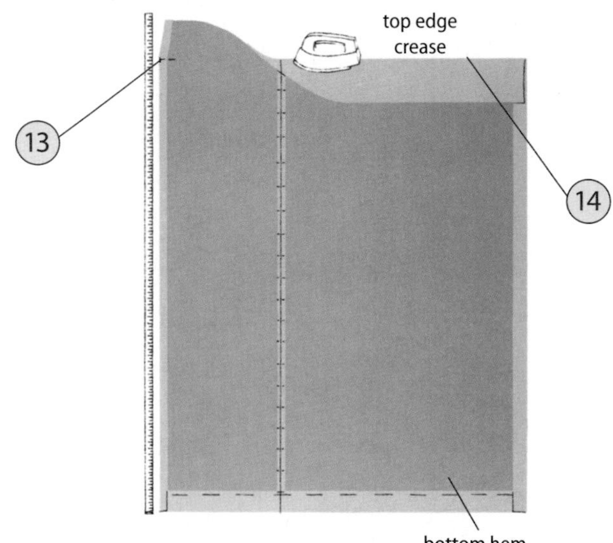

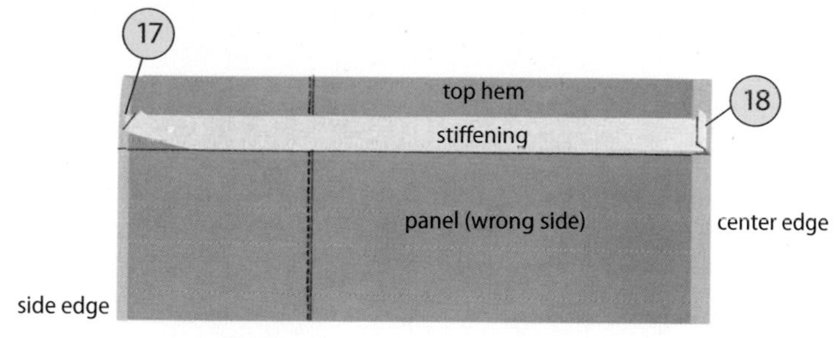

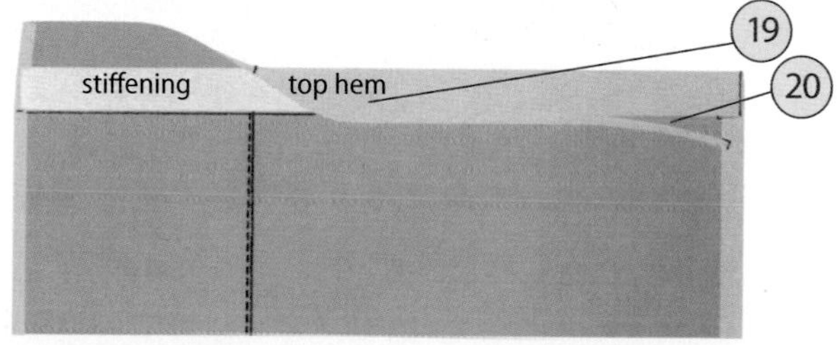

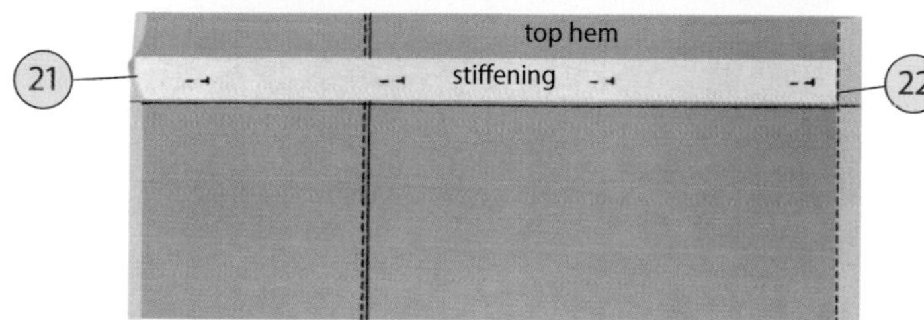

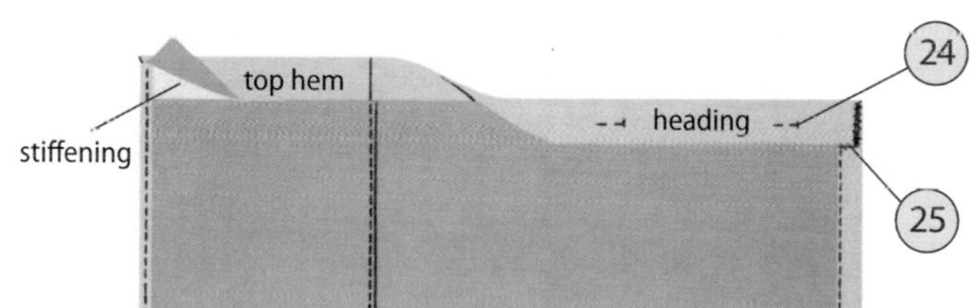

16. If you plan to pleat the draperies or curtains, cut the stiffening 1½ inches longer than the width of the panel from the side edge to the center edge.

17. Place the stiffening just above the heading crease made in Step 14, aligning one end with the side edge of the panel.

18. Turn the 1½ inches of excess stiffening at the center edge and press.

19. Fold the top hem over the stiffening and press.

20. Cut off any excess fabric below the stiffening.

21. Unfold the top hem and tuck the stiffening ends under the folded hems at both sides of the panel. Pin the stiffening in place.

22. Machine or hand stitch, using the slip stitch, along the side and the center hems from the top edge to within 2 inches of the bottom hem. Remove the pins inserted in Step 21.

23. Turn the top hem over the stiffening to cover it.

24. Turn over the covered stiffening and pin.

25. Finish the sides of the heading along the hemmed edges on both sides of the panel with the hemming stitch or slip stitch. Remove the pins.

26. Repeat Steps 16–25 for the second panel of the pair.

Making Draperies and Curtains

Cutting and Preparing Lining

27. Cut lining fabric following the instructions in Steps 2–5.

28. To join sections of lining, if necessary, place one piece on top of the other, wrong sides out, then pin. Repeat for each additional section required. Machine stitch ½ inch from the selvages and clip into the selvages at regular intervals to prevent the seams from puckering. Press the seams open.

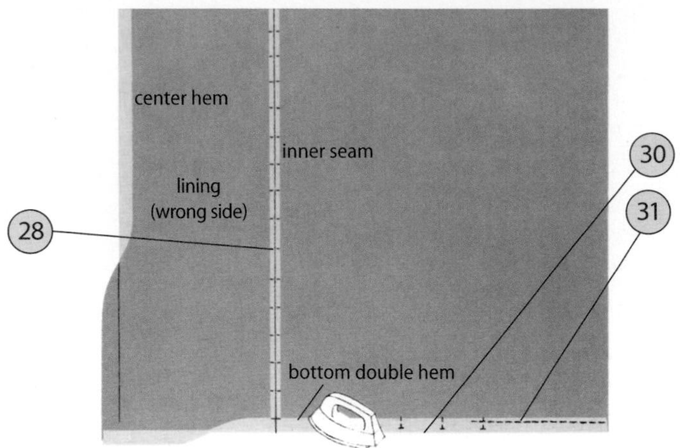

29. Turn up the bottom edge of the fabric 1¾ inches to start a double hem. Press.

30. Turn the pressed hem up another 1¾ inches and press again. Pin.

31. Machine stitch close to the top edge of the double hem, removing the pins as you sew.

32. Turn up the edge that will be on the center of the window 1½ inches to form a single hem, then press. Before making the center hem, turn the lining around—if necessary—so that any inner seam on the lining does not overlap an inner seam on the drapery.

33. Repeat Steps 28–32 for the second panel of the lining.

Attaching the Lining to the Center Edge Seam

34. Place the fabric panel, wrong side down, on a flat surface.

35. Position the lining, wrong side up, 1½ inches above the bottom hem of the panel.

36. Unfold the center hems of both the lining and drapery fabrics and align the edges. Pin.

37. Turn the excess lining fabric at the top down so that the fold aligns with the heading crease line made in Step 14. Pin.

38. Machine stitch the lining to the drapery along the center edge crease line of the lining to within 3 inches of the stitching of the bottom hem. Remove the pins inserted in Steps 36 and 37.

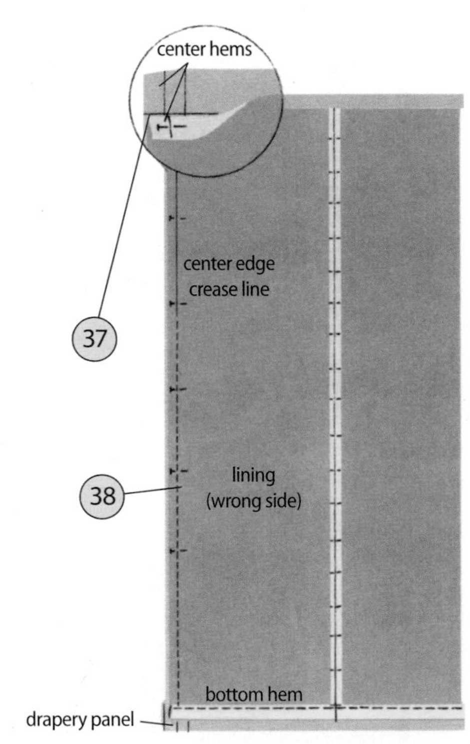

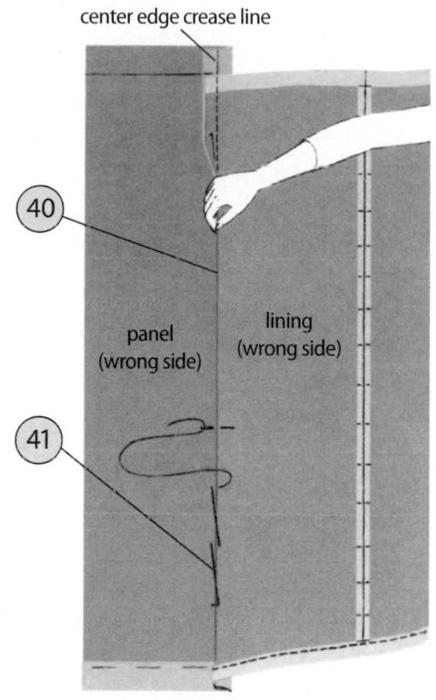

39. Spread the joined pieces out on a flat surface, wrong sides up.

40. Fold both center edge seam allowances along the stitches made in Step 38 and tuck them under so that the edges are flush against the remaining center crease on the drapery panel.

41. Tack the folded edge of the lining to the panel with diagonal basting stitches catching as few threads of the panel and the lining as possible in the stitches. Begin sewing 10 inches above the bottom edge—spacing the stitches at 6- to 8-inch intervals—and stop 10 inches below the top edge of the lining.

42. Repeat Steps 34–41 on the second panel of the pair.

Making the Heading for Lined Panels

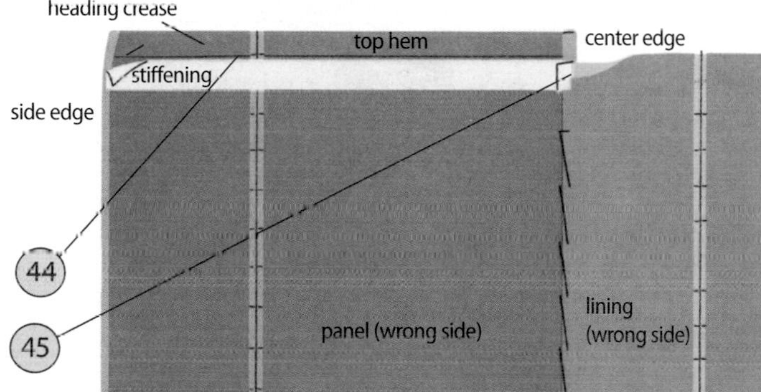

43. Cut stiffening for the heading 1½ inches longer than the width of the panel.

44. Place the stiffening just below the heading crease made in Step 14, aligning one end of the stiffening with the side edge of the panel.

45. Turn the 1½ inches of excess stiffening at the center edge and press it flat.

46. Tuck the stiffening ends under the folded hems at both sides of panel.

47. Fold down the top hem of the panel along the crease, to cover the stiffening. Trim off any excess fabric below the stiffening. Pin.

48. Repeat Steps 43–47 for the second panel of the pair.

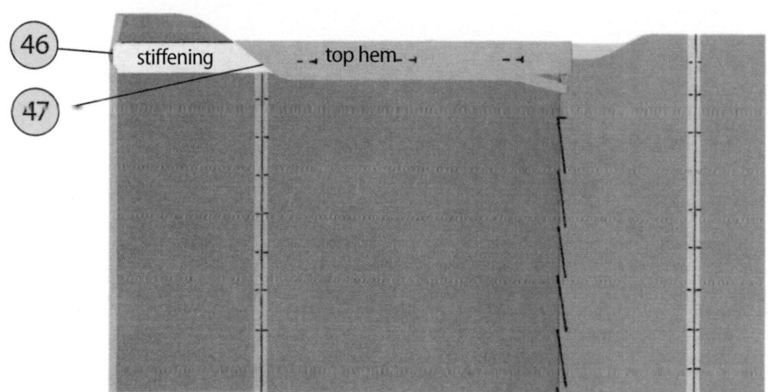

Making Draperies and Curtains

Attaching and Finishing the Lining

49. To attach the lining to the rest of the drapery panel, fold the lining lengthwise to the halfway point on the first full width of fabric in the panel. If there is a lining seam near the fold, fold the lining at the seam.

50. Make a tacking loop 15 inches below the top edge of the drapery as follows: Thread a needle with a single strand of strong thread that matches the color of the drapery fabric. Using the thread unknotted, and at least 15 inches long, insert the needle into the back of the drapery fabric, catching as few threads of fabric as possible. Then take a tiny stitch through the back of the lining fabric. Remove the needle and tie the thread ends into a knot.

51. Make several more tacking loops down the panel, spacing them 12 inches to 18 inches apart.

52. Fold the lining vertically again along the inner seam (if any) of the drapery fabric and repeat Steps 50 and 51. If there are additional widths of fabric, tack them similarly in the centers and at the inner seams.

53. Fold under the top edge of the lining to about ¼ inch below the top of the drapery. Pin.

54. Baste along the top edge with large stitches. Remove the pins.

55. Fold under the side edge of the lining to within about ½ inch of the edge of the drapery. Using the slip stitch or the hemming stitch, hand sew along the fold of the lining to within 2 inches of the drapery hem. Remove the pins. Press.

56. Repeat Steps 49–55 for the second panel of the pair.

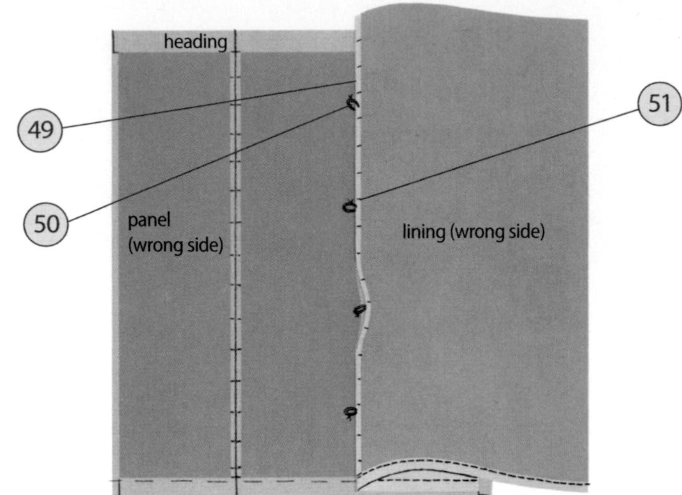

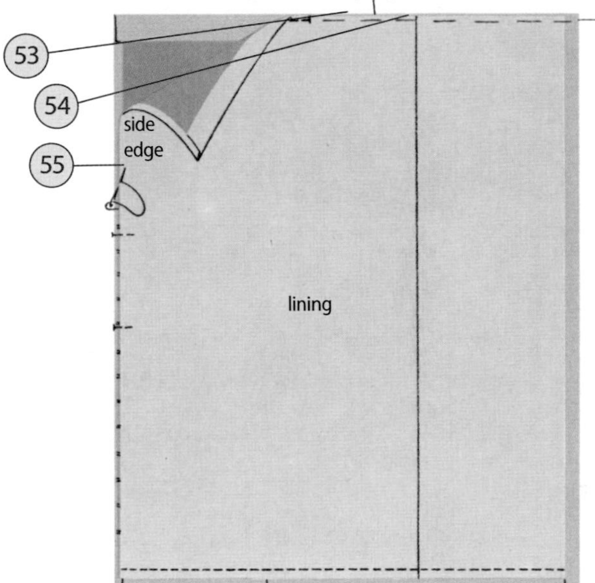

Crisp and delicate shades

An Austrian shade and a Roman shade represent two extremes in window coverings: from lush formality to no-nonsense crispness. The Austrian shade is best made of a lightweight fabric that will shirr gracefully and fall in puffy folds. The Roman shade should be of a sturdy fabric reinforced by lining; the combination has sufficient body to fold evenly and to hang plumb. Carefully placed underpinnings of tapes and the rings that guide the draw cords make both types behave as they should, as shown on the following pages.

Photograph courtesy of Calico Corners—*Calico Home*

The Roman Shade

Preparing the Fabric

1. To determine the finished shade length, measure from inside the top of the window frame to the sill. To find the number of pleats, divide the window length by four and a half—rounding off fractions to the next full number—and add two and a half. To find the fabric length, multiply the number of pleats by 5 inches and add 16½ inches.

2. To determine the finished shade width, measure between the jambs and subtract ½ inch. To calculate the fabric width required, add 4 inches.

3. To determine the length for the lining subtract 6½ inches from the shade fabric length *(Step 1)*. To determine the length of the heavyweight nonwoven interfacing, subtract ½ inch from the fabric length *(Step 1)*. The width of both lining and interfacing will be the same as the finished shade width *(Step 2)*.

4. Using the fabric length and width measurements calculated in Steps 1 and 2, cut the shade fabric. To make a shade that is wider than one fabric width, cut two equal strips for the added width required and attach one strip to each side of the center panel. Match at the selvages and stitch the strips to the center panel just inside the selvages. Press open the seams.

5. Place the fabric wrong side down and fold up the bottom edge 6½ inches to form a facing for the bottom flap. Pin.

shade fabric (wrong side)
4
shade fabric
5
6
seam
seam
bottom flap facing fabric (wrong side)
fold

Preparing the Lining and the Interfacing

6. Cut the lining and interfacing, using the measurements in Step 3. If needed, repeat Step 6 to join widths of lining. To join interfacing, cut an extra panel and a strip of ½-inch twill tape of the same length. Butt the two panels over the tape. Pin and sew with a machine zigzag stitch. Remove the pins.

7. Place the interfacing with the tape up and fold up the bottom edge 6 inches. Press.

8. Place the lining, wrong side down, on the interfacing and align all the edges. Pin and hem lower edge together.

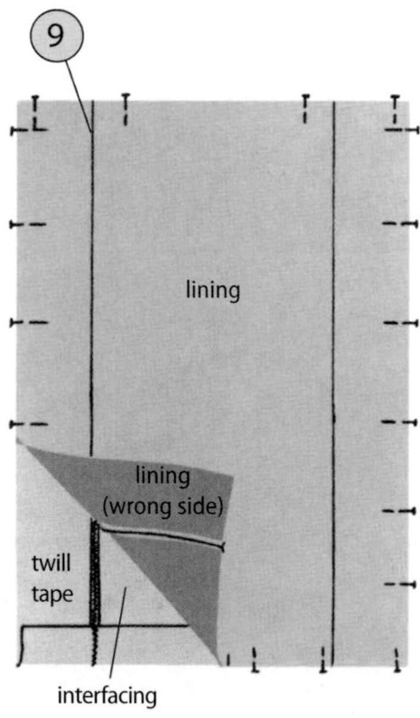

The Roman Shade

Pressing the Pleats

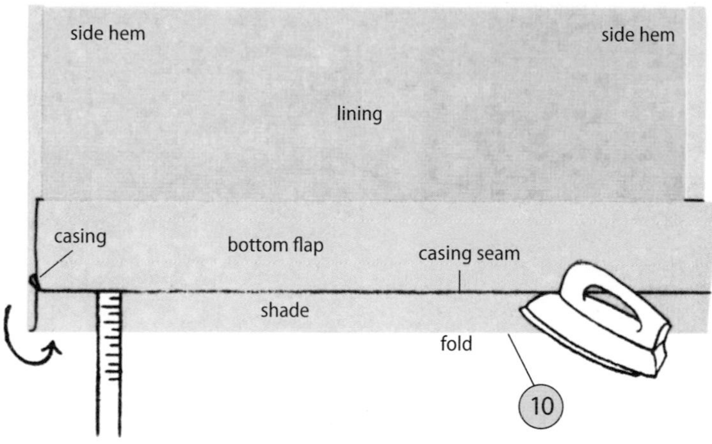

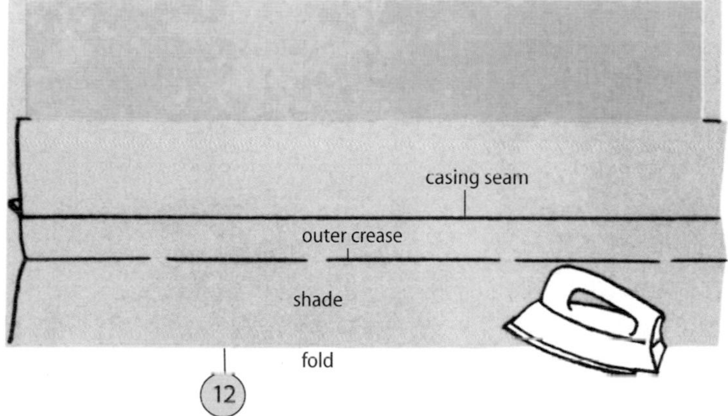

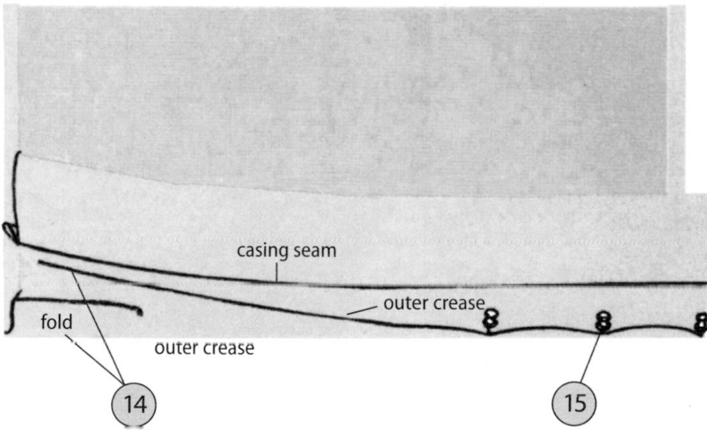

9. Place the shade, wrong side up, on a large flat surface—such as a cutting board—into which you can insert pins.

10. Using a ruler, fold up the bottom 2½ Inches.

11. Press a crease along the fold with a steam iron.

12. Fold the bottom up again 5 inches beyond the crease pressed into the fabric in Step 9.

13. Press in a crease along the fold.

14. Bring the edge of the first crease *(Step 11)* over and align it with the edge of the second crease *(Step 13)* to create an inner fold midway between the two.

15. To be sure that the creased edges lie directly on top of each other, insert pushpins through all the layers near the edge.

The Roman Shade

16. Fold down the bottom flap to expose the inner fold made in Step 14.

17. Steam press a crease along the inner fold.

18. Fold up the bottom flap again and remove the pushpins.

19. To create the next outer fold, fold up the bottom flap 5 inches beyond the outer crease made in Step 12. Press a crease along the fold.

20. Repeat Steps 16–18 to create the next inner fold. Then fold up the bottom flap and remove the pushpins.

21. Continue to repeat Steps 19 and 20 to create the remaining pleats.

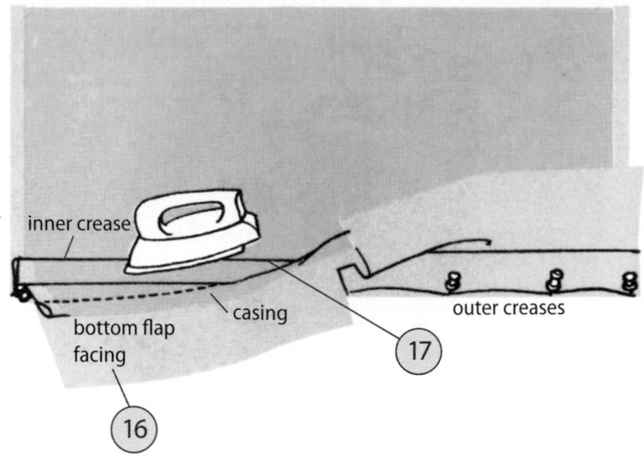

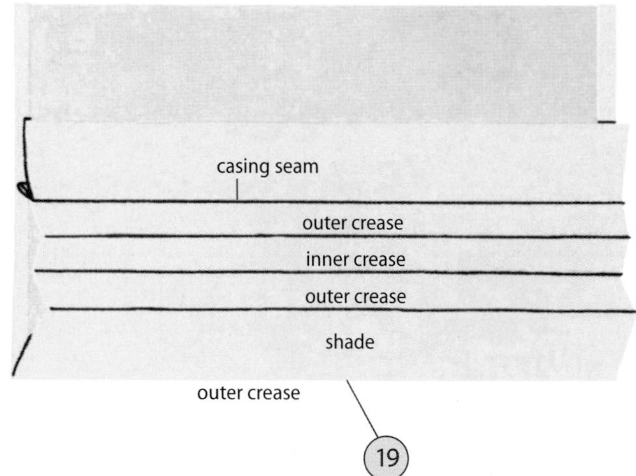

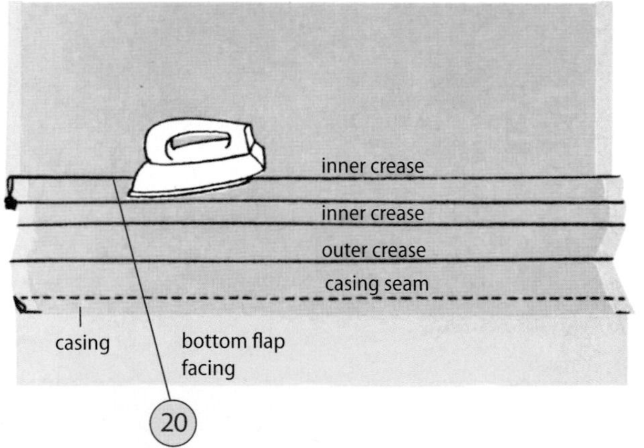

Preparing to Attach the Tapes

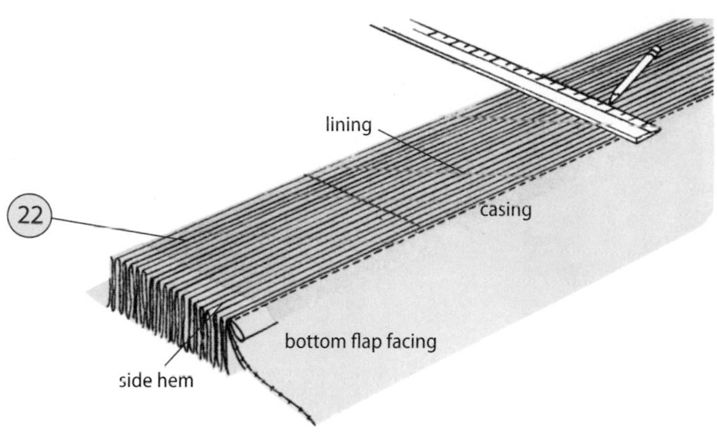

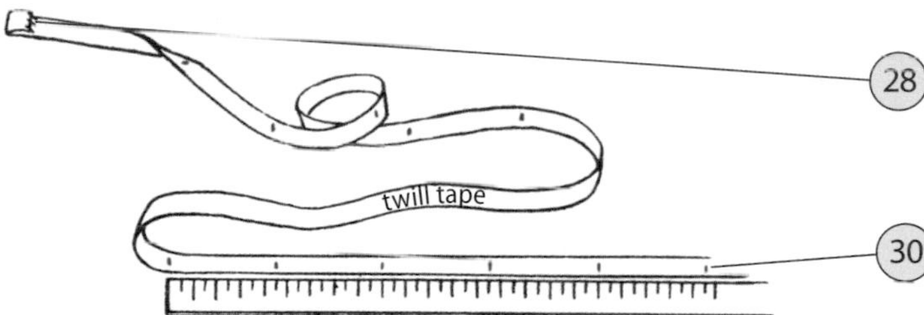

22. The tapes that will be attached at each side hem will need no placement guide lines. For the other tapes that will be attached above the cutout spaces of the dentils, mark guide lines by folding the shade into pleats on the crease lines.

23. To mark the guide lines, place a ruler on top of the pleated fabric parallel to the side edges and aligned with the mid-point of the first cutout space in the dentil-edged bottom flap.

24. Draw a line with pencil or chalk across the pleated fabric using the ruler as a guide.

25. Repeat Steps 23 and 24 to mark guide lines across the pleated fabric at the mid-point of each cutout space unless the spaces are less than 5 inches apart—in that case, make the guide lines at alternate spaces.

26. To determine the length of the tapes, multiply the number of pleats into which the shade is divided *(Step 1)* by 4½ inches. Then add 3 inches.

27. Cut a strip of ⅝-inch-wide cotton twill tape of this length for each guide line marked on the shade and for each side hem.

28. Fold one end of each tape under 1 inch and anchor it with overcast stitches.

29. Place the tapes folded ends down.

30. Measuring from the folded end, mark off 4½-inch intervals along the length of each tape.

The Roman Shade

Finishing the Shade

31. Extend the pleats and place a strip of tape—with the fold underneath—just inside one side hem. Align the folded tape end along the stitching above the bottom flap. Pin and attach the bottom of the tape with overcast stitches.

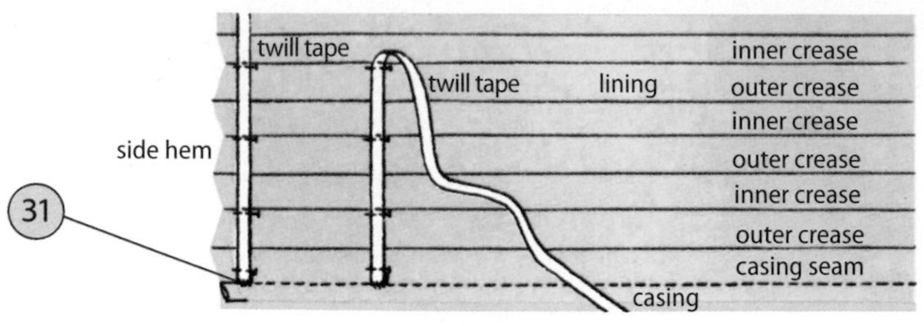

32. Match the first mark on the tape with the second creased fold above the bottom flap and pin. Continue matching the tape to every second crease until you have pinned to within one crease of the top edge.

33. Repeat Steps 31 and 32 to anchor and pin a tape to the shade over each marked guide line and just inside the second side hem.

34. Attach a curtain ring to the bottom of each tape with fastening stitches.

35. Attach each of the tapes and a curtain ring to the shade at every pinned marking. To do this, first make horizontal fastening stitches through the tape and all layers of the fabric. Remove the pin but do not cut the thread. Then place a ring over the stitches and anchor it with vertical fastening stitches. Tie off and cut the thread.

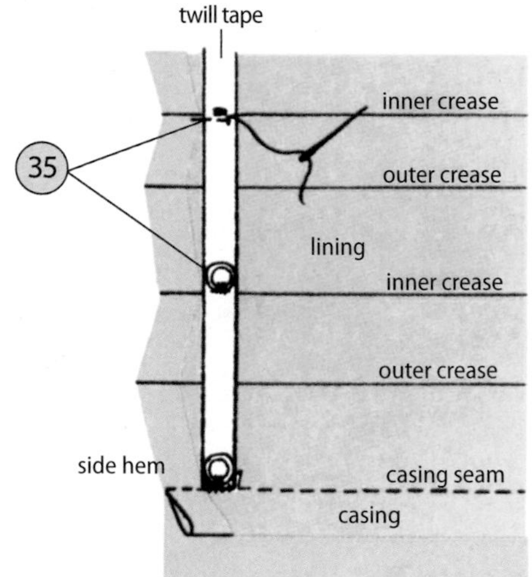

36. Above the top ring, smooth each tape flat against the shade and pin. Then trim off any excess tape extending above the top edge of the shade.

37. Stitch all the layers together—including the tapes—with machine zigzag stitching along the top edge. Remove the pins.

38. Finish and hang the shade.

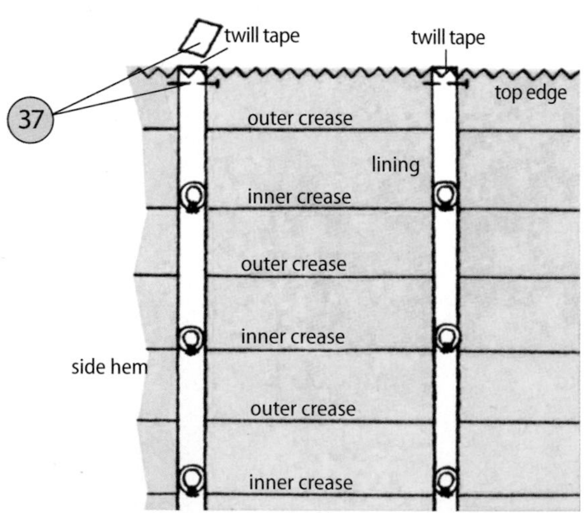

The casual charm of café curtains

Most versatile of all window coverings, café curtains can be made in multiple tiers of varying depths, any of which can be opened or closed independently. They lend themselves to almost any heading that suits the mood of the room—scalloped, saw-toothed, or gathered. Sometimes they are gathered top and bottom.

Diagrams on page 86 explain how to measure for café curtains, and directions follow for making various styles.

Calculations for making café curtains

Before measuring your windows for café curtains, mount the rod or rods you expect to use. Whatever heading one-tier café curtains may have—shaped, pleated, hand shirred, or gathered through a tunnel of fabric called a casing—the rod can be attached anywhere on the window frame.

Two-tier café curtains, as well as one-tier curtains that are gathered through casings at both ends of each panel, will generally hang from rods attached to the top and middle of the frame.

When the rod or rods have been mounted, make the measurements indicated below, then apply them to the formulas on the chart at right to estimate how much fabric you will require.

Separate formulas are given for each curtain style. Insert the measurements called for, as identified by the letters on the drawing below, and perform in sequence the mathematical operations indicated by the standard symbols.

For fabric with a repeated pattern that needs matching, determine the length of one repeat by measuring along a selvage from one design detail to the next identical design detail.

The width of the rod or rods dictates the number of fabric widths you will need for curtains. Whether a rod is mounted across the front of the window frame *(A)* or between the jambs *(B)*, measure the width from one end to the other—including the bent or bracketed return sections, if any. Record all measurements in inches.

The length of curtains varies with the style as well as with the measurement from the rods to the hems. For one-tier café curtains and the bottom panels of two-tier curtains, measure (in inches) from the lower edge of the rod to the sill or the lower edge of the apron *(C or D and G or H)*. For the top panels of two-tier curtains, measure from the lower edge of the higher rod to 2 inches below the lower rod *(E or F);* for shaped top headings add 2 inches. For curtains with both top and bottom casings, measure from the lower edge of the top rod to the upper edge of the bottom rod *(I or J)*.

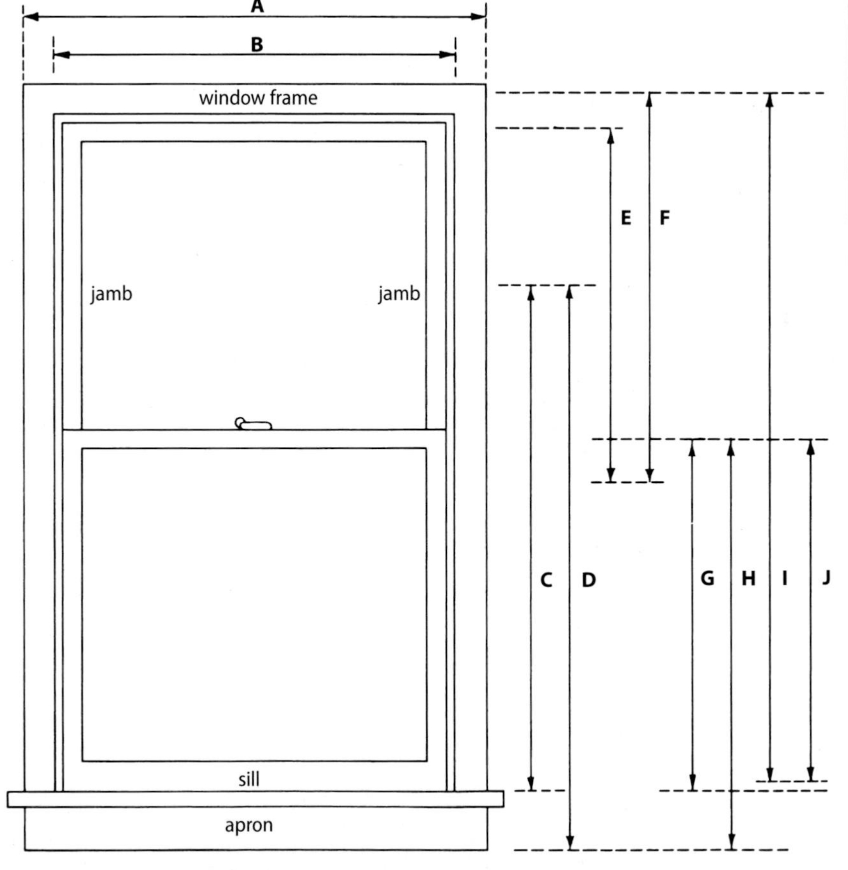

Estimating Materials

One-Tier Café Curtains

Width	For medium- to heavyweight fabrics	Number of fabric widths required for a pair of curtains **= A or B × 2½ ÷ Fabric Width in Inches***
	For lightweight or sheer fabrics	Number of fabric widths required for a pair of curtains **= A or B × 3 ÷ Fabric Width in Inches***
Length	For fabrics that do not require matching a pattern	Total length required for one curtain in inches **= C or D + 15**
	For fabrics that require matching a pattern	Total length required for one curtain in inches **= C or D + 15 + Length of Pattern Repeat in Inches**
Yardage	Total yardage required = **Number of Widths × Total Length of One Curtain in Inches ÷ 36**	

Two-Tier Café Curtains

Width	For medium- to heavyweight fabrics	Number of fabric widths required for a pair of curtains **= A or B × 2½ ÷ Fabric Width in Inches***
	For lightweight or sheer fabrics	Number of fabric widths required for a pair of curtains **= A or B × 3 ÷ Fabric Width in Inches***
Length	For fabrics that do not require matching a pattern	Total length in inches required **= Length for One Top Curtain (E or F) + Length Required for One Bottom Curtain (G or H) + 30**
	For fabrics that require matching a pattern	Total length in inches required **= Length for One Top Curtain (E or F) + Length Required for One Bottom Curtain (G or H) + 30 + Two Times Length of Pattern Repeat in Inches**
Yardage	Total yardage required = **Number of Widths × Total Length Required in Inches ÷ 36**	

Café Curtains with Top and Bottom Casings

Width	For medium- to heavyweight fabrics	Number of fabric widths required for a pair of curtains **= A or B × 2½ ÷ Fabric Width in Inches***
	For lightweight or sheer fabrics	Number of fabric widths required for a pair of curtains **= A or B × 3 ÷ Fabric Width in Inches***
Length	For fabrics that do not require matching a pattern	Total length required for one curtain in inches **= I or J + 24**
	For fabrics that require matching a pattern	Total length required for one curtain in inches **= I or J + 24 + Length of Pattern Repeat in Inches**
Yardage	Total yardage required = **Number of Widths × Total Length Required for One Curtain in Inches ÷ 36**	

*Round off fractions to the nearest full width.

Making Café Curtains

Cutting and Preparing the Fabric

1. Place the fabric, wrong side down, on a large table. Straighten one edge by drawing a crosswise thread and cutting along the drawn thread or by drawing and cutting along a chalk line, following the instructions for draperies and curtains.

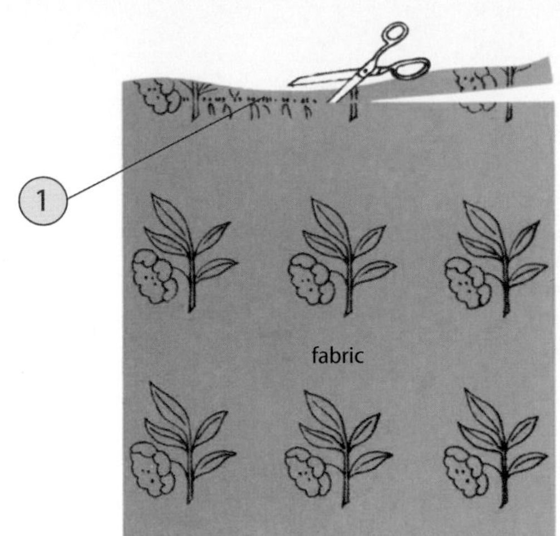

2a. For fabric that does not require matching a pattern, use the desired panel length measurement *(page 87)* to mark and cut off as many sections as you need for your window. Make all cuts along crosswise threads or chalk lines.

2b. For fabric with a pronounced pattern, cut off a section equal to the panel length as determined by the formula on page 87. Examine fabric and window to decide where pattern repeats should fall, then trim the section. Cut off a total amount equal to one full pattern repeat, but trim some from the top and some from the bottom as necessary to get the pattern positioned suitably.

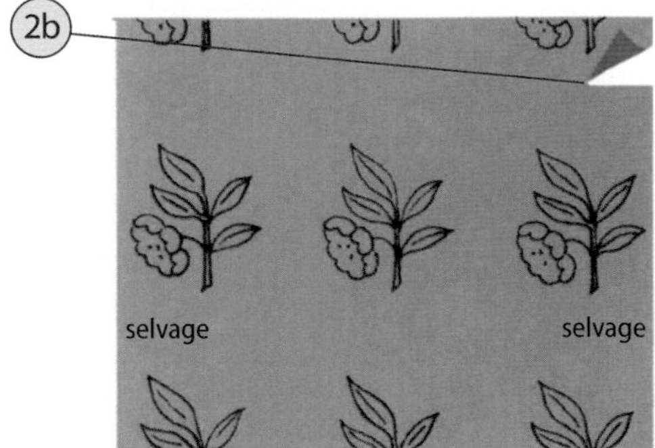

3. To straighten the fabric grains, follow the instructions for draperies and curtains *(Step 4, page 73).*

4. To divide a fabric section into two half-widths, or to make a panel from two or more fabric sections, follow the instructions for draperies and curtains *(Steps 5–8, page 73)*. Make the joining seams narrow—especially if the fabric is sheer.

Hemming the Sides of the Panels

5. Place one curtain panel wrong side up and press any inner seam.

6. Make a double hem 1 inch deep on each side of the panel by folding up each edge 1 inch and pressing in a crease, then folding each edge another 1 inch and pressing it again.

7. Machine stitch along the inner edges of the hems.

8. Repeat Steps 5–7 on the second panel of the pair.

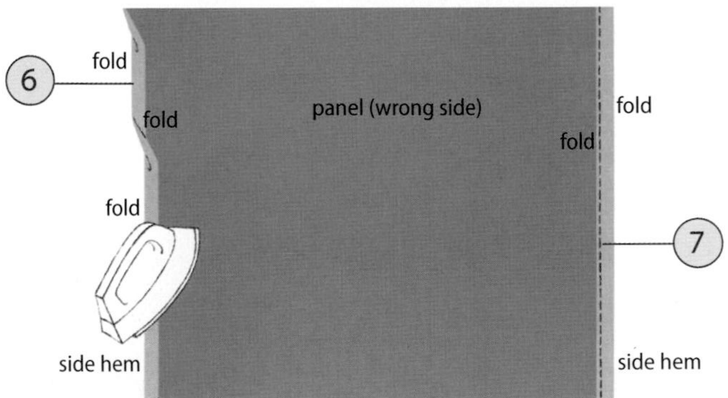

Making Casing Tops

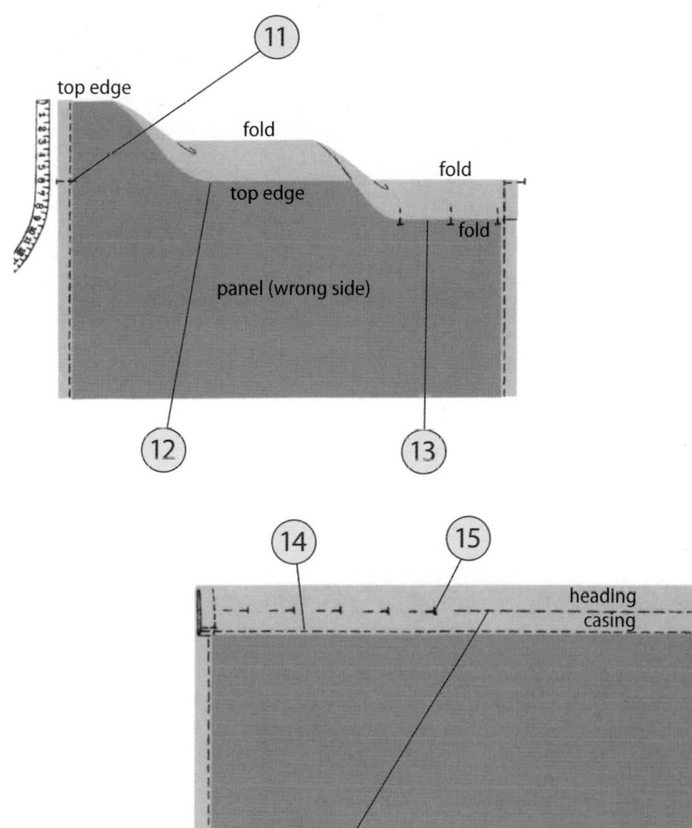

9. To find the depth necessary for casing tops, measure the diameter of your round rod by placing a ruler in front of it; then double the figure. If you have a flat rod, measure its depth and add ⅜ inch.

10. To determine the number of inches of fabric you need to make a double hem for the casing and heading—i.e., the top section that will extend above the casing—multiply the figure calculated in the previous step by four.

11. Measure this distance from the top edge on both sides of the panel and pin.

12. Make a double hem for the casing and heading by folding the top of the panel down to the pin markings and pressing in a crease.

13. Fold the panel down again, aligning the crease made in the preceding step with the pins. Press in another crease along the fold and remove the pin markings. Then pin along the double hem.

14. Stitch as close to the inner edge of the hem as possible. Make sure to backstitch at each end. Remove the pins.

15. To make the casing, insert pins at 2-inch intervals midway between the panel top and the line of stitching.

16. Stitch along the row of pins, removing the pins as you sew. Make sure to backstitch at each end.

17. Repeat Steps 11–16 on the second panel of the pair.

Making Café Curtains

Making Backed and Stiffened Tops

18. For pleated headings and shaped tops, place one panel, wrong side up, on a flat surface and measure the finished width.

19. Cut a strip of stiffening ¼ inch shorter than the width of the panel, using a 4-inch-deep stiffening for the shaped tops, a 3-inch one for the pleated headings.

20. Align one edge of the stiffening with the top edge of the panel, and center the stiffening so that the ends fall just inside the side edges. Pin. Fold down the top of the panel along the bottom edge of the stiffening, then press on the fold.

21a. To make the headings for pleats, fold down the covered stiffening again and press. Remove the pins inserted in Step 20, then insert pins near the sides of the heading.

22a. Machine or hand stitch down each side edge and along the bottom of the heading only as far as the inner edge of the hem on the side of the panel. Use the slip stitch or a hemming stitch if you hand sew. Remove the pins.

23a. Repeat Steps 19–21 and 22a and 23a on the second panel of the pair. To plot the pleats, follow the instructions in draperies and curtains *(page 81)*. To finish the hem, skip to Step 58a.

21b. To make the headings for shaped tops, first turn the panel wrong side down. Then fold over the covered stiffening along the bottom edge of the heading and press on the fold, avoiding pins.

22b. Remove the pins inserted in Step 21. Pin the heading and stiffening together at the sides.

23b. Repeat Steps 19, 20, and 21b–22b on the second panel of the pair.

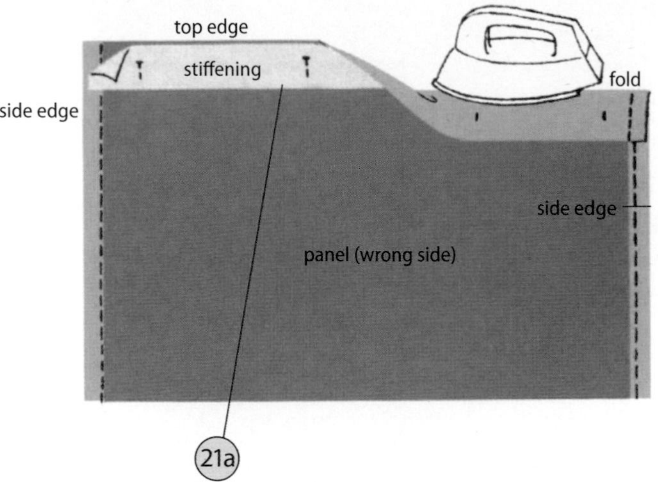

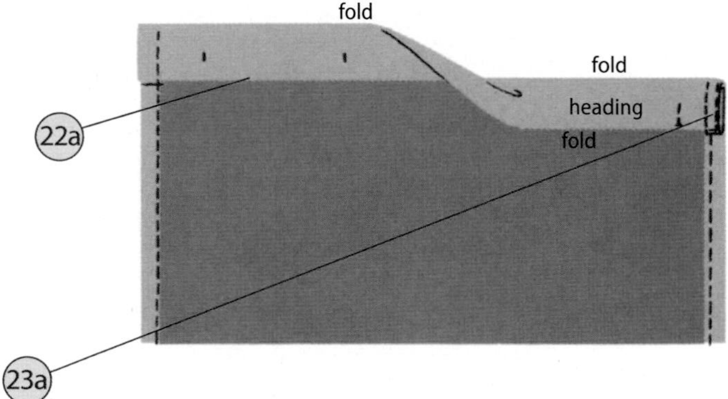

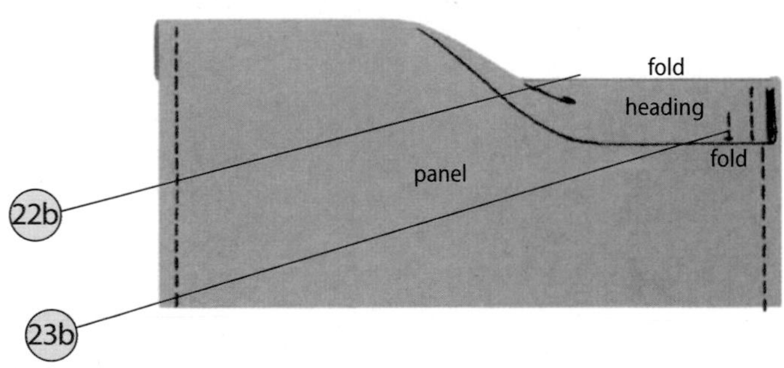

Making Unpleated Shaped Tops

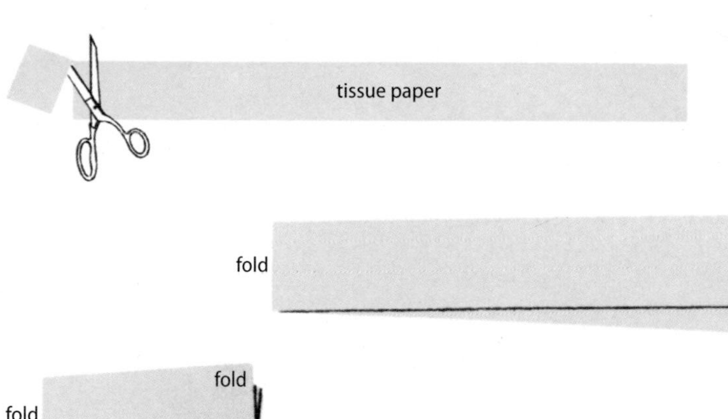

24. To make shaped tops with evenly spaced identical designs but no pleats, cut out a strip of tissue paper the length and width of the panel heading *(Steps 19 and 20)*.

25. If your rod has side returns and you want the top of the curtains to be unshaped along the returns, measure the length of one return and cut this distance off the paper strip.

26. Fold the paper strip in half across its width, into quarters, then eighths.

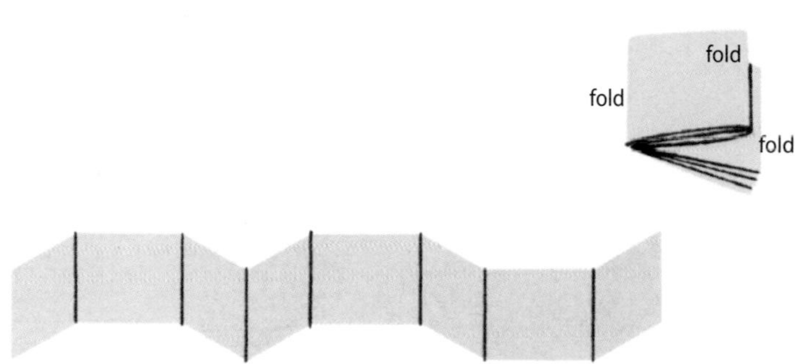

27. Unfold the strip to examine the spacing. If you want more divisions, fold the paper again as many times as necessary.

28. Draw a line across the bottom of the strip ¾ inch from the edge to determine the bottom point for your design.

29. Starting at the top corner of one end and finishing at the top corner of the other end, draw the design you want between the folded segments and above the pencil line made in Step 28.

30. Cut out the design to create a paper pattern.

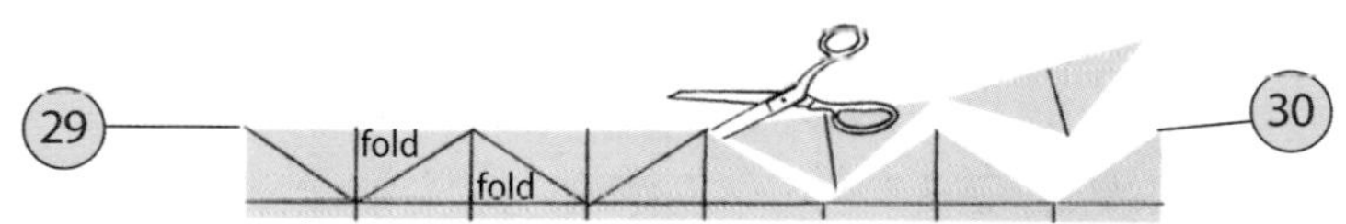

Making Café Curtains

31. With the panel wrong side down, position the paper pattern on the heading ¼ inch below the top edge, aligning the ends with the side edges of the panel. If you provided for a return in Step 25, align the right-hand end of the pattern with the right-hand side edge of the panel that you plan to hang at the left of the window. Pin.

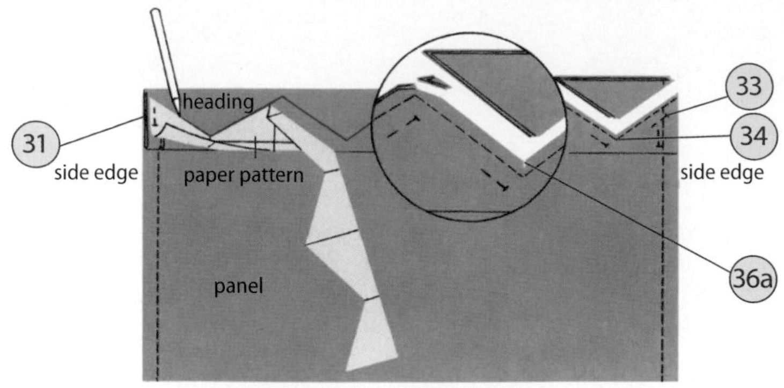

32. Trace the outline of the design onto the heading with dressmaker's chalk. Remove the pattern.

33. Pin the layers of heading together, avoiding the chalk lines.

34. Machine stitch on the chalk lines. Remove all the pins.

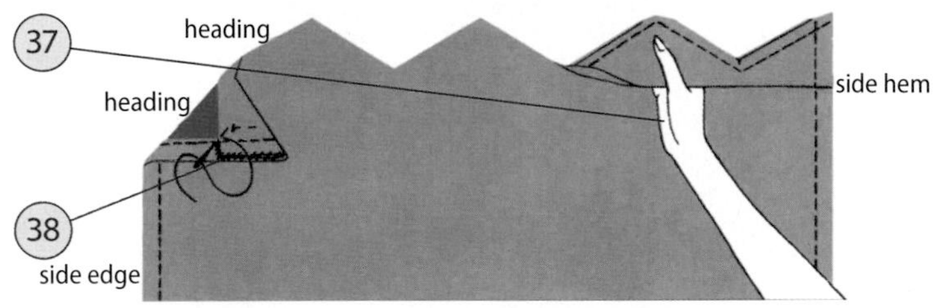

35. Cut out the design ¼ inch above the stitching.

36a. For straight-edged designs, cut off outside corners diagonally and clip into the seam allowance at the bottom of inside corners.

36b. For curved designs, notch the outside curves and clip along inside curves.

37. Turn the stitched top edge inside out by lifting up the heading from the front of the panel and turning it over onto the back. Push out the shaped tops with your fingers. Bring out corners by gently pulling them with the tip of a needle. Press.

38. Pin along each side of the heading, and finish the sides, following Step 22a.

39. Repeat Steps 31–38 on the second panel of the pair. If you provided for a return in Step 25, however, align the left-hand end of the pattern with the left-hand side edge of the panel. Skip to Step 60.

Making Pleated Shaped Tops

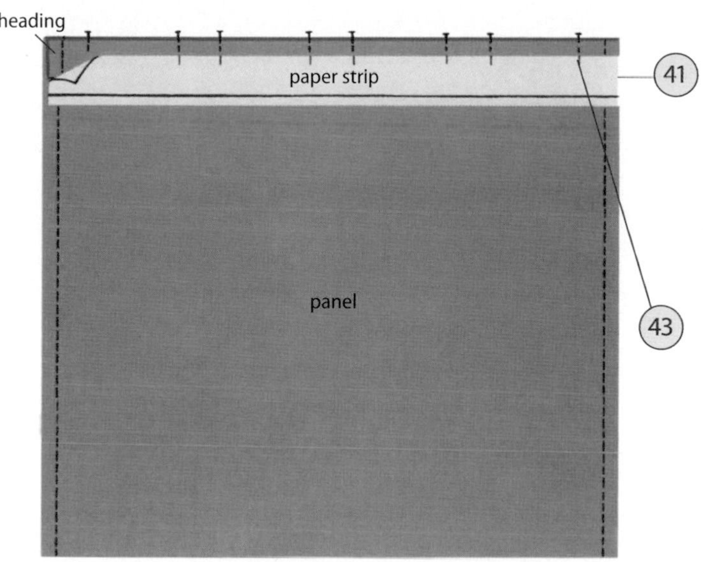

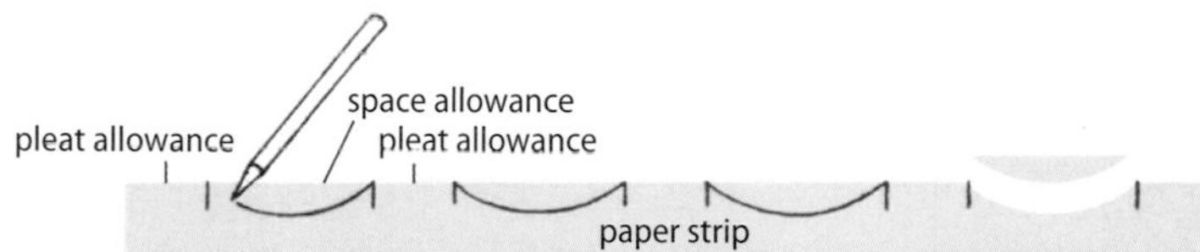

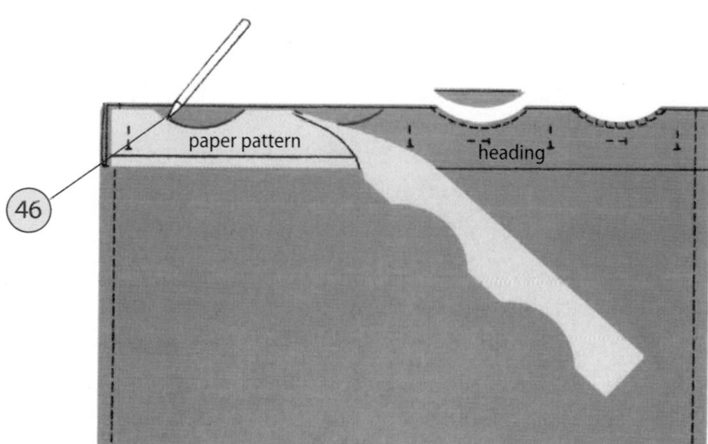

40. To make curtains with headings that combine pleats with cutout shapes, first plot the pleats with pins.

41. Before stitching the pleat allowance seams, cut a strip of tissue paper to make a pattern for the shaped cutouts and draw a line across the bottom by repeating Steps 24 and 28.

42. Place the paper strip over the heading of the pinned panel and align the top edges.

43. Draw a vertical pencil line over each pin inserted in Step 40, then remove the paper strip from the panel. Remove the pins.

44. Using a ruler, compass, or saucer, draw the shape of the cutout design you want within each of the individual space allowances between the pencil-marked pleat allowances. Make sure to keep the bottom point of each shape above the bottom pencil line.

45. Cut out the paper pattern along the drawn designs.

46. Pin the paper pattern to the heading of the panel, aligning the top and side edges. Then trace the outlines for the cutout shapes onto the fabric with dressmaker's chalk. Remove the pattern.

47. Repeat Steps 32–37 to finish and stitch the cutout shapes. Using the paper pattern as a guide, reinsert the pin markings for the pleats. Then stitch and shape the pleats.

48. Repeat Steps 46 and 47 on the second panel of the pair. Skip to Step 57.

Making Café Curtains

Making Self-Fabric Loops

49. To determine the length of each loop, first measure the circumference of your rod by wrapping a tape measure around it. Decide how far below the rod you want the curtains to hang and multiply this distance by two; then add the circumference plus 2 inches for seam allowances.

50. Decide how wide you want each loop to be, multiply that figure by two and add ½ inch for seam allowances.

51. With the measurements determined in Steps 49 and 50, cut out as many loops as you need from the curtain fabric.

52. To make each loop, fold a loop strip in half lengthwise, wrong sides out, and pin. Stitch ¼ inch inside the long edge and one short end. Remove the pins.

53. Use the eraser end of a pencil to turn the loop strip right side out. Bring out the corners with the tip of a needle. Press.

54. Turn in the raw edges of the unstitched end ¼ inch and sew them together by hand, using a slip stitch.

55. To attach each loop, place the curtain panel wrong side up on a flat surface. Fold a loop strip in half crosswise and position it on the panel where desired, overlapping the stitched ends ¾ inch below the top edge of the panel. If the loop will be attached behind a pleat, center the loop strip over the pleat allowance seam.

56. Pin the loop strip in place, then attach it to the panel by making hemming stitches all around the edges.

57. Before finishing the hems for any style of curtain, hang the panels in place on the rod.

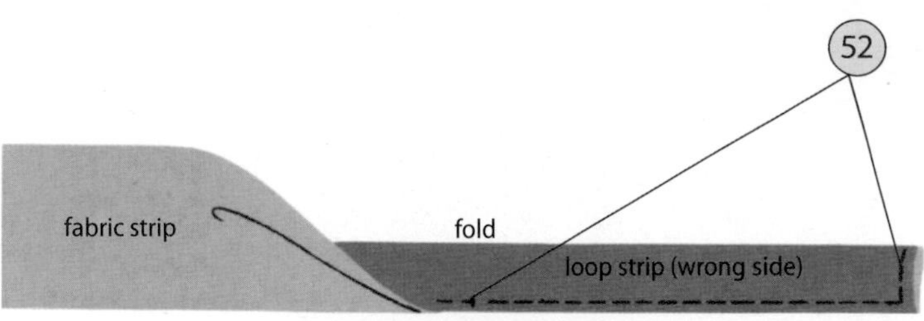

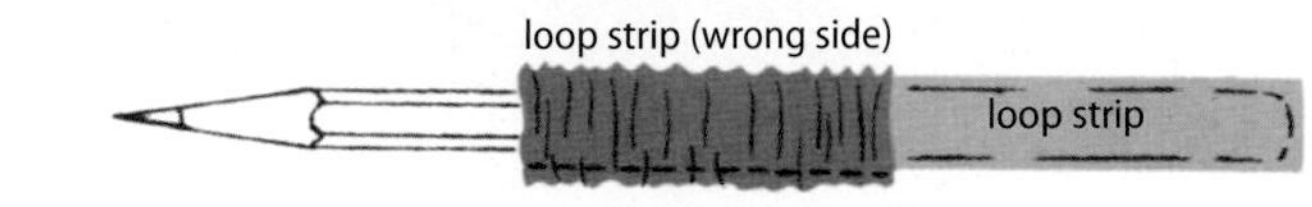

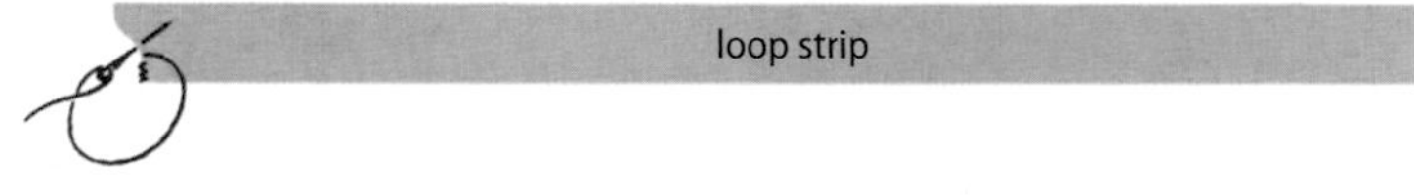

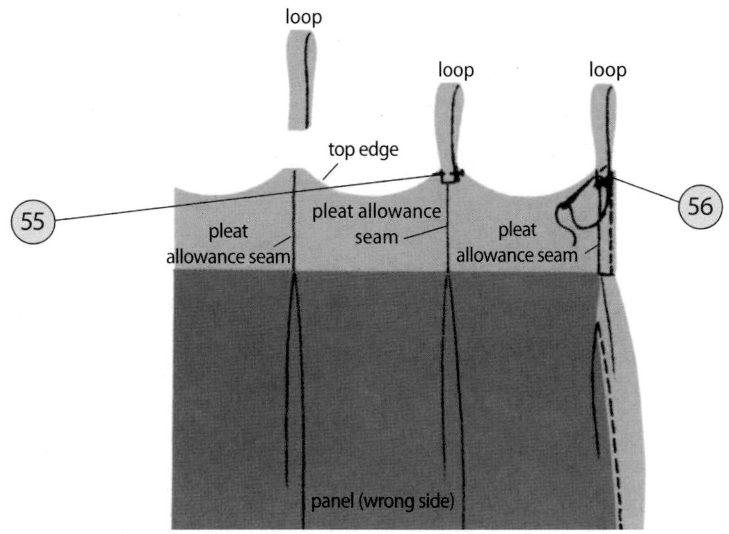

Chapter 3: Curtains and Drapes

Making Café Curtains

Finishing the Hems

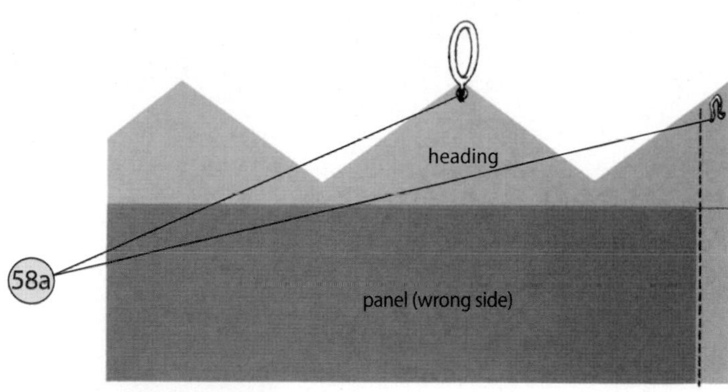

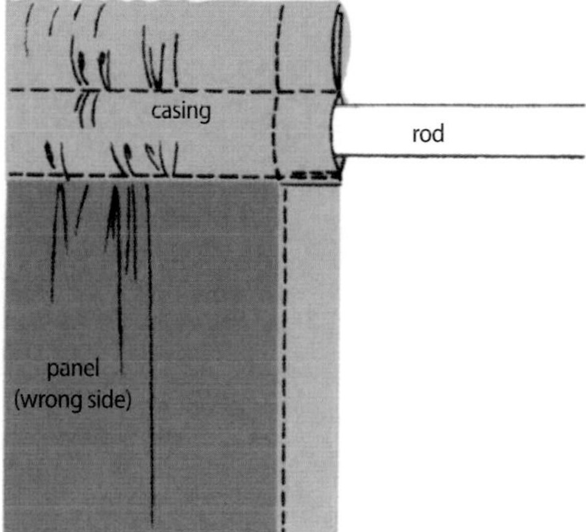

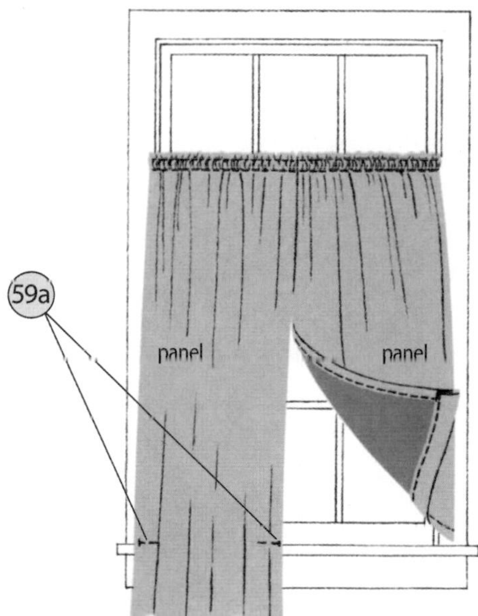

58a. For curtains with continuous shaped tops, sew a ring at the uppermost point of each design segment or insert a pin hook so that the top bend is ¼ inch below the uppermost point. Insert the rod through the rings or hang the hooks from the rod.

58b. For curtains with a casing at the top, insert the rod so that two layers of the hem are in front of it when the rod is hung.

58c. For curtains with self-fabric loops, simply insert the rod through the loops.

58d. For curtains with fully pleated or shaped pleated headings, attach or insert hooks, then attach the hooks to the rod.

59a. To make a bottom hem for any curtain except one with a bottom casing, first insert pins on both sides of each panel at the level you want the bottom of the hem to reach. Remove the panels from the rod.

59b. To make bottom casings on curtains, first insert pins on both sides of each panel just above the bottom rod. Remove the panels from the rod.

60a. Trim off each panel 4 inches below the pin marks.

60b. Turn each panel top side down, then multiply the casing depth (Step 9) by six and measure this distance from the pins to the unfinished edge. Trim off excess fabric.

61a. Turn each panel top side down, then make a 2-inch-wide double hem, following the instructions in Steps 12 and 13. Press.

61b. Divide the figure determined in Step 60b by three and use chalk to mark off this distance from the pins toward the unfinished edge. Turn the edge up to the chalk marks and press in a crease. Then turn up the crease, aligning it with the chalk marks. Repeat Steps 14–16 to stitch the double hem for the bottom heading and casing.

Photograph courtesy of Calico Corners—*Calico Home*

Slipcovers

4

A Perfect Fit for Covers and Spreads

From the very beginning (the oldest known slipcover dates from about 1670) slipcovers have served a number of purposes: to protect fine furniture from everyday wear and tear; to dress it up for special occasions; and to give new life to an old piece. In Victorian times slipcovers were ill-fitting, makeshift affairs, thrown on to keep off summer dust or perhaps to hide the scars of hand-me-down furniture.

Today, some 300 years after their first appearance, slipcovers are still going strong; indeed they are enjoying something of a renaissance as fashion worthy of attention in their own right. "If a slipcover is properly made it is indistinguishable from a permanent cover," says New York decorator Billy Baldwin. Most contemporary decorators generally take the same view—but not all. "I don't like slipcovers to look like upholstery," counters San Francisco's Michael Taylor. "They should be loose, airy, baggy; that way they relax the room."

Either way, slipcovers are eminently practical; a removable slip cover is more easily cleaned than upholstery. And they are infinitely versatile; the homeowner restless for change can switch covers with the seasons (replacing a warm, wintry corduroy with an airy cotton for summer, for instance) or with the mood (moving from tailored to frilly, for example). Slipcovers are not necessarily cheap, for they can be made in the finest and most expensive of fabrics, but they are more economical than upholstery because it takes less time and money to switch slipcovers than to reupholster a piece of furniture.

What fabric to use for the slipcover? It should be strong enough to hold its shape but pliant enough to curve over arms and backs and—if the slipcover is to have a ruffled or pleated skirt—to hang in folds. Linen, chintz, and damask lend themselves

Slipcovers are akin to a pretty dress for your furniture—they go over fabric, frame, and cushions that must be in good shape beneath the slipcover. Slipcovers can be made to fit like a glove and look as if they are upholstered.

to slipcovering very well; so do corduroy, cretonne, various other silks and cottons, and many man-made fabrics—except for those that stretch.

Figuring importantly in the final effect, too, is the type of fabric *under* the slipcover. If the furniture upholstery itself is slippery, like satin, it will not hold an overlying fabric in place. Nubby upholstery will show through a slipcover that is lighter in weight than itself. And velvet abrades easily under a slipcover—something to bear in mind if the velvet upholstery has not already had its day and will be wanted for future use. For that matter, some decorators even urge their clients to have new furniture upholstered in plain muslin or, better yet, neutral twill or ticking, and then to use a custom-made slipcover for the furniture's regular attire. The advantage of these never-to-be-seen upholstery fabrics is that any of them serves well under any slipcover, and survives any number of redecorations. And they are not so ugly that they cannot be lived with for the duration of an incumbent slipcover's trip to the cleaners.

Making a slipcover, like any sewing for the home, requires patience, forethought, and care. Particularly crucial to success are the blocking and cutting of the fabric. But even those important operations are not so formidable as might be imagined. "I think it's easier to make a slipcover than a dress," says New York upholsterer Henrietta Blau. "Your chair won't move. It won't breathe while you're measuring, pinning, and cutting. And it doesn't need a coffee break."

Calculations for making slipcovers

The chart below gives rough estimates of the number of yards of fabric a sofa or chair slipcover will require. To use the chart, add the estimate for body and cushion fabric to the estimated yardage for welting and the desired style of skirt.

These figures are based on requirements for standard pieces of furniture covered in solid-colored or small-patterned fabrics. For special sizes and shapes of furniture and for more precise fabric estimating—particularly with stripes or large pattern repeats—you should measure your own furniture by the system that professionals call blocking. Blocking also serves as a guide to cutting fabric into rectangular sections—blocks—to pin and shape on the furniture.

In blocking, furniture is measured and slipcovers are cut as rectangles—whatever the finished shapes of the sections will be. The entire center section of a sofa or chair forms a single block. This block extends up from the bottom of the outside back over and down the inside back, across the platform with the cushions removed to the bottom of the front base, which is known as the drop. Each arm is treated as three blocks—an inside, an outside, and a top and front surface. On a wing chair, each wing is covered by two blocks—an inside and an outside. On an armless sofa or chair, each side section forms a block.

Each cushion is figured in two blocks—the front boxing together with the top section and the bottom section. The other three sides of the boxing are picked up from leftover fabric. If there is a separate pleated or ruffled skirt, it constitutes another block.

With the techniques shown on the next page, you can block furniture of any size or shape by measuring it in sections as outlined by the seams in the upholstery. Be sure, though, to leave a tuck-in allowance twice the depth of any groove or indentation between sections, and to provide 3/8-inch seam allowances all around every block after you fit it to the sofa or chair.

Approximate Yardage Required for Slipcovers

Furniture	Number of Cushions	Body and Cushion Fabric	Straight Skirt or Lining Fabric	Ruffled Skirt or Lining Fabric	Pleated Skirt or Lining Fabric	Welting Fabric	Welting Cord
		54"	54"	54"	54"	54"	Length
Sofa	Six	19	1¼	2½	3	2½	64
	Four	17	1¼	2½	3	2	50
	Three	15	1¼	2½	3	1¾	46
	Two	12	1¼	2½	3	1½	38
	One	12	1¼	2½	3	1¼	34
	None	9	1¼	2½	3	¾	20
Love Seat	Four	14	1¼	1½	2½	1¾	46½
	Two	11	1¼	1½	2½	1¼	34½
	One	11	1¼	1½	2½	1	30½
	None	8	1¼	1½	2½	¾	18½
Armchair	Two	8	1	1	2	1	27
	One	7	1	1	2	¾	21
	None	5	1	1	2	⅔	15

Blocking the Slipcover

Marking the Skirt Attachment Line

1. Remove all cushions from the sofa or chair.

2. Locate the front board in the wooden frame underneath the upholstery by pressing your fingers into the drop near its bottom edge.

3. Decide how high on the board you want the seam that attaches the skirt to the drop, and make a chalk mark. (The skirt should be longer than the drop.)

4. Using a ruler, measure from the floor to the first chalk mark. Make similar marks at the same height at 6- to 8-inch intervals all around the sofa or chair. Connect the marks with chalk lines.

5. Measure the width of the skirt attachment line on each side, and mark its center point.

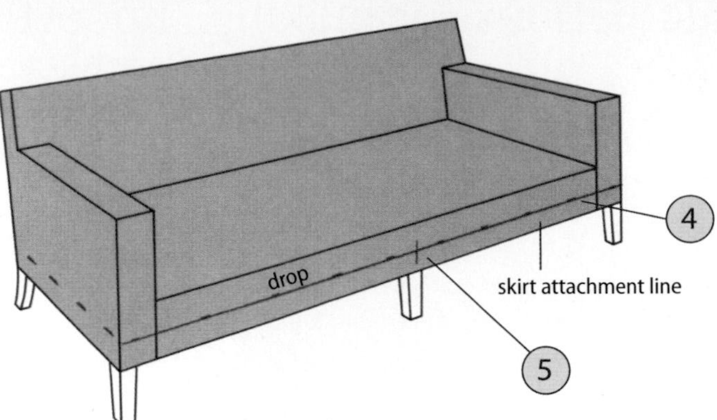

Measuring the Center Block

6a. For a slipcover with a straight skirt, measure straight up from the floor to the skirt attachment line at one back corner. Then follow the contours to measure to the top of the outside back. Add a 4-inch seam, hem and fitting allowance.

6b. For a slipcover with a ruffled or pleated skirt, measure from the skirt attachment line to the top of the outside back following the contours. Add a 2-inch seam and fitting allowance.

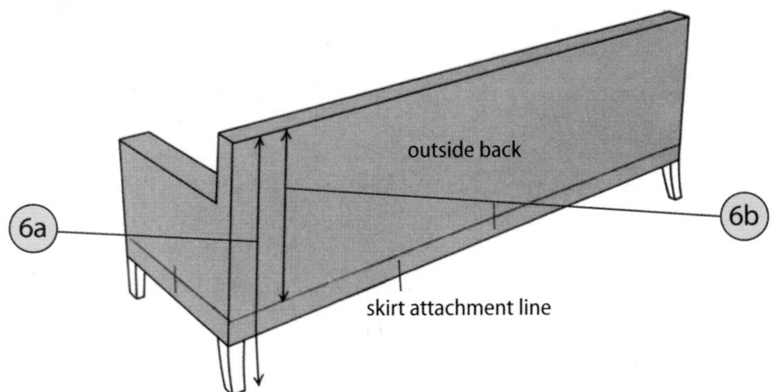

7. Measure the inside back of the sofa or chair from the top of the outside back to the platform. Add a 2-inch seam and fitting allowance.

8. Measure the platform from the inside back to the drop edge. Add a 6-inch tuck-in allowance.

9a. For a slipcover with a straight skirt, measure from the edge of the platform to the floor. Add a 2⅝-inch seam and hem allowance.

9b. For a slipcover with a ruffled or pleated skirt, measure from the edge of the platform to the skirt attachment line and add a ¾-inch seam allowance.

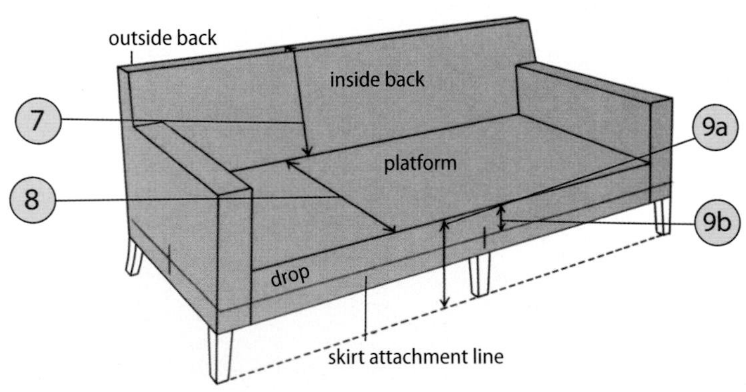

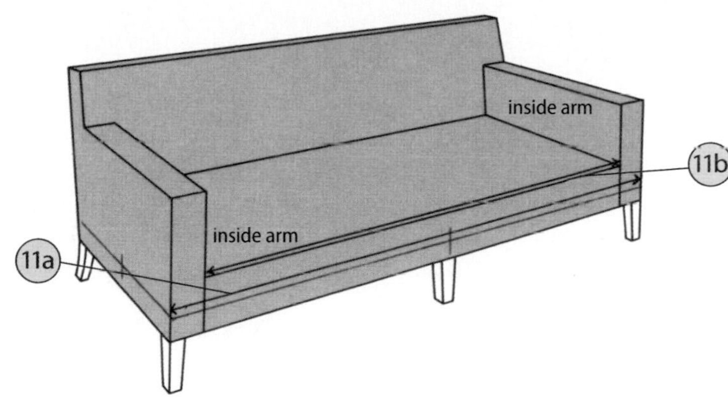

10. Add the measurements made in Steps 6–9 to determine the length of the center block.

11a. For a slipcover with a straight skirt, determine the width of the center block by adding an 8-inch allowance for corner pleat fold backs and for fitting to the width of the front skirt attachment line *(Step 5)*.

11b. For a slipcover with a ruffled or pleated skirt, determine the width of the center block by measuring the platform from inside arm to inside arm. Add a 13-inch tuck-in and seam allowance.

Measuring the Arm Blocks

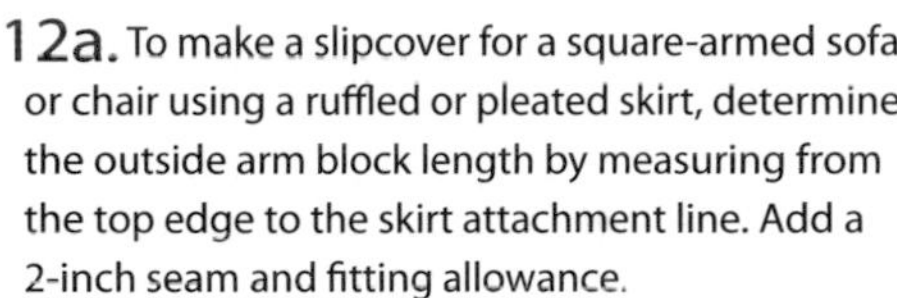

12a. To make a slipcover for a square-armed sofa or chair using a ruffled or pleated skirt, determine the outside arm block length by measuring from the top edge to the skirt attachment line. Add a 2-inch seam and fitting allowance.

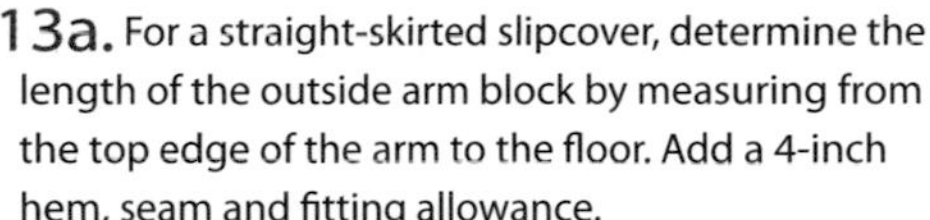

13a. For a straight-skirted slipcover, determine the length of the outside arm block by measuring from the top edge of the arm to the floor. Add a 4-inch hem, seam and fitting allowance.

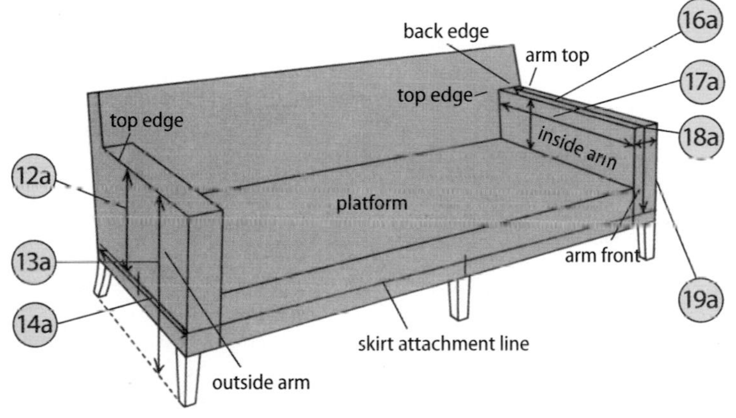

14a. For a straight skirted slipcover, determine the width of the outside arm block by adding an 8-inch pleat and fitting allowance to the skirt attachment line width *(Step 5)*.

15a. For a ruffled or pleated slipcover, determine the width of the outside arm block by measuring the outside arm at its widest point and adding a 2-inch seam and fitting allowance.

16a. To determine the length of the inside arm block, measure from the top edge of the arm to the platform. Add a 2-inch seam allowance.

17a. To determine the width of the inside arm, measure its widest point and add a 4-inch seam and fitting allowance.

Blocking the Slipcover

18a. To determine the length of the block covering the top and front of the arm, measure from the back edge of the arm forward and down to the skirt attachment line. Add a 4-inch seam and fitting allowance.

19a. To determine the width of the arm top and front block, measure the arm at its widest point and add a ¾-inch seam allowance.

12b. To make a slipcover for a curved-arm sofa or chair, first draw a horizontal chalk line on the arm at the outermost point on the curve to represent the top edge for the outside and inside arm.

13b–17b. Follow Steps 12a–17a, using the chalk line whenever you need to make a measurement from the top edge of the arm.

18b. To determine the width of the arm front block, measure the arm at its widest point and add a ¾-inch seam allowance.

19b. To determine the length of the block covering the front of the arm, measure from the top of the arm to the skirt attachment line. Add a 2-inch seam and fitting allowance.

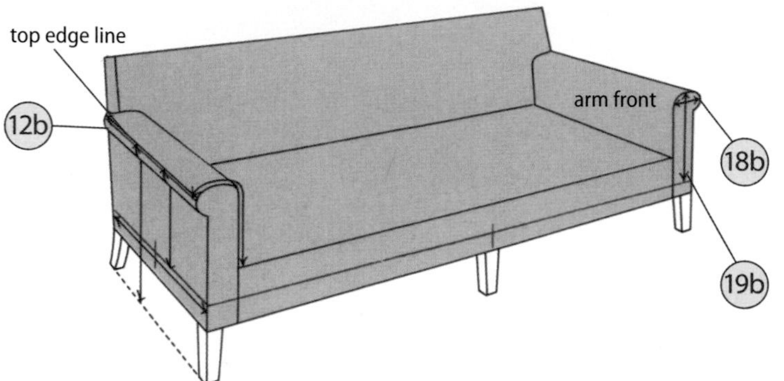

Measuring Cushion Blocks

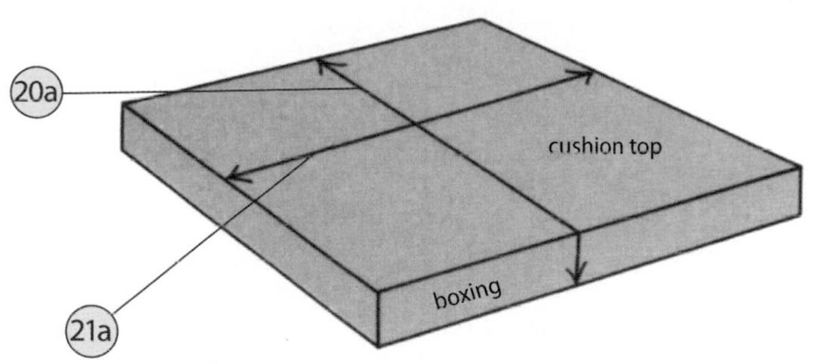

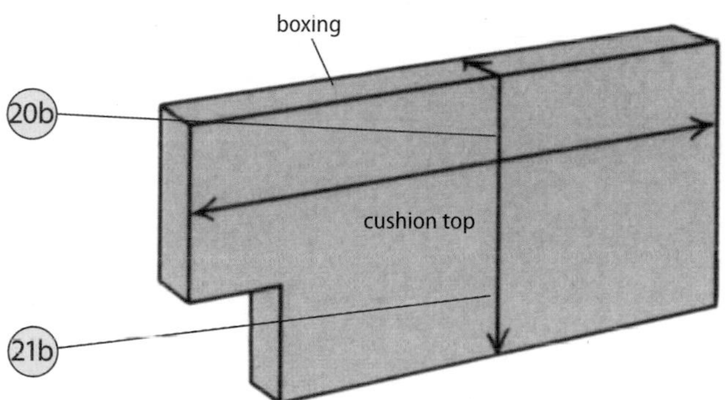

20a. To determine the length of each rectangular cushion top block, measure the top of the cushion at its longest point. Add the depth of the boxing and a 2-inch seam and fitting allowance.

21a. To determine the width of each rectangular cushion top block, measure the cushion at its widest point and add a 4-inch allowance for seams and for boxing turn-ins.

22a. To determine the length and width of each rectangular cushion bottom block, measure the bottom of the cushion at its longest and widest points. Add a 4-inch seam and fitting allowance to each dimension. Do not block the boxing of the cushion at this stage.

20b. To determine the length of each T-shaped or semi T-shaped cushion top block, follow Step 20a.

21b. To determine the width of each T-shaped or semi T-shaped cushion top block, measure the cushion top at its widest point. Add a 2-inch seam and fitting allowance.

22b. To determine the length and width of each T-shaped or semi T-shaped cushion bottom block, follow Step 22a.

Measuring Ruffled and Pleated Skirt Blocks

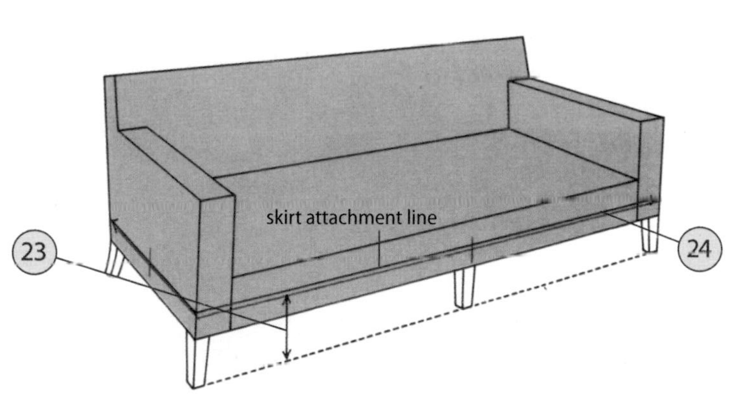

23. To determine the length of the skirt block for a ruffled or pleated skirt, measure from the skirt attachment line to the floor and add 1⅞ inches.

24. To determine the width of the skirt block, add the widths of the skirt attachment lines on all four sides of the sofa or chair. For a pleated skirt, multiply this figure by three and add 12 inches for seam allowances. For a ruffled skirt, multiply by two and a half and add 12 inches.

Determining Yardage and Cutting Guides

Planning for Plain Fabrics and Small Patterns

1. Starting near the top of graph paper, and using a scale of one small square for every 6 inches, draw a horizontal line to the width—in scale—of your fabric. Draw vertical lines from each end to represent the side edges of the fabric.

2. Mark off the length—to scale—of the center block *(Step 10, page 105)* and draw a horizontal line. Label this rectangle "center block," and draw a grain-line arrow parallel to its lengthwise edges.

3a. If the width of the center block is the same or less than the fabric width, skip to Step 4.

3b. If the center block is wider than one fabric width, draw another rectangle of equal length beneath the first one. Divide the extra width required by two and add a ¾-inch seam allowance. Measure this distance in from each side of the rectangle and draw vertical lines to indicate the additional center block sections.

4. Mark off each successive slipcover block, arranging them side by side wherever possible. Draw grain-line arrows and label the blocks as you go. Use more graph paper if necessary.

5. To calculate the number of yards of fabric that your slipcover will require, count the number of lengthwise squares and divide by six.

6. Add the number of yards recommended for welting in the chart on page 99.

7. Use the chart on page 99 to determine the number of yards of sateen-type skirt-lining fabric you need.

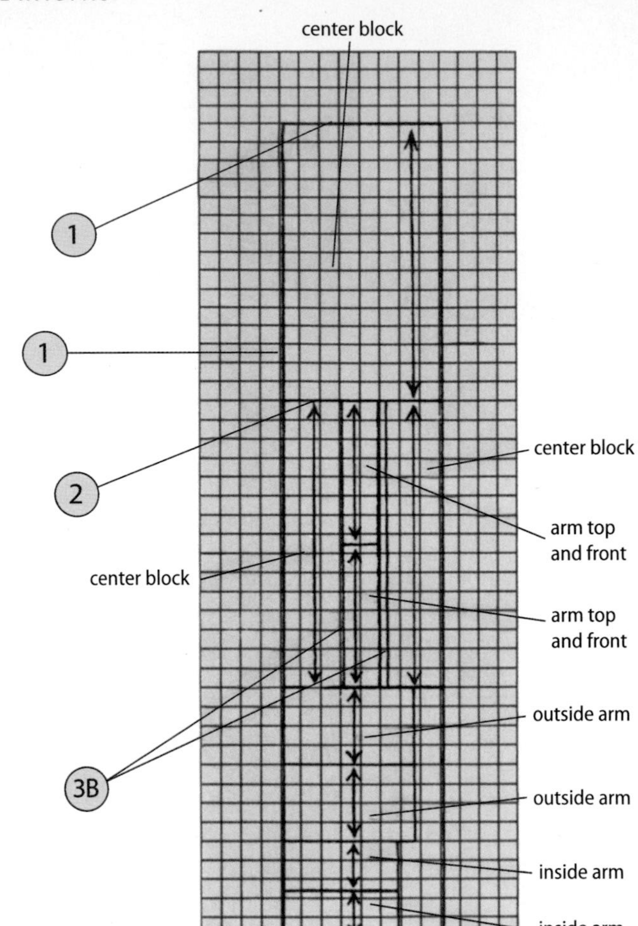

Indicating Stripes and Large Pattern Repeats

8. Repeat Step 1 to draw a rectangular scale model of your slipcover fabric on graph paper.

9. On your fabric, determine the position of repeated dominant patterns. Then mark their locations—in scale—on the rectangle representing the fabric. Use circles to indicate the focal points of large motifs and lines to indicate pattern repeats of stripes, plaids or checks.

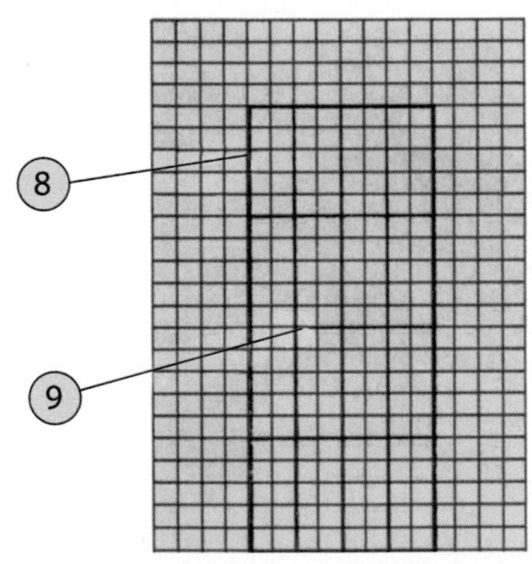

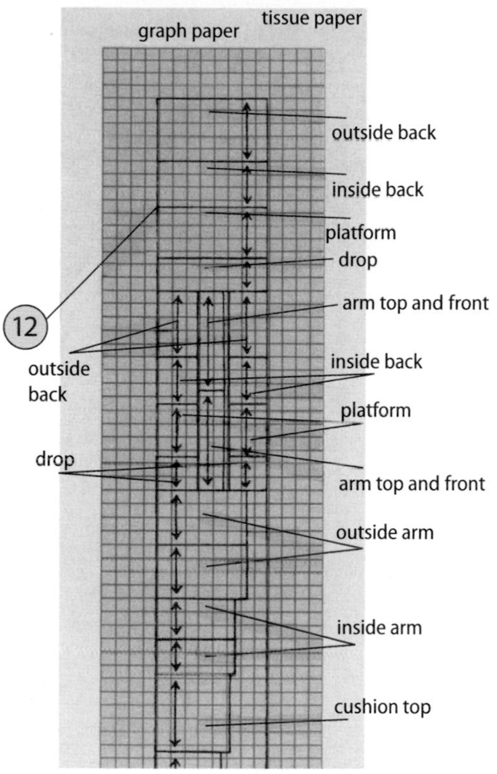

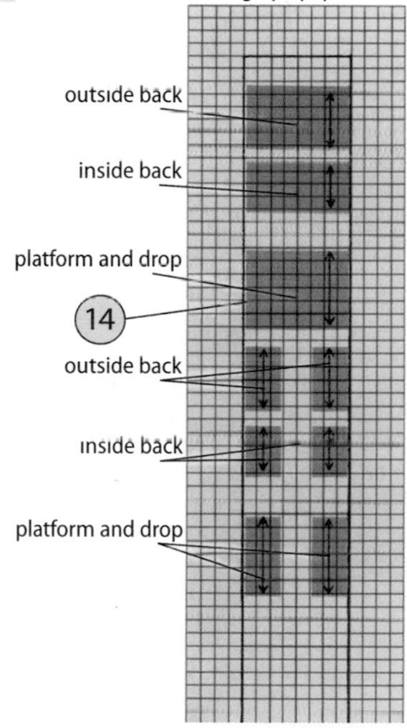

10. To plan how the pattern repeats on your slipcover fabric will match between the blocks of the slipcover, place tissue paper over the marked graph paper.

11. Start from the top of the rectangle that represents the fabric and draw in each of the blocks you need for your slipcover—following the directions in Steps 2–4.

12. Use the measurements of the separate sections of the center block to divide the full-width and partial center blocks, if any, horizontally into separate sections for the drop, platform, inside back, and outside back. Label the sections and draw grain-line arrows parallel to their lengthwise edges.

13. Cut out the tissue-paper blocks. Separate the inside and outside back from the platform and drop sections of the center block to make matching easier; however, do not separate the platform and drop sections.

14. Arrange the tissue-paper blocks on the graph paper, aligning them with the pattern repeat lines or focal point circles so that patterns will match along the seams as well as on such identical sections as cushions or arms, wherever possible, and large motifs will be centered on the prominent blocks of the slipcover.

15. When you have worked out an arrangement you like, tape the tissue-paper blocks to the graph paper.

16. Repeat Steps 5–7 to calculate the number of yards of fabric that your slipcover will require.

Cutting the Slipcover

Preparing the Fabric Blocks

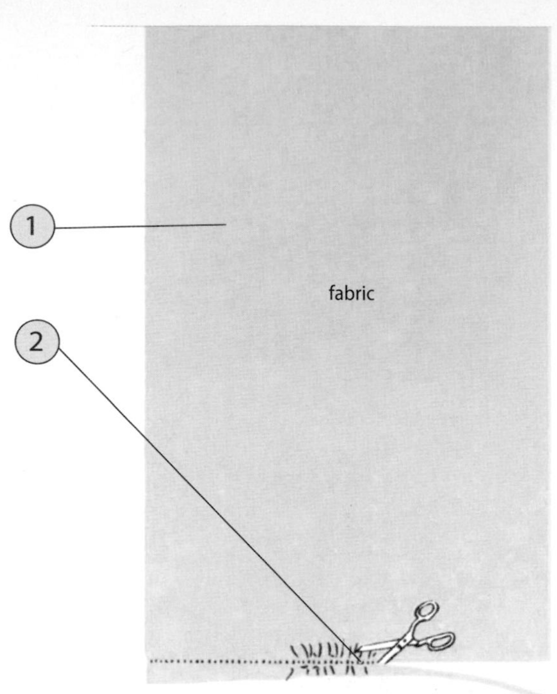

1. Place the fabric, wrong side down, on a large flat surface.

2. Straighten one edge, following the directions for draperies and curtains *(page 88)*.

3. Using the graph paper as a guide, chalk and cut out all of the blocks—but do not separate the sections of the center block horizontally even if your pattern is striped or has a large repeat. Be sure to use the actual — not the scaled-down — measurements of the blocks.

4. Label each block on its wrong side, and draw a grain-line arrow pointing to its top edge. If the fabric grains need straightening, follow the directions for draperies and curtains.

5. For a slipcover with a straight skirt, mark off the distance from the floor to the skirt attachment line on each outside arm block. Add a 1⅞-inch hem and seam allowance. Then draw lines across the width of the blocks at that point, and cut along the lines. Label the skirt sections on their wrong sides, and draw grain-line arrows pointing to their top edges.

Joining Center Block Widths

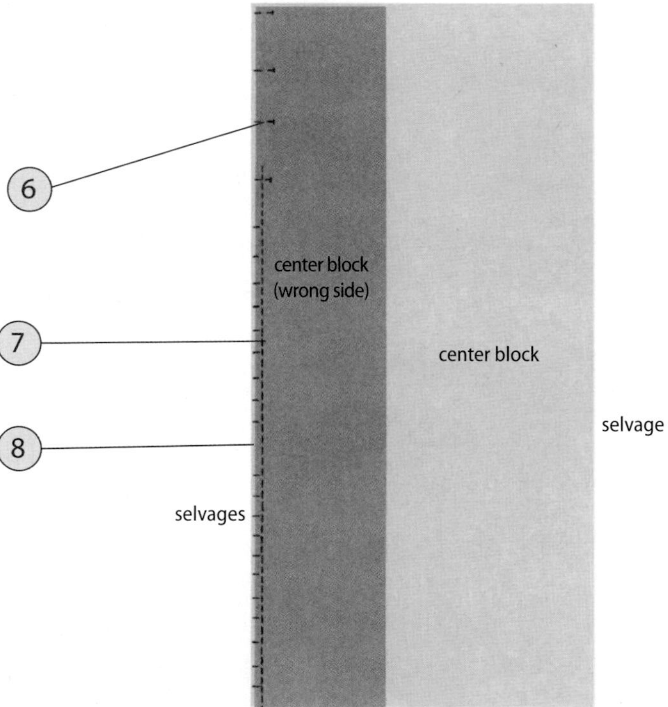

6. To make a center block that is wider than the fabric width, first lay the wide segment of the center block on a flat surface, wrong side down. Over it, lay one of the narrow center block segments, wrong side up. Align the segments along the selvages and pin.

7. Machine stitch ⅜ inch from the edges of the selvages.

8. Clip into the selvages at regular intervals to prevent the seams from puckering.

9. Press the seam allowances open.

10. Align the second narrow segment with the second selvage of the wide center block segment and pin the edges together. Repeat Steps 7–9.

Separating Center Block Lengths

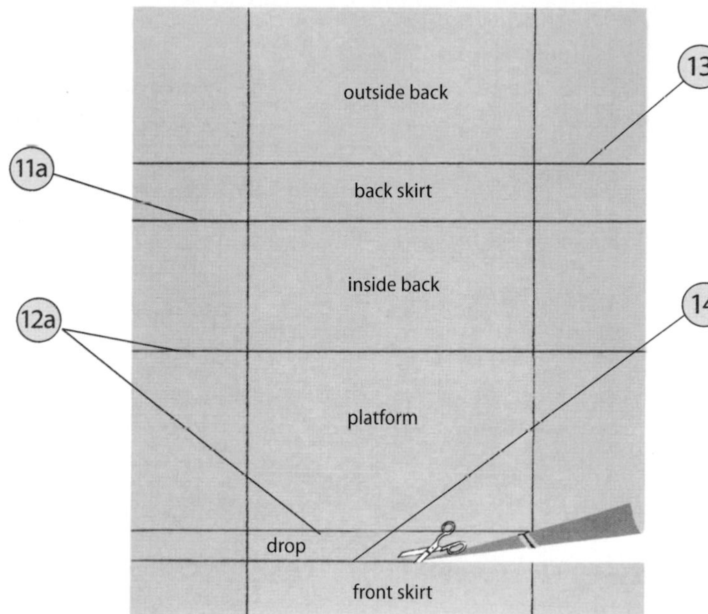

11a. To divide the center block of a solid-colored or small-patterned fabric into separate lengths for pin fitting the slipcover, first mark off the length of the outside back from the top of the block. Draw a chalk line across the block at this point.

12a. Mark off the length of the inside back and the platform sections of the block and draw horizontal lines at each marking.

11b. To divide the center block of a striped or large-patterned fabric, use the graph paper model made in Steps 10–15 on page 105 as a guide.

12b. Draw horizontal chalk lines across the center block to indicate the outside back, inside back, platform and drop sections.

13. For a slipcover with a pleated or ruffled skirt, skip to Step 15. For a slipcover with a straight skirt, indicate the back skirt on the outside back section. Measure above the line dividing the outside back from the inside back the distance from the floor to the skirt attachment line *(Step 4, page 100)*. Add a 1⅞-inch hem and seam allowance and draw a horizontal line at this point.

14. Draw a line the same distance above the bottom edge of the drop section.

15. Cut the center block apart along the horizontal chalk lines. Label each section on the wrong side, and draw a grain-line arrow pointing to its top edge.

16. Fold each section of fabric in half widthwise, and mark the center of its top and bottom edges with pins.

Pin Fitting the Slipcover

Positioning the Sections

1. With the wrong side of the drop section fabric facing in, match the center pin on the section to the center mark on the front skirt attachment line.

2. Align the drop section to extend ⅜ inch below the skirt attachment line and ⅜ inch above the platform edge.

3. Smooth the fabric over the upholstery, and pin it in position.

4. Lay the platform section wrong side down on the platform of the sofa or chair, aligning the center pin on the section with the center pin on the drop.

5. Align the front edge of the platform section with the top edge of the drop section. Then pin the sections together ⅜ inch inside their raw edges.

6. Smooth the platform section toward the arms and back of the sofa or chair and fold up the excess fabric at the back and side edges. Then, using the end of a ruler, tuck 2 or 3 inches of the folded fabric at the back of the platform section into the crease between the inside back and the platform of the sofa or chair.

7. With the wrong side of one outside arm section of the fabric facing in, match the center pin on the section to the center mark on one side skirt attachment line.

8. Align the outside arm section to extend ⅜ inch below the skirt attachment line.

9. Smooth the fabric over the upholstery, and pin it in position. Then trim away any fitting allowance that extends more than 1 inch beyond the side edges of the outside arm of the sofa or chair.

10. Repeat Steps 7–9 on the other outside arm.

11. With the wrong side of the outside back section of the fabric facing in, match the center pin on the section to the center mark on the back skirt attachment line.

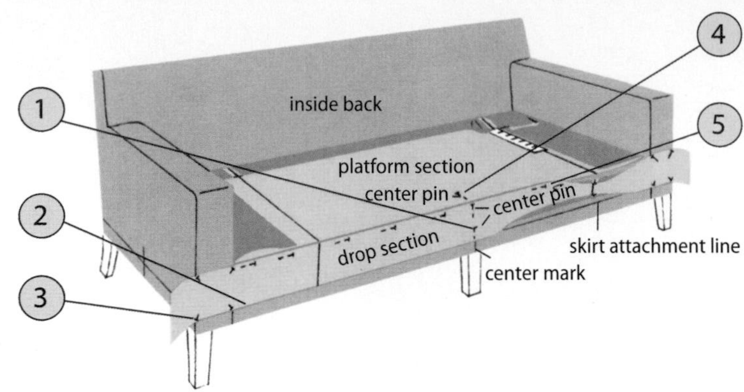

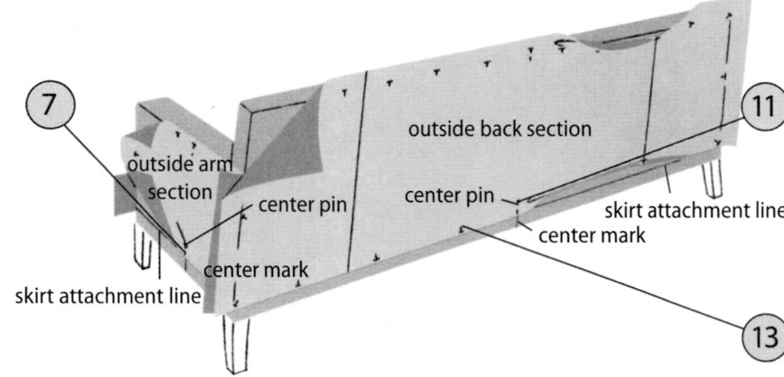

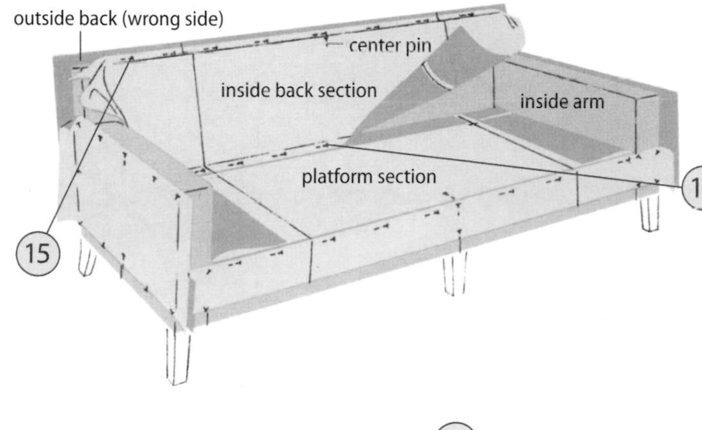

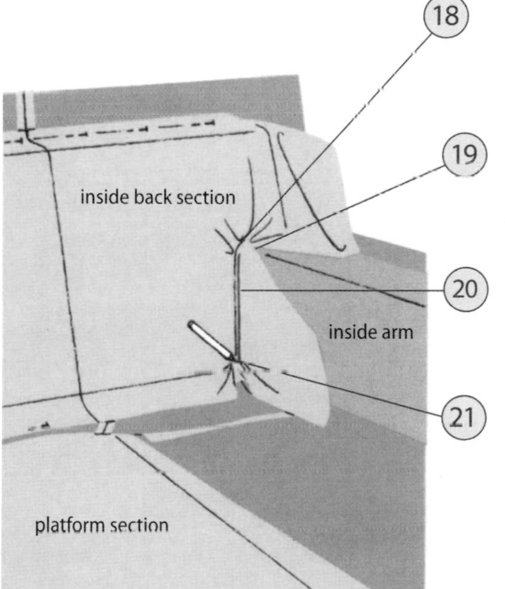

12. Align the outside back section to extend ⅜ inch below the skirt attachment line.

13. Smooth the fabric over the upholstery, and pin it in position. Then trim away any fitting allowance that extends more than 1 inch beyond the side edges of the outside back of the sofa or chair.

14. Still working from the back, place the inside back section on the sofa or chair with the fabric wrong side in. Align the center pin on the section with the center pin on the outside back section.

15. Align the top edge of the inside back section to extend ⅜ inch above the upper edge of the outside back of the sofa or chair. Then pin the inside back and outside back sections together, pinning as closely as possible to the upper edge of the outside back of the sofa or chair.

16. Smooth the inside back section toward the arms and platform.

17. Fold the platform section fabric so that the raw back edge aligns with the bottom edge of the inside back section. Then pin the two sections together ⅜ inch inside their raw edges. Stop pinning several inches from the inside arm on each side.

Fitting the Inside Back Over the Arm

18. At the top of the inside arm, tuck the inside back section into the indentation between the inside arm and the inside back of the sofa or chair.

19. Slash the inside back section to within ¾ inch of the indentation as shown. The cut should align approximately with the top edge of the inside arm.

20. Continue to tuck the inside back section into the indentation from the slash to the platform.

21. With dressmaker's chalk, trace along the indentation from the slash to the platform.

Pin Fitting the Slipcover

22. Pull the fabric out of the indentation, and trim away the excess ¾ inch outside the chalk line.

23. Tuck the trimmed fabric back into the indentation, and then tuck the inside back section into the indentation over the top of the arm.

24. Trace along the indentation at the top of the arm with chalk.

25. Pull the fabric out of the indentation, and trim away the excess ¾ inch outside the chalk line.

26. Slash the inside back section at the corner of the inside back and the top of the arm to within ¼ inch of the chalk line.

27. Repeat Steps 18–26 on the other side of the inside back.

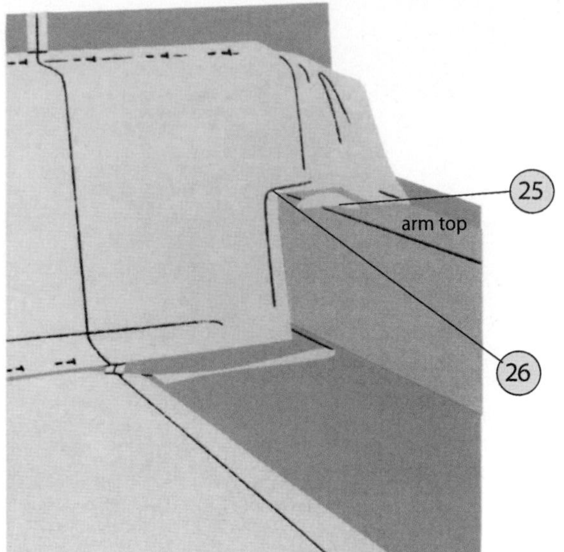

Fitting the Inside Arm

28. Fold the inside back section away from the arm.

29. Arrange the platform fabric at the side over the fabric at the back; measure its width. Trim any width in excess of 6 inches. This is the side tuck-in allowance.

30. With your hand, press the front edge of the platform. If the furniture has a spring edge—i.e., the front of the platform can be pushed down—follow the instructions on page 115. Then skip to Step 44. If the platform has a hard front frame, determine the thickness of the wood with your fingers.

31. Make a diagonal cut in the side tuck-in allowance starting approximately ½ inch from the inside arm at the front edge of the platform frame and extending to 1 inch from the inside arm at the back edge of the front frame.

32. Trim the front portion of the side tuck-in allowance even with the depth of the cut made in the preceding step.

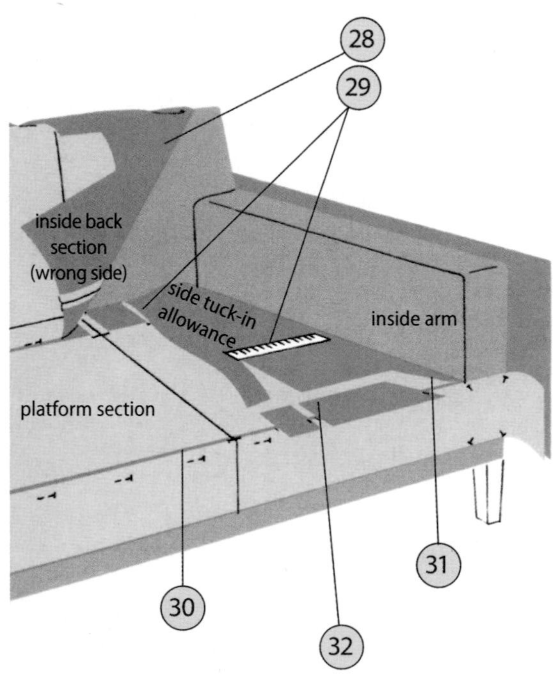

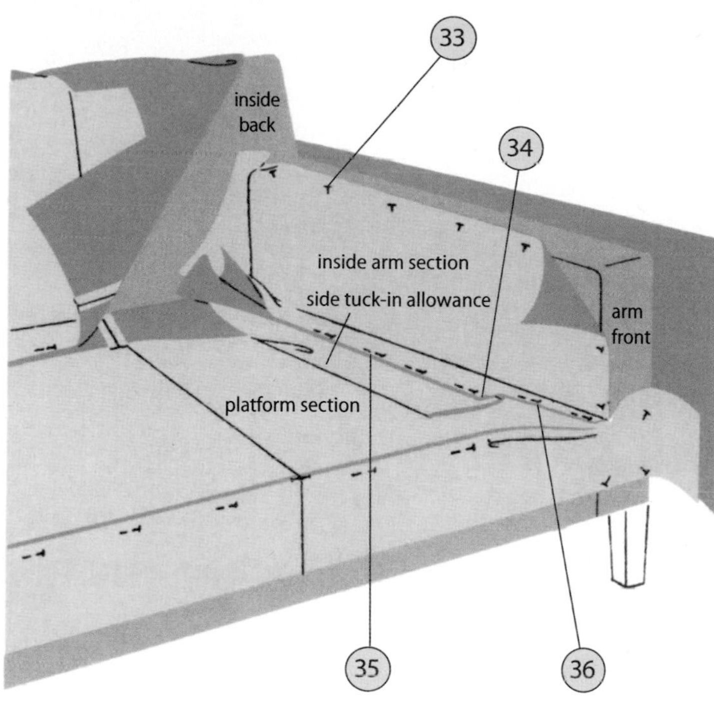

33. Position the inside arm section so that the side edge is 1 inch beyond the arm front and the bottom edge extends 1½ inches onto the platform. Pin.

34. Cut the corner of the inside arm to match the cut in the platform.

35. Fold back the side tuck-in allowance on the platform section until its raw edge matches that of the inside arm section. Pin the sections together ⅜ inch inside their raw edges. Stop pinning several inches from the inside back.

36. Pin the cutout portions of the inside arm and platform sections together ⅜ inch inside their raw edges.

Pin Fitting the Arm Top and Front Section

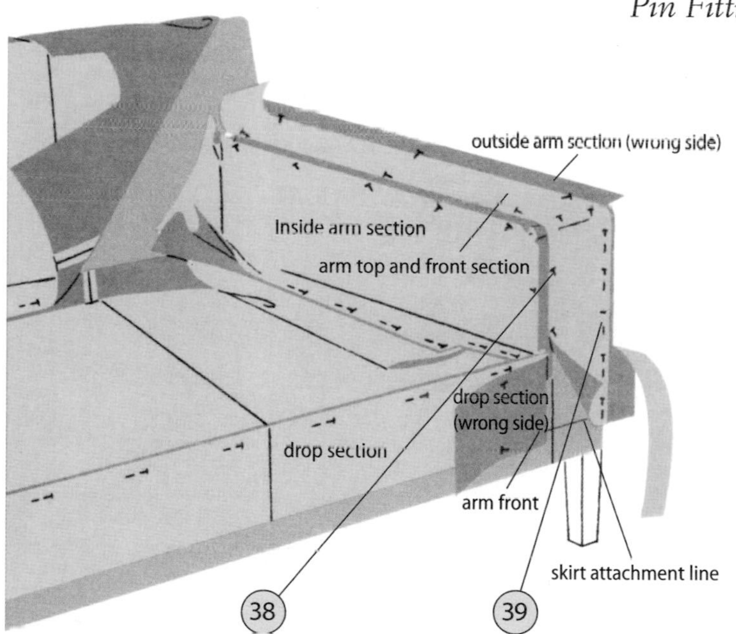

37. Remove the pins from the end of the drop section and pin back the fabric to expose the arm front.

38. For a square-armed sofa or chair, position the arm top and front section with the bottom edge extending ⅜ inch below the skirt attachment line and the side edges extending ⅜ inch beyond the side edges of the sofa or chair arm. Smooth the fabric over the upholstery and pin it in position.

39. Pin the inside arm, the drop, and the outside arm to the arm front section ⅜ inch inside the raw edges of the arm front section.

40. Trim the inside arm, the drop, and the outside arm fitting allowances to align with the arm front seam allowance.

Pin Fitting the Slipcover

41. Pin the inside arm and the outside arm to the arm top ⅜ inch inside its long raw edges.

42. Trim the inside arm fitting allowance to align with the arm top seam allowance all the way to the back edge.

43. Make a small horizontal tuck in the fabric on each side of the top and front arm section to fit the fabric tightly over the curve. Baste the tucks in place.

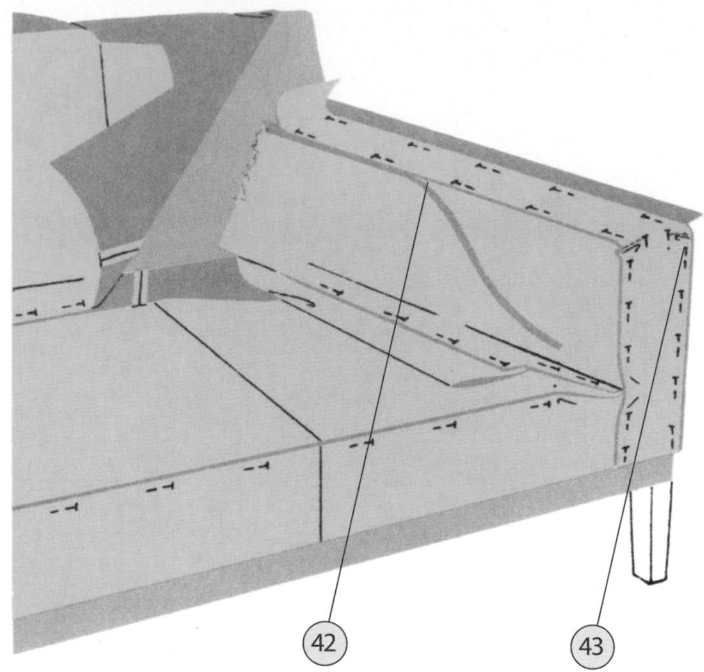

Fitting the Arm at the Inside Back

44. With the end of the ruler, tuck the back of the inside arm section into the indentation between the inside arm and the inside back.

45. With chalk, mark the wrong side of the fabric at the edge of the indentation.

46. Pull the fabric out of the indentation and cut ¾ inch outside the chalk line.

47. Finish pinning the arm top to the inside arm.

48. Trim the back edge of the arm top section even with the back edge of the inside arm.

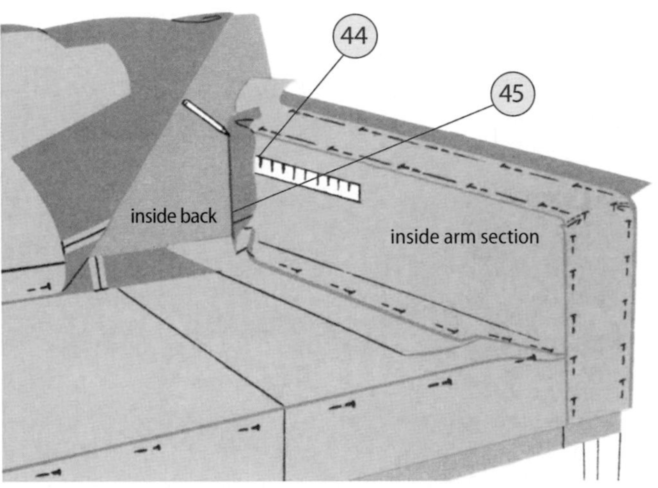

Joining the Inside Back and Arm

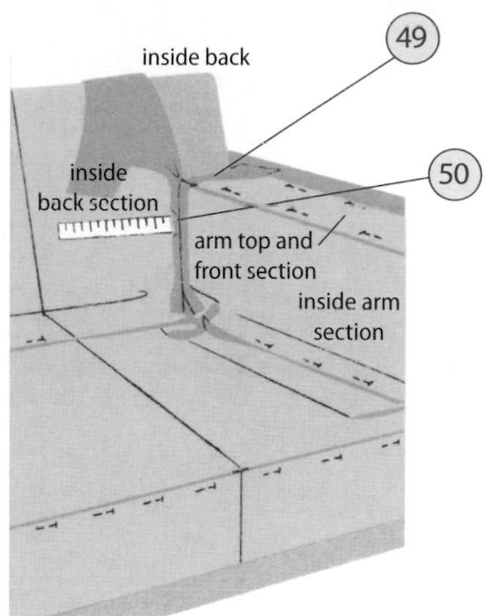

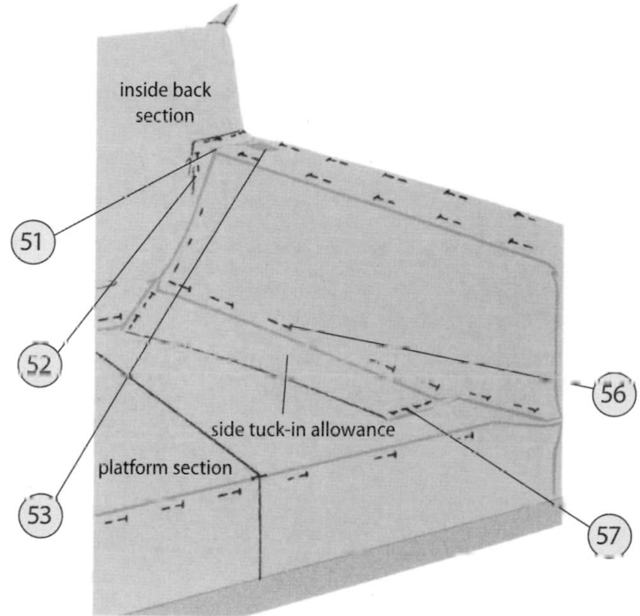

49. Using the ruler, tuck the inside arm and top and front arm sections into the indentation between the arm and the inside back of the sofa or chair.

50. Tuck the inside back section into the indentation at the inside arm and top arm of the sofa or chair.

51. Make a horizontal clip in the inside back section at the junction between the inside arm and top arm sections to fit the fabric smoothly over the arm.

52. Pin the inside back section to the arm top and inside arm sections as closely as possible to the indentation in the sofa or chair.

53. Trim away any excess fitting allowance on the top arm section even with the inside back seam allowance.

54. Pull the pinned sections out of the indentation at the bottom corner of the inside back and inside arm.

55. Finish pinning the bottom edge of the inside back section to the back edge of the platform section ⅜ inch from their raw edges.

56. Finish pinning the inside arm section to the side tuck-in allowance of the platform section ⅜ inch from their raw edges.

57. Pin together the layers of the folded side tuck-in allowance ⅜ inch inside their raw edges at both the back and front ends.

Pin Fitting the Slipcover

Fitting the Outside Arm and Outside Back

58. Smooth the unpinned edge of the inside back section and pin it in place.

59. Make a dart in the inside back section at the junction between the top and the side edges.

60. Pin the outside arm and the inside back sections together on a line with the top of the arm.

61. Starting at the top of the sofa or chair, pin the inside back and the outside arm sections to the outside back section. Insert the pins close to the back edge of the sofa or chair.

62. Trim the seam allowance for the dart made in Step 59 to ⅜ inch.

63. Trim the outside arm and the inside back seam allowances to ⅜ inch. Continue trimming the outside arm seam allowance up to the front arm edge.

64. Repeat Steps 28–63 on the other side of the sofa or chair.

65. On the zipper side, measure 24½ inches from the floor, following the contour of the outside back edge. Mark with chalk.

66. Above the chalk mark, trim the outside back and inside back seam allowances to ⅜ inch, and below, to 1 inch.

67. On the side that will have a zipper, spread apart the outside back seam allowance and mark the zipper opening seam line with chalk.

68. Make cross marks on the seam allowance near the top and center of the outside arm.

69. Examine the seam allowances on the slipcover to be sure that all of them have been trimmed to ⅜ inch, except the one for the zipper opening.

70. Spread each seam apart and make cross marks on the seam allowances at 3- or 4-inch intervals to serve as stitching guides.

71. Remove the pins from the zipper opening and carefully remove the slipcover from the chair.

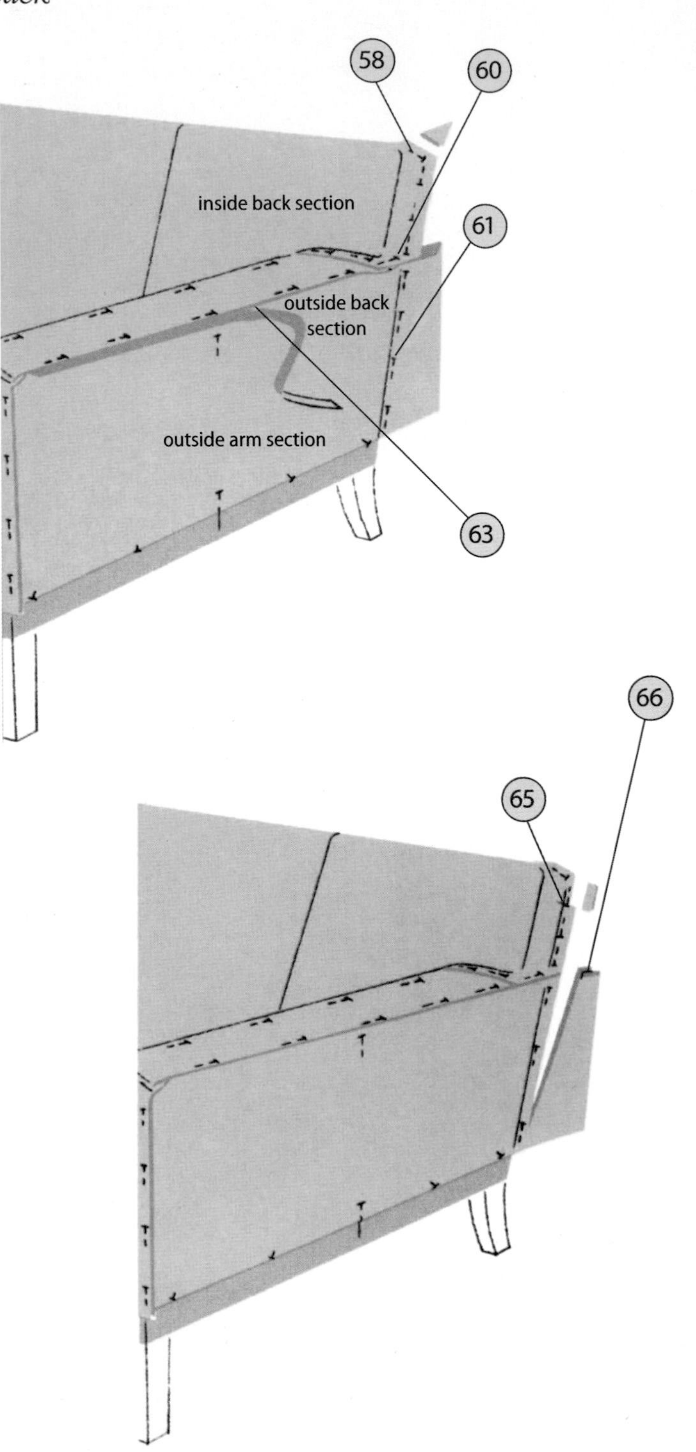

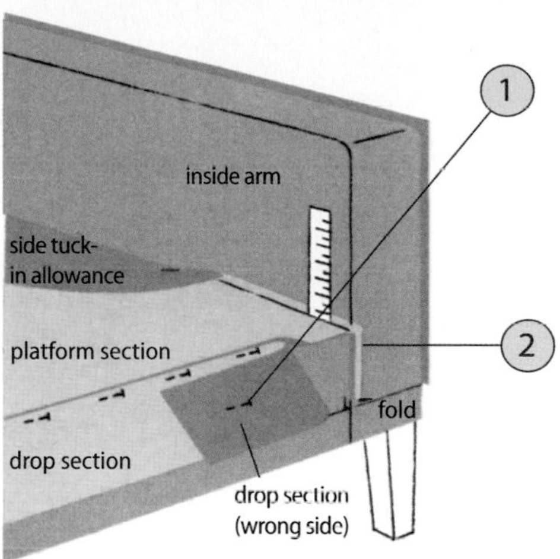

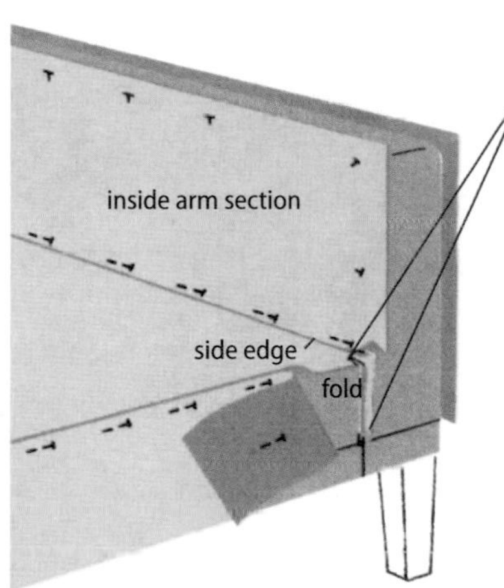

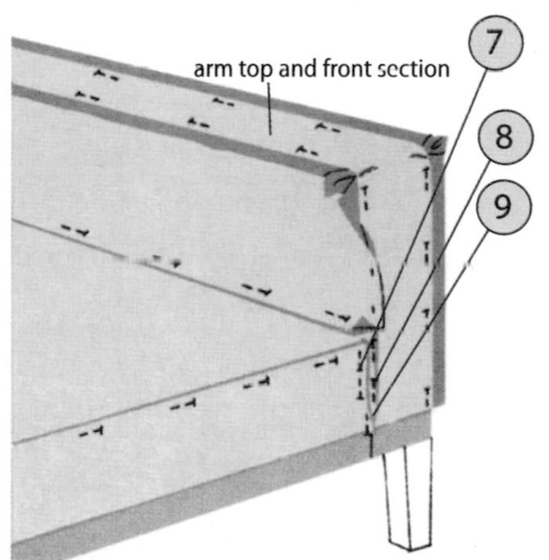

1. Remove the pins from one end of the drop section of the slipcover and fold back the fabric to expose the groove between the platform and the inside arm of the sofa or chair. Pin the drop section out of the way.

2. Using the end of a ruler, push the fold of the side tuck-in allowance on the platform section down 3 inches into the groove between the inside arm and the platform. The front edges of the tuck-in allowance should protrude ⅜ inch beyond the drop and arm front, and the side edge should extend ½ inch above the platform of the sofa or chair.

3. Make ¼-inch clips at the side edge of the platform section and in the fold of the tuck-in, as shown.

4. Position the inside arm, wrong side down, so the front edge of the section protrudes 1 inch beyond the front of the arm, and the bottom edge extends ½ inch onto the platform. Pin.

5. Align the raw side edge of the tuck-in with the raw bottom edge of the inside arm.

6a. For a curved arm, pin the arm front section in position according to the instructions on page 116, Steps 1–6.

6b. For a square arm, pin the arm top and front section in position as shown on page 111, Step 38.

7. Pin the drop to the adjacent layer of the tuck-in allowance.

8. Pin the arm front to the adjacent layer of the tuck-in.

9. Pin the arm front to the drop below the tuck-in fold.

10. Repeat Steps 1–9 at the other end of the platform.

11a. For a curved arm, finish pin fitting the arm front as shown on page 116, Steps 7–10.

11b. For a square arm, finish pin fitting the arm front as shown on page 112, Steps 39–43.

Pin Fitting a Curved-Arm Sofa or Chair

1. Remove the pins from the front of the arm sections, and fold out of the way.

2. Position one arm front section, wrong side down, so that the bottom edge extends ⅜ inch below the skirt attachment line. Pin.

3. Trace the shape of the arm front onto the fabric by running chalk along the edges of the arm front at the prominent edge of the welt or seam.

4. Remove the arm front section. Correct the chalk lines, smoothing the curve.

5. Pin the second arm front section of the slipcover to the chalked section, wrong sides together. Trim the two sections ⅜ inch outside the chalk lines. Remove the pins.

6. Pin one trimmed arm front section, wrong side down, to the arm front of the sofa or chair so that the bottom edge extends ⅜ inch below the skirt attachment line, and the side and top edges protrude ⅜ inch beyond the arm front.

7. Unfold the inside and outside arm sections, and smooth them toward the arm front. Pin the sections in position.

8. Pin the inside and outside arm sections together along the chalk line drawn on the outermost edge of the sofa or chair arm *(page 111, Step 37)*. Trim the seam allowances to ⅜ inch.

9. Baste three or four small tucks into the top front of the inside arm section.

10. Pin the drop, the inside arm, and the outside arm sections of the slipcover to the arm front ⅜ inch inside the raw edges of the arm front section.

11. Trim the inside arm, the drop, and the outside arm section fitting allowances to align with the arm front section seam allowances.

12. Repeat Steps 6–11 on the other arm front section of the slipcover.

13. Proceed with Step 44, page 112.

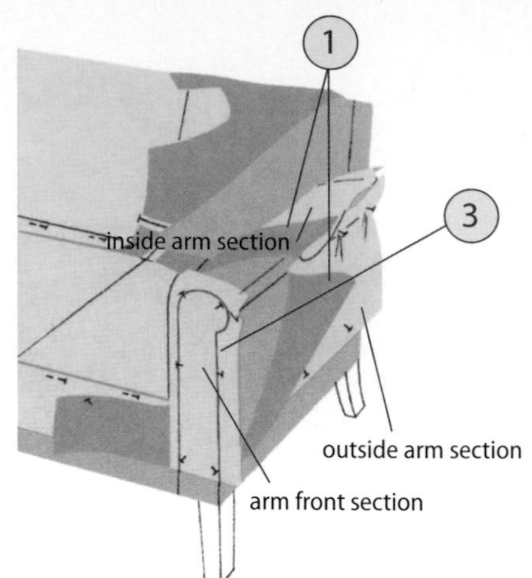

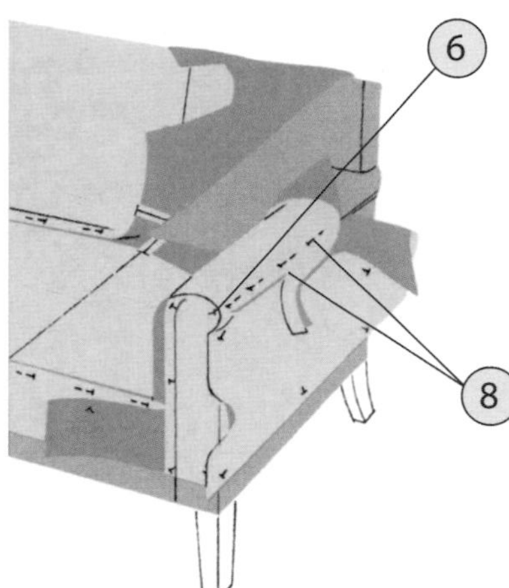

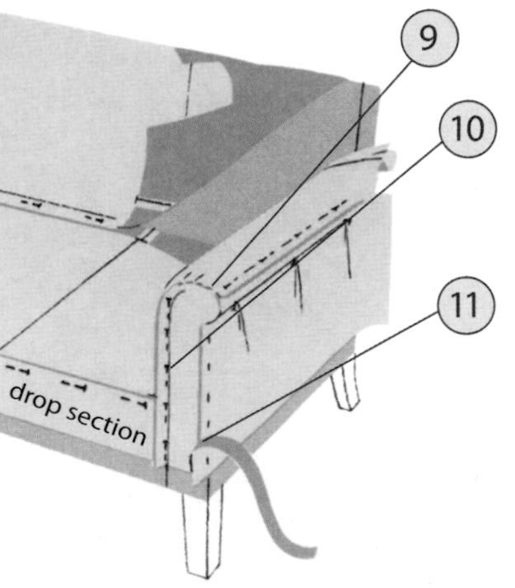

Joining the Platform and Inside Arm Sections

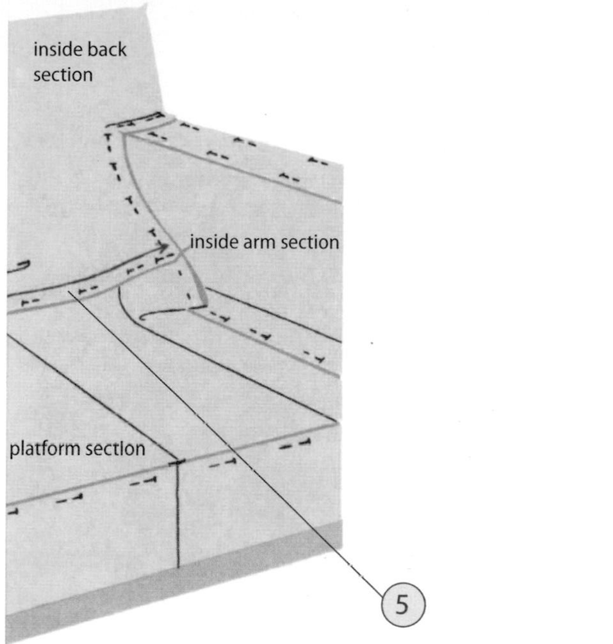

1. To sew the slipcover, remove the pins from one seam at a time.

2. For an unwelted seam, skip to Step 4. For a seam that is to be welted, attach the welting to the larger of the sections that you plan to join—sewing it to the side of the fabric that will be visible in the finished slipcover.

3. Turn the slipcover, wrong side out, and repin the seam ⅜ inch inside the raw edges.

4. Machine stitch the seam ⅜ inch inside the raw edges of the fabric; remove the pins as you go.

5. Stitch the seam between the inside back section and the platform section from one inside arm to the other.

6a. For a hard-edged sofa or chair, stitch the seam between the inside arm and platform sections from the inside back to the indentation at the front of the tuck-in allowance.

7a. Stitch along the front indentation of the platform section—sewing from the fold in the side tuck-in allowance to the front edges of the platform and inside arm sections; pivot at the corner.

8a. Repeat Steps 6a and 7a on the other side of the platform.

9a. Use a welt seam to stitch the drop section to the platform section from one inside arm to the other.

10a. Use a welt seam to stitch the arm top and front section to the inside arm and drop sections from the inside back to the bottom of the drop.

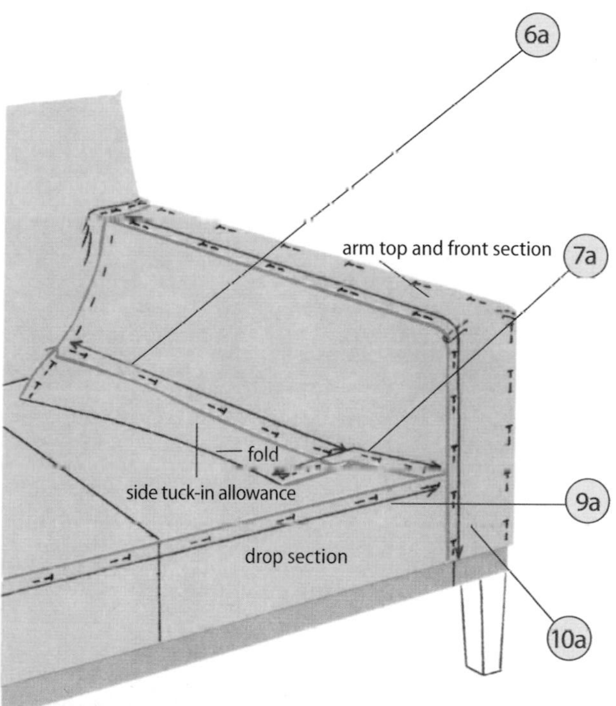

Stitching the Slipcover

6b. For a sofa or chair with a spring edge, stitch the seam between the inside arm section and the side tuck-in allowance of the platform section from the inside back to the drop.

7b. Repeat Step 6b on the other side of the slipcover.

8b. Stitch welting to the front edge of the platform section between the clips at the beginning of each side tuck-in allowance.

9b. Stitch the inner layer of the side tuck-in allowance to the adjacent portion of the drop from the fold to the platform edge. Without breaking threads, stitch the front of the platform section to the top of the drop section. Then stitch the inner layer of the other side tuck-in allowance to the other end of the drop.

10b. Use a welt seam to stitch the arm top and front section to the inside arm section and the outer layer of the side tuck-in allowance. Then stitch from just beneath the fold in the side tuck-in allowance to the bottom edges of the drop and arm front sections.

11. Stitch the inside back section to the arm top and inside arm sections from the outside arm to the side tuck-in allowance of the platform section. Then stitch together the layers of the tuck-in allowance.

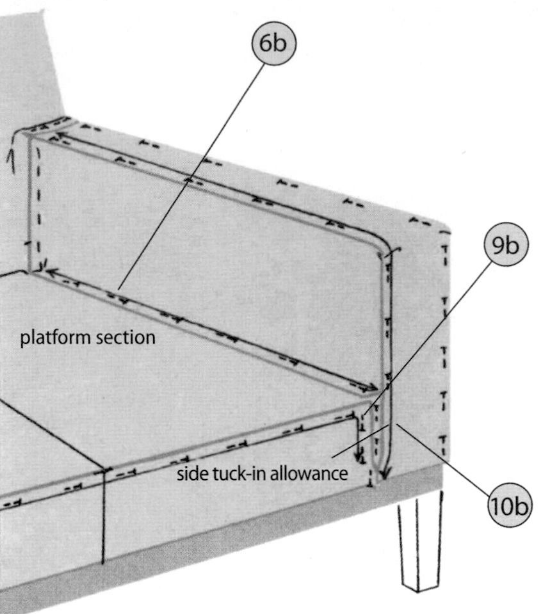

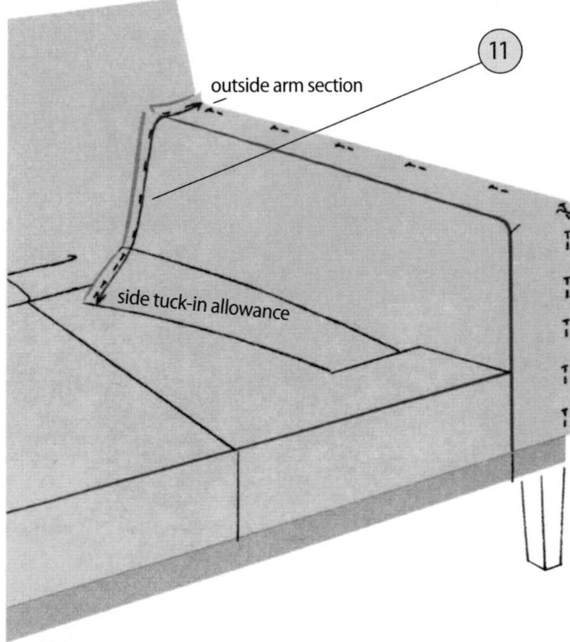

Chapter 4: Slipcovers

Stitching the Slipcover

Joining the Outside Arm and Outside Back Sections

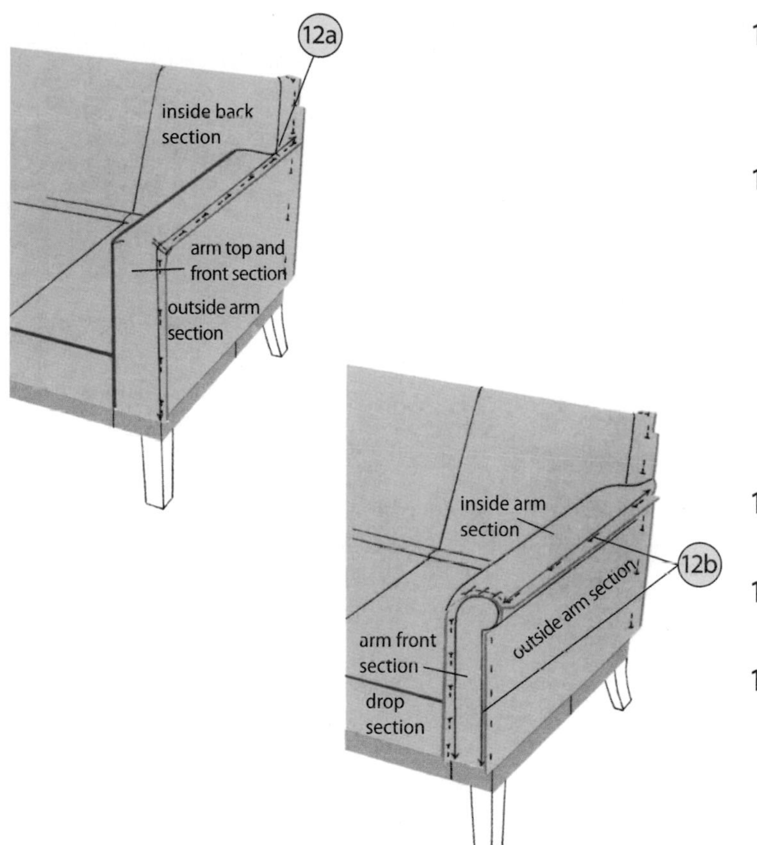

12a. For a sofa or chair with a square arm, use a welt seam to stitch the outside arm section to the inside back section and the arm top and front section from the outside back to the bottom of the arm front.

12b. For a sofa or chair with a curved arm, use a welt seam to stitch the outside arm section to the inside arm section from the outside back to the arm front. Then, using a welt seam, stitch the arm front section to the outside arm and inside arm sections. For a hard-edged sofa or chair, stitch the bottom of the arm front to the drop following the instructions in Step 10a. For a spring-edged sofa or chair, stitch the bottom of the arm front to the side tuck-in allowance and then to the bottom of the drop *(Step 10b)*.

13. Stitch the dart at the junction between the top and side of the inside back section.

14. Repeat Steps 9–13 on the other side of the slipcover.

15. Stitch welting to the top and side edges of the outside back section. Then, starting at the bottom of the side that will not have a zipper, stitch the outside back section to the outside arm and inside back sections. Stop stitching at the top of the zipper opening.

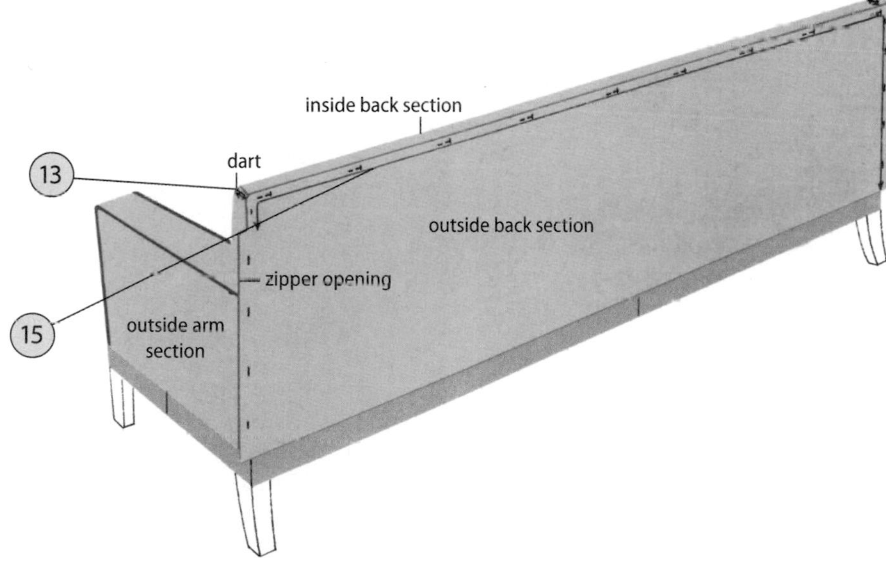

Stitching the Slipcover

Joining the Skirt Sections

16a. At the zipper opening allow a 1¼-Inch seam allowance outside the edges of the first and last pleats. Then skip to Step 17.

16b. For a ruffled skirt, machine stitch the widths together ½ inch inside their raw edges. Then skip to Box D.

16c. For a slipcover with a straight skirt, lay the body of the slipcover wrong side down on a large, flat surface.

17. Replace the pins marking the centers of the outside back, drop, and outside arm sections with chalk marks.

18. Align the center pin on one skirt section with the center mark on the corresponding slipcover section.

19. Align the top edge of the skirt section with the bottom edge of the slipcover.

20. At the corners of the slipcover, mark the skirt section 1 inch outside the corner welting. At the corner where the zipper opening will be, mark the skirt section even with the zipper opening seam allowance.

21. Trim the ends of the skirt section even with the marks made in the preceding step.

22. Repeat Steps 18–21 on each skirt section.

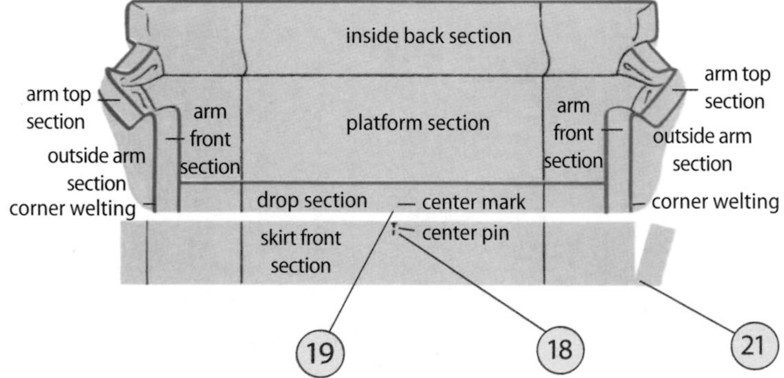

Stitching the Slipcover

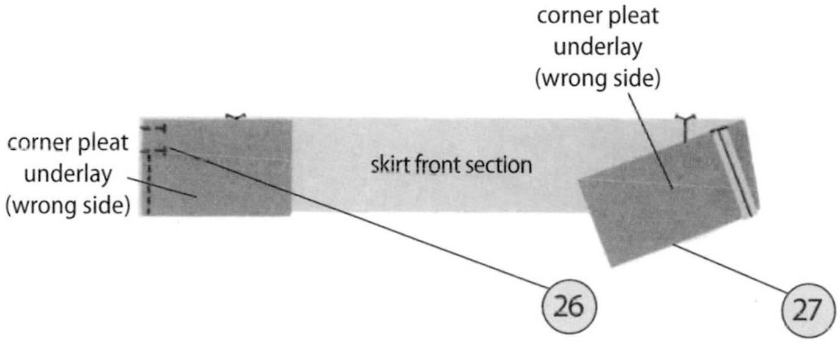

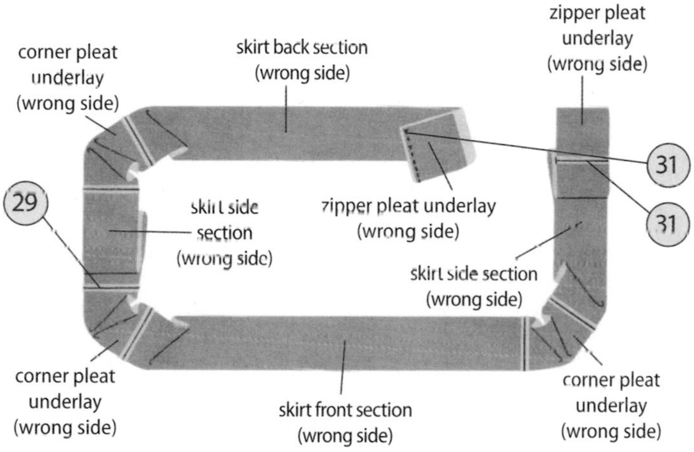

23. To make underlays for pleats at the closed corners of the slipcover, cut scraps of slipcover fabric into three rectangles 16 inches wide and the length of the skirt. Mark the center of one wide edge of each rectangle with chalk.

24. To make underlays for the zipper opening pleat, cut two rectangles 9¼ inches wide and the same length as the skirt.

25. Place the skirt front section wrong side down and set a pleat underlay over it, wrong side up.

26. Align one end of the underlay with one end of the skirt section. Pin.

27. Machine stitch ½ inch inside the raw edges of the fabric, removing the pins as you go. Press the seam allowances open.

28. Repeat Steps 25 and 27 on the other side of the skirt front section.

29. Pin and stitch the skirt side sections to the unstitched ends of the corner pleat underlays already attached to the skirt front.

30. Pin and stitch one end of the remaining corner pleat underlay to the end of the skirt side section that will not have a zipper. Then pin and stitch the back skirt section to the other end of the underlay.

31. Pin and stitch one end of a zipper pleat underlay to the end of the back skirt section that will have a zipper. Then attach the other zipper pleat underlay to the skirt side section that will have a zipper.

Stitching the Slipcover

Lining the Skirt

32. Measure the total width of the skirt sections joined in Steps 16–31.

33. To make the skirt lining, decide the number of widths needed by dividing the skirt width by the width of the lining fabric. Round the figure to the next highest full number. Subtract 3 inches from the skirt length to find the lining length. Cut out the lining.

34. Machine stitch the lining widths together ½ inch inside their raw edges.

35. Place the skirt wrong side down with the lining on top, wrong side up. Align the bottom edges. Pin.

36. Machine stitch ½ inch inside the raw edges.

37. Turn the skirt away from the lining, and press the seam allowances toward the skirt.

38. Fold up the lining with its wrong side against the wrong side of the skirt. Match the top edges of the skirt and lining. Pin.

39. Press the bottom edge of the skirt.

40. Stitch the lining and skirt together ¼ inch inside their top edges, removing the pins as you go.

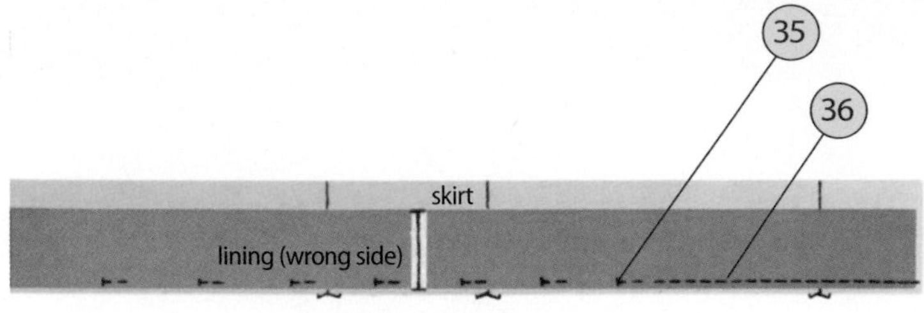

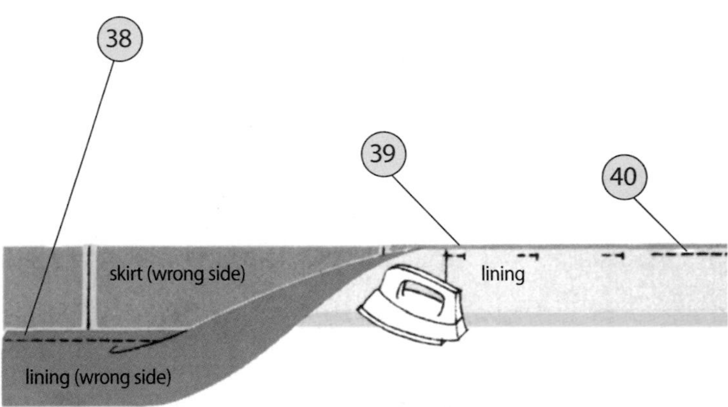

Making the Pleats or Ruffles

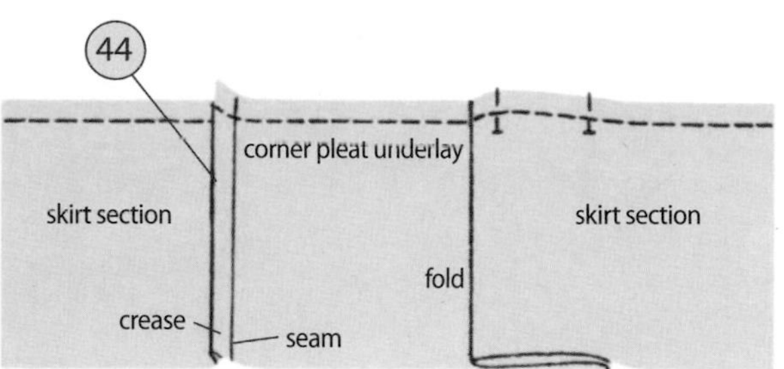

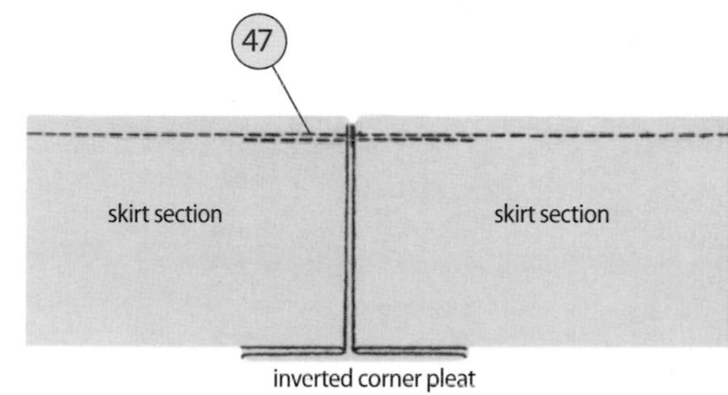

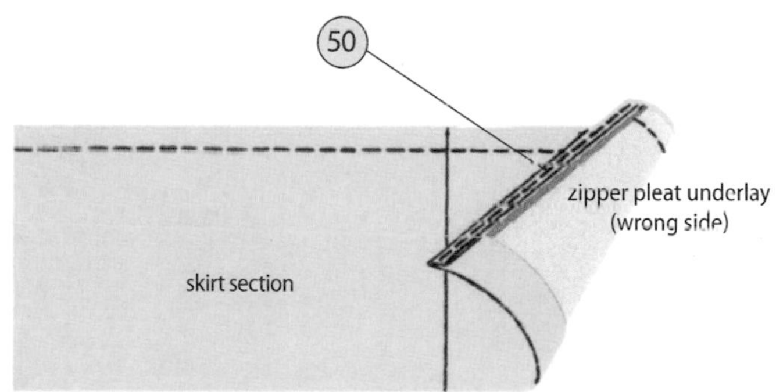

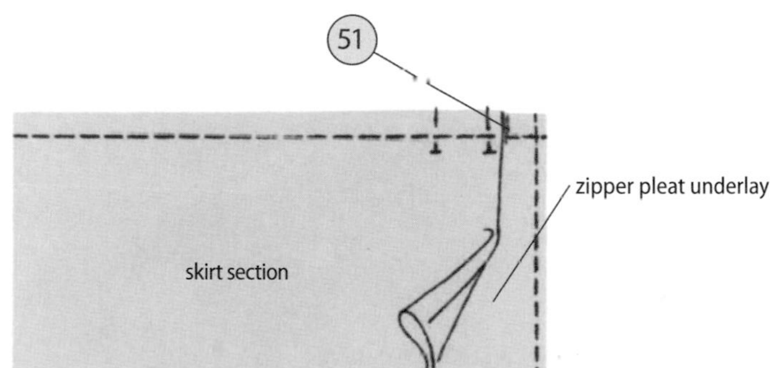

41. For a slipcover with a pleated skirt, make box pleats following the instructions on page 67. Then skip to Step 56.

42. For a slipcover with a ruffled skirt, gather the ruffles like on page 39, but in this case make the gathering stitches ¼ inch from the top edge of the skirt. Start and end the ruffling 2 inches inside the ends of the skirt. Then skip to Step 56.

43. For a slipcover with a straight skirt, place the skirt on a flat surface, lining side down.

44. To make an inverted pleat at one closed corner of the skirt, first form a lengthwise crease in one skirt section with your fingers. Make the crease ½ inch outside and parallel to the seam between the skirt section and a corner pleat underlay.

45. Fold the fabric to align the crease with the chalk mark in the center of the underlay. Pin.

46. Repeat Steps 44 and 45 on the other side of the corner pleat underlay.

47. Press the inverted corner pleat, then machine stitch it in place ¼ inch inside its top edge.

48. Repeat Steps 44–47 to make the inverted corner pleats on the two remaining closed corners of the slipcover.

49. To make an inverted corner pleat on one edge of the zipper opening of the slipcover, fold the unattached end of one of the zipper pleat underlays under by ¼ inch.

50. Machine stitch close to the fold.

51. Measure in from the fold 1 inch and make a mark with chalk.

52. Make a half pleat in the manner described in Steps 44, 45 and 47.

53. Repeat Steps 49–52 to make a half pleat on the other zipper opening edge.

Stitching the Slipcover

Attaching the Skirt to the Body of the Slipcover

54. Sew welting to the bottom edge of the body of the slipcover. Start the welting on the outside back, at the zipper opening edge. End the welting at the zipper opening seam line marked on the wrong side of the outside arm section.

55. Place the skirt on a flat surface, lining side down, and position the body of the slipcover on top of it, wrong side up. Align the top edge of the skirt with the bottom edge of the slipcover.

56. At the zipper opening, match the folds of the pleats or the ends of the ruffled portion of the skirt to the ends of the welting sewed around the bottom of the slipcover in Step 54. Pin.

57. Match the center of each skirt section to the center marks on the corresponding slipcover sections. Pin.

58. For straight and pleated skirts, match the centers of the inverted corner pleats with the corners of the slipcover. Pin.

59. Finish pinning the skirt to the slipcover.

60. Machine stitch the skirt to the slipcover ⅜ inch inside their raw edges, removing the pins as you go.

61. Insert the zipper in the zipper opening, following the instructions on page 55, Steps 1–13. For a skirt with pleats at the zipper opening edges, make this exception in Step 13: when sewing the unattached edge of the zipper to the outside arm and side skirt, stop stitching at the welt between the two sections. Break the threads. Then turn the pleat out of the way, and resume stitching below the welt to the bottom edge of the skirt.

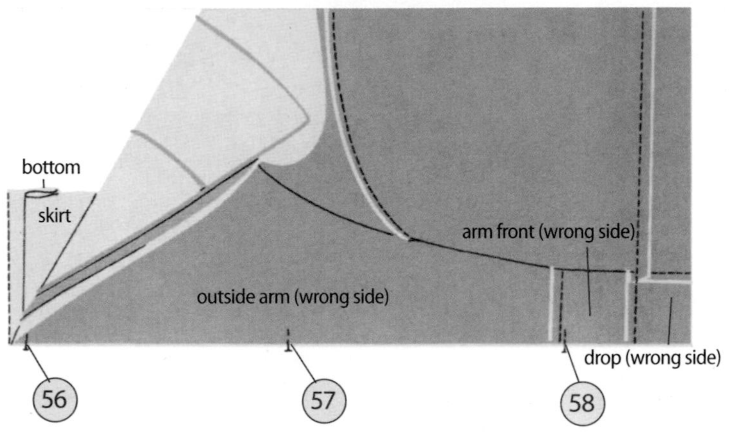

Stitching the Slipcover

Cutting the Cushion Sections

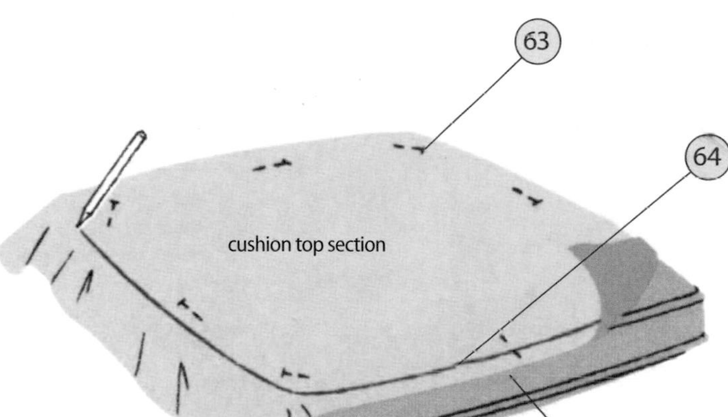

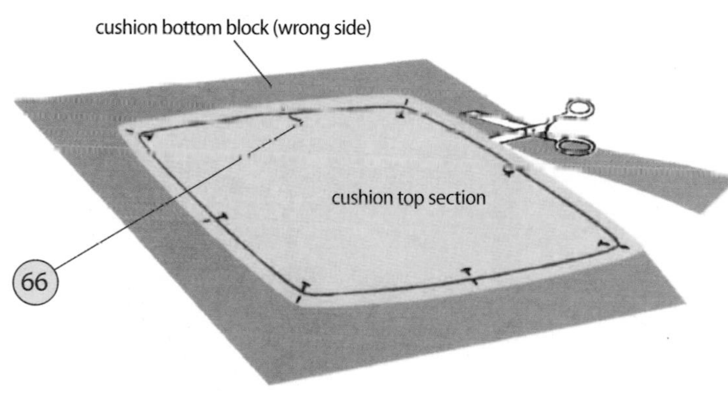

62a. To separate the front boxing from each seat cushion, measure the depth of the box from the lower edge of the top block. Add a ¾-inch seam allowance. Draw a chalk line across the block at this point. Then cut along the line.

62b. To separate the top boxing from each back cushion, measure the depth of the box from the upper edge of the top block. Add a ¾-inch seam allowance. Draw a chalk line across the block at this point. Then cut along the line.

63. Lay the cushion top section, wrong side down, on the cushion with the edge cut in the preceding step protruding ⅜ inch beyond the front edge of a seat cushion or the upper edge of a back cushion. Pin the section to the cushion.

64. With dressmaker's chalk. trace around the perimeter of the cushion at the prominent edge of the welt or seam line. Remove the section from the cushion.

65a. For a rectangular cushion, fold the fabric in half—wrong side in—and match up the chalk lines as closely as possible. Then trim ⅜ inch outside the chalk lines on the top layer.

65b. For a cushion that is T-shaped, or semi T-shaped, trim the cushion top section ⅜ inch outside the chalk lines.

66. Place the cushion bottom block, wrong side up, and set the cushion top section over it, wrong side down. Be sure the arrows on the wrong sides of the sections face the same direction. Pin.

Stitching the Slipcover

67. Trim around the edges of the cushion top section.

68. To make the boxing for the sides of each cushion, cut scrap fabric into two rectangles the depth of the cushion front box and the length of the cushion sides. Label each piece with chalk on its wrong side.

69. Determine the length the zipper should be by measuring the back edge of a seat cushion or the lower edge of a back cushion. Add 8 inches.

70. Cut two strips of fabric that are the depth of the box sides and front and the length of the zipper tapes.

Sewing the Cushion Covers

71. Stitch welting around the outside edges of the cushion top section and the cushion bottom section.

72. Sew the zipper into the strips cut in Step 70, following the instructions on pages 53 and 54, Steps 3–13.

73. Align the ends of the zippered boxing with the ends of the side boxing. Pin. Follow the instructions on page 54, Steps 15–18.

74. Pin the front or upper boxing to the corresponding edge of the cushion top. For a rectangular cushion, start and stop pinning at the corners. For a T- or semi T-shaped cushion, start and stop pinning 2 inches from the front or upper corners of the cushion top.

75. Center the zippered boxing section along the lower or back edge of the cushion top section.

76. Pin the zippered and side box sections to the edges of the cushion top. For a rectangular cushion, stop pinning the sides 4 inches short of the upper or front edge of the cushion top section. For a T-shaped or semi T-shaped cushion, stop pinning 2 inches short of the upper or front edge of the cushion top section.

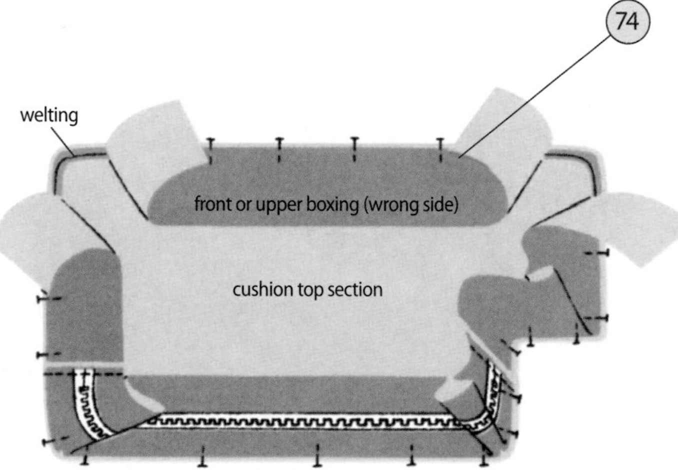

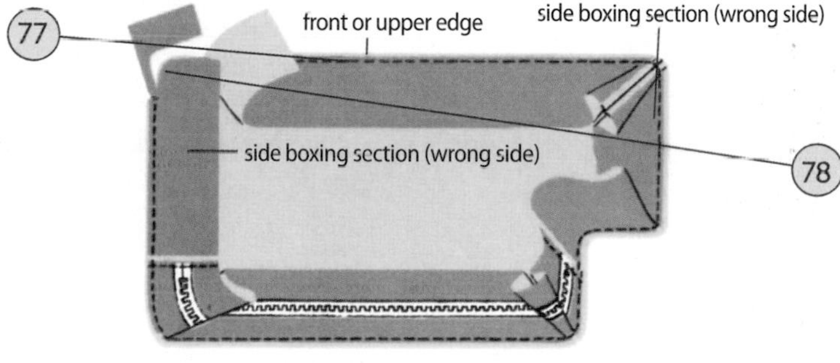

77. Stitch the boxing sections to the cushion top section between the pins.

78a. For a rectangular cushion, make seams to connect the sides of the boxing to the front or upper boxing section 2 inches short of the front or upper edge of the cushion top section. Trim the seam allowance to ⅜ inch, and press the seam allowance open.

78b. For a T-shaped or semi T-shaped cushion, trim the ends of the side boxing sections even with the front or upper edge of the cushion top seam allowance. Then trim the ends of the upper or front boxing section even with the side edges of the cushion top seam allowance. Make seams connecting the boxing at the front or upper corners of the cushion top section. Press the seam allowances open.

79. Finish stitching the boxing to the cushion top section.

80. Pin and machine stitch the cushion bottom to the unattached edges of the box.

Photograph courtesy of Calico Corners—*Calico Home*

Bedrooms 5

Tailored to the bed

Beds, like the people who sleep in them, have idiosyncrasies of height and girth; that is why making a bed-spread requires such accurate measurements and careful estimates of yardage, which vary with the style of the spread—fitted, ruffled, or pleated.

Lighter than comforters or duvets, coverlets create a beautifully layered bed like the picture at left. Falling just below the mattress, coverlets are lined and can be made with your choice of fill weights. They can be tailored or fancy, casual or formal, quilted or unquilted. Matelassé fabrics make beautiful coverlets.

And, be sure to dress your bed all the way to the floor with a beautiful custom bed skirt designed to complement your coverlet, comforter, or duvet. Custom bed skirts are made for your bed, so they fit perfectly.

Calculations for bedcovers and skirts

The chart below lists the fabric and lining yardage needed for a fitted bedcover and a bed skirt, and the drawings at right show how to measure your bed to make them. The chart estimates are generous and provide ample fabric for welting and even for non-standard sizes.

With plain fabric, simply find the figures on the chart that best correspond to your bed. With patterned fabric, measure the depth of the skirt or drop *(C, F, or G on pages 132–133)* and add 2½ inches for a bed skirt or 5½ inches for a bedcover. Then measure the pattern repeat lengthwise from one design detail to the next one. If the repeat is longer than the total depth, use the column headed Long Repeats. If the repeat is shorter, use the column headed Short Repeats.

Estimating Yardage

Style of Cover	Bed Sizes	Plain Fabric 54-Inch Width	Fabric with Design Repeats 54-Inch Width		Lining 54-Inch Width
			Long Repeats	Short Repeats	
Fitted Bedcover	Twin	8	7 × Repeat ÷ 36 (Then add 3½)	14 × Repeat ÷ 36 (Then add 3½)	8
	Double	12	8 × Repeat ÷ 36 (Then add 7)	16 × Repeat ÷ 36 (Then add 7)	12
	Queen	12	8 × Repeat ÷ 36 (Then add 7)	16 × Repeat ÷ 36 (Then add 7)	12
	King	12	8 × Repeat ÷ 36 (Then add 7)	16 × Repeat ÷ 36 (Then add 7)	12
Fitted Bed Skirt	Twin	4½	6 × Repeat ÷ 36 (Then add 2½)	12 × Repeat ÷ 36 (Then add 2½)	7
	Double	6	6 × Repeat ÷ 36 (Then add 2½)	12 × Repeat ÷ 36 (Then add 2½)	8½
	Queen	6	7 × Repeat ÷ 36 (Then add 2½)	14 × Repeat ÷ 36 (Then add 2½)	11
	King	8	7 × Repeat ÷ 36 (Then add 2½)	14 × Repeat ÷ 36 (Then add 2½)	13

continued

Style of Cover	Bed Sizes	Plain Fabric 54-Inch Width	Fabric with Design Repeats 54-Inch Width		Lining 54-Inch Width
			Long Repeats	Short Repeats	
Pleated Bed Skirt	Twin	10	14 × Repeat ÷ 36 (Then add 2½)	28 × Repeat ÷ 36 (Then add 2½)	12½
	Double	12	14 × Repeat ÷ 36 (Then add 2½)	28 × Repeat ÷ 36 (Then add 2½)	17
	Queen	12	15 × Repeat ÷ 36 (Then add 2½)	30 × Repeat ÷ 36 (Then add 2½)	17
	King	13	15 × Repeat ÷ 36 (Then add 2½)	30 × Repeat ÷ 36 (Then add 2½)	18
Ruffled Bed Skirt	Twin	8	10 × Repeat ÷ 36 (Then add 2½)	20 × Repeat ÷ 36 (Then add 2½)	10½
	Double	10	10 × Repeat ÷ 36 (Then add 2½)	20 × Repeat ÷ 36 (Then add 2½)	12½
	Queen	10	12 × Repeat ÷ 36 (Then add 2½)	24 × Repeat ÷ 36 (Then add 2½)	15
	King	11	12 × Repeat ÷ 36 (Then add 2½)	24 × Repeat ÷ 36 (Then add 2½)	16

Basic Bed Measurements

Measuring the Box Spring for a Bed Skirt
Before measuring the box spring, remove the mattress. For accuracy, use a steel measuring tape or a yardstick.

Measuring platform length: Measure the platform—the top surface of the box spring—from the foot to the head of the bed *(measurement A on the diagram at left)*.

Measuring platform width: Measure across the platform from one side edge to the other *(B)*.

Measuring platform height: Measure down from the top edge of the platform to within ½ inch of the floor *(C)*.

Calculating the fabric for the platform cover: For the length of the platform fabric, add 9½ inches to A (this includes a 6-inch overhang and a 3-inch fold-over hem at the head and a ½-inch seam at the foot). To find the width of the platform fabric if your fabric is wider than the bed, add 1 inch to B. To achieve the width of the platform fabric if your fabric is narrower than the bed, you will have to add two side panels equally on each side of a central panel. The central panel will be the width of your fabric. To find the width of each side panel, subtract 1 inch from the width of your fabric, then subtract the result from B. Divide this figure by two and add 1 inch for seam allowances.

Calculating the fabric for the facings: The foot and side edges of the platform require 5-inch-wide facings. To find the length of each side facing, add 9½ inches to A. To find the length of the foot-end facing, add 1 inch to B.

Calculating the fabric for the skirt: For the length of the skirt, first multiply A by two and add B. Then add at least 7 inches for hems. For a pleated skirt, multiply this figure by three; for a ruffled skirt, multiply by two; for a fitted skirt, add 32 inches for corner pleats. To determine the number of fabric widths you should cut, divide the final skirt-length figure by the width of your fabric. To find the depth of the skirt, add 2½ inches for hem and seam to C.

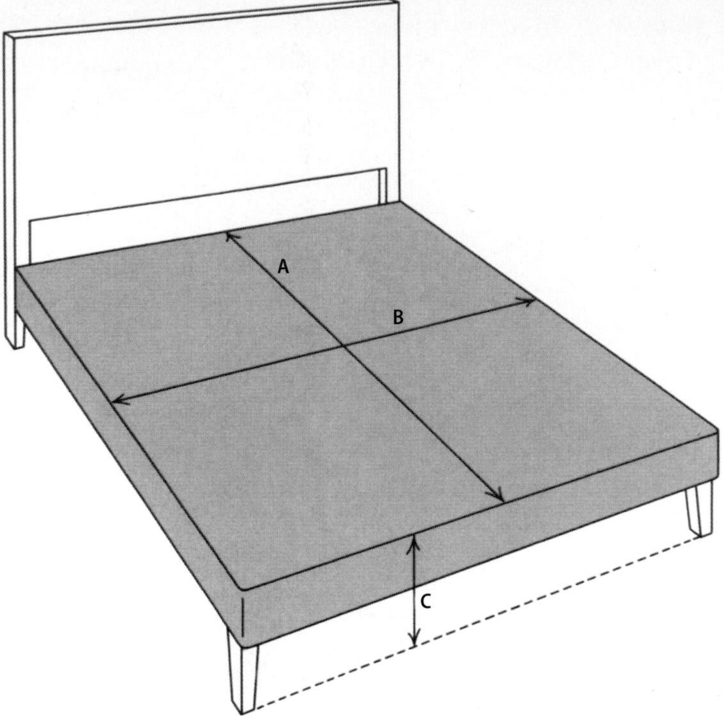

Chapter 5: Bedrooms

Basic Bed Measurements

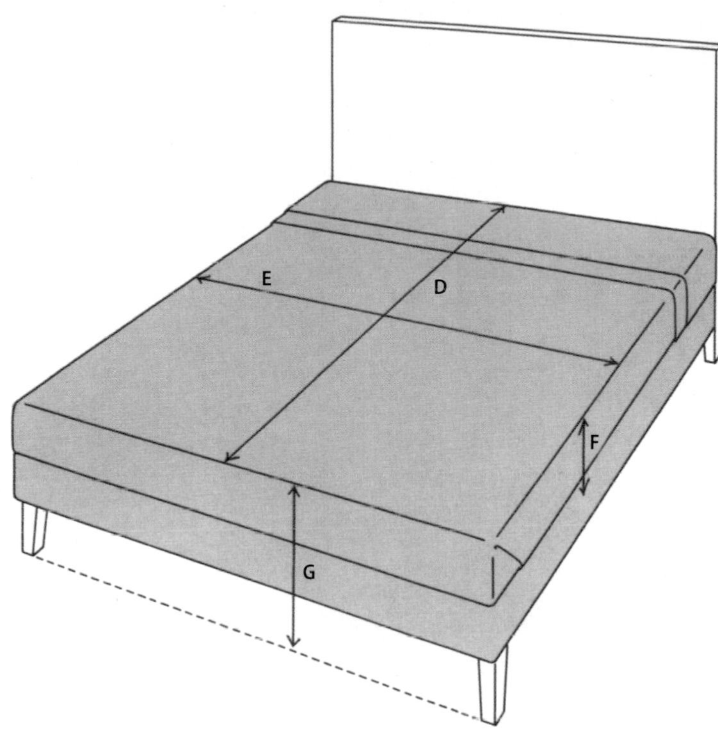

Measuring the Bed for a Fitted Bedcover
Before measuring, make the bed with the sheets and blankets you normally use but leave the pillows off. For accuracy, use a steel measuring tape or a yardstick.

Measuring the mattress length: Measure the top of the made-up mattress from the foot of the bed to the head *(measurement D in the diagram at right)*.

Measuring the mattress width: Measure across the top of the made-up mattress from one side edge to the other *(E)*.

Measuring the bed height: For a short bedcover, measure down one side from the top of the made-up mattress to at least 2 inches below the point where the mattress meets the box spring *(F)*. For a full-length bedcover, measure from the top of the mattress to within 1/2 inch of the floor *(G)*.

Calculating the fabric for the bedcover top: For the bedcover-top fabric length, add 27 1/2 inches to D (this includes a 24-inch tuck-in under the pillows, a 3-inch hem at the top and a 1/2-inch seam allowance at the foot). To find the width of the top if your fabric is wider than the bed, add 1 inch to E. If your fabric is narrower than the bed, add two side panels equally on each side of a central panel. The central panel will be the width of your fabric. To find the width of each side panel, first subtract 1 inch from the width of your fabric, then subtract the result from E. Divide this figure by two and add 1 inch for seam allowances.

Calculating the fabric for the drops: The foot and side edges require three panels of fabric called drops. To find the length of the two side drops, add 34 inches to D (for a 24-inch pillow tuck-in and 5-inch hems at the head and foot ends). To find the length of the foot drop, add 10 inches to E. To find the depth of each drop if you are making a short bedcover, add 5 1/2 inches to F (for 5-inch hems at the bottom and a 1/2-inch seam allowance at the top). If you are making a full-length bedcover, add the 5 1/2 inches to G.

How to make the basic coverings

Plain or fancy, home furnishings gain that costly, made-to-order-by-an-expert look when they are given the attention ordinarily reserved for haute couture gowns. Elementary shapes can be embellished with details borrowed from the couturier's techniques—or they can be used simply as they are. Either way, they must fit precisely to be properly haute couture.

To guarantee such precision in home furnishings, follow the instructions for measuring the items to be covered by the shapes—pillows, tables, window valances and beds. It is best to make larger shapes like bed covers or table throws in muslin first; a mistake in measuring the intended fabric can be costly. Before measuring any piece of fabric remove the selvages, so that none is included in the measurements. Figure on a seam allowance of ½ inch, rather than the ⅝ inch generally used in dressmaking calculations.

Fabric Needed for Bed Covers

The tables below indicate the approximate yardage of 54-inch-wide material that will be required to make coverlets or bedspreads for beds of the four most common standard sizes.

Coverlets

Bed Size	54-Inch Material
Twin	5¾ Yards
Double	5¾ Yards
Queen	6¼ Yards
King	9¼ Yards

Bedspreads

Bed Size	54-Inch Material
Twin	6¼ Yards
Double	7¾ Yards
Oueen	8¼ Yards
King	10¼ Yards

How to Measure a Bed

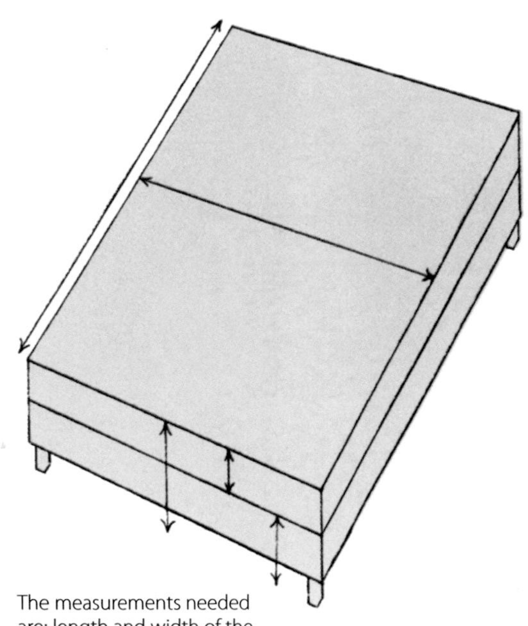

The measurements needed are: length and width of the mattress top; height (with the bed made); mattress depth from blanket top to box-spring top; length, width, and height of the box spring.

Measuring and Cutting the Coverlet

1. To find the length of each of the three coverlet panels, measure the length of the bed top and add 10 inches. If the coverlet is to tuck under and over pillows, add another 16 inches.

2. To find the width of each side panel, measure the width of the bed top, add 18 inches for the side drops, divide the total by four, and then add 1 inch for seam allowances to each side panel.

3. To find the width of the center panel, double the figure found in Step 2 and subtract 1 inch.

4. Cut the three panels to the dimensions calculated in Steps 1–3.

Cutting Curved Corners

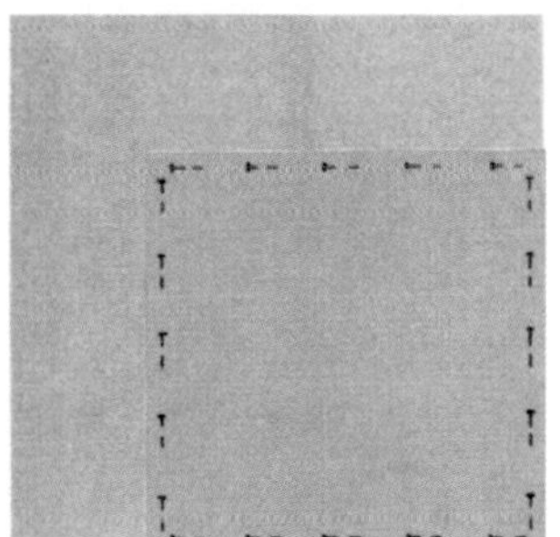

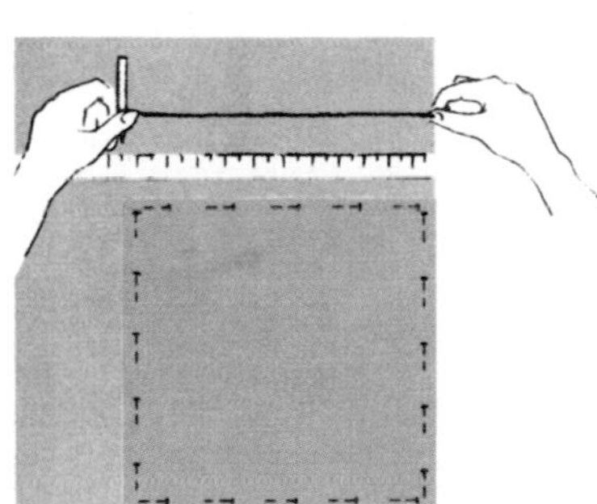

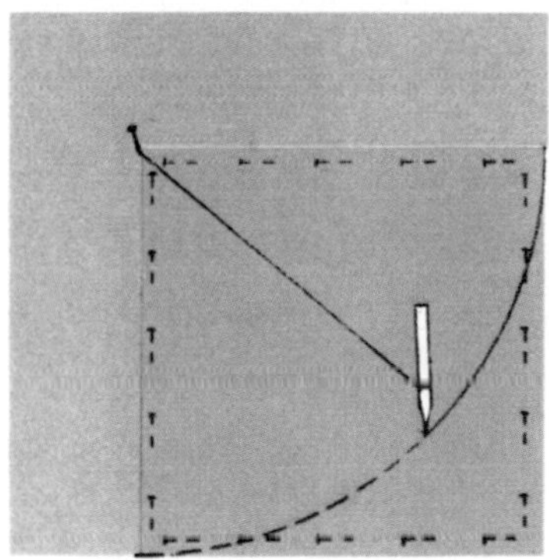

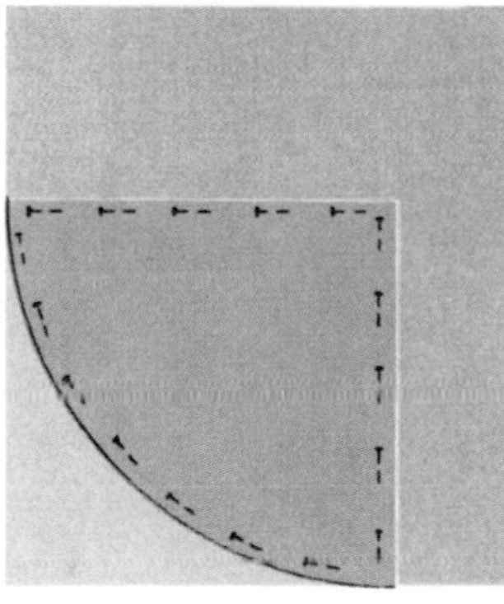

5. To curve the bottom corners, cut a square of shelf paper 9½ inches on each side and pin to a bottom corner of the coverlet, aligning the paper edges with the fabric corners.

6. Tie one end of a piece of string to a pencil and the other end to a thumbtack so that the separation is 9½ inches.

7. Insert the thumbtack at the corner of the paper square that is diagonally opposite the coverlet corner, and holding the string taut, draw an arc on the paper.

8. Cut paper and fabric along the arc drawn in Step 7. Remove the pins and the paper pattern.

9. Pin the paper pattern to the other bottom corner of the coverlet and cut the fabric along the arced edge of the pattern. Remove the pins and pattern.

The Basic Coverlet

Sewing the Coverlet

10. With the panels wrong sides out, pin the side panels to the center panel, ½ inch in from the edges at 2-inch intervals. Baste ⅜ inch in from the edges. Machine stitch, leaving a ½-inch seam allowance.

11. Remove the bastings and press the seams open.

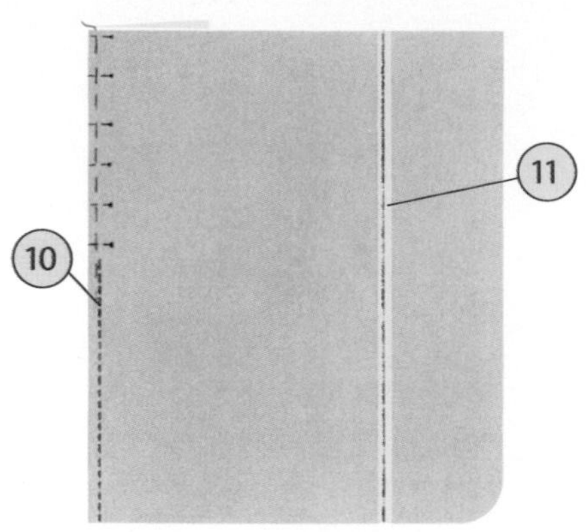

Lining the Coverlet

12. Measure, cut, and sew together three lining panels from preshrunk sheets just as for the coverlet.

13. With the coverlet fabric wrong side down, place the lining on it wrong side up. Pin the lining to the coverlet along the sides and foot ½ inch in from the edges at 2-inch intervals. Baste ⅜ inch in from the edges.

14. Remove pins and starting at one top corner, machine stitch—with a ½-inch seam allowance—along one side edge, around the foot and along the other side edge. Notch the curved corners. Remove the bastings.

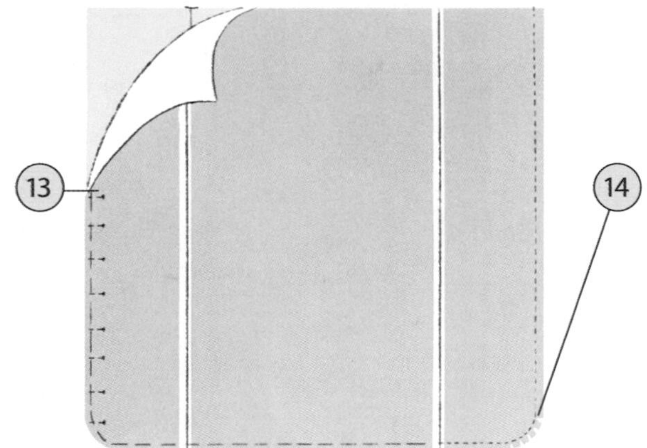

Finishing the Coverlet

15. Turn the coverlet right side out through the opening at the top of the coverlet and lining.

16. At the coverlet top, turn inside ½ inch of lining and coverlet fabric. Pin along the top ¼ inch in from the folded edges at 2-inch intervals. Baste ¼ inch in from the edges.

17. Remove the pins and slip stitch.

18. Roll the edges of the coverlet between the thumb and fingers to get a neat seam and baste all around the sides and foot.

19. Press the coverlet and remove all bastings.

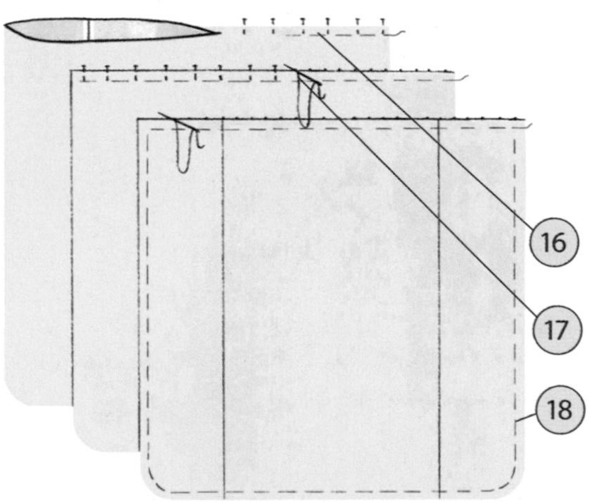

The Basic Bedskirt

Measuring and Cutting the Bedskirt

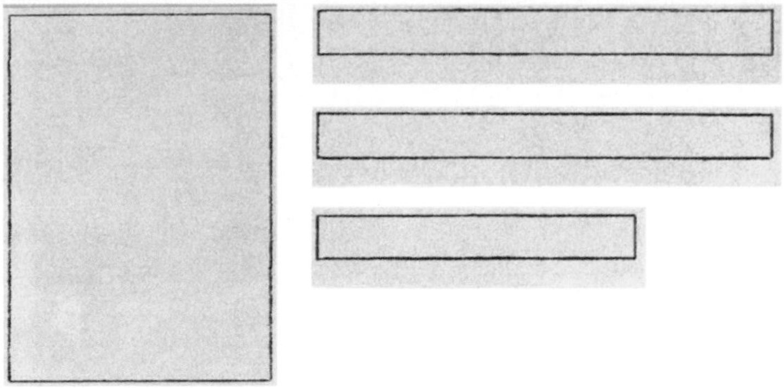

1. Cut the bedskirt top 1½ inches longer and 1 inch wider than the length and width of the box spring.

2. Cut each bedskirt side as long as the bedskirt top and 3 inches deeper than the box-spring height.

3. Cut the bedskirt foot as long as the width of the bedskirt top and as deep as each bedskirt side.

Sewing the Bedskirt

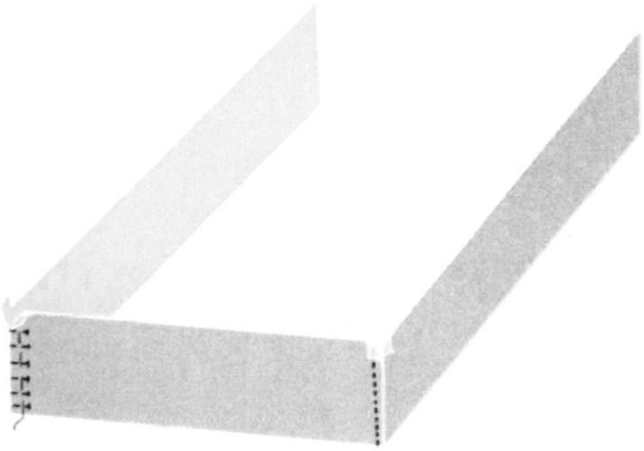

4. With the bedskirt sides and foot wrong side out, pin the foot end of each side to one end of the foot ½ inch in from the edges at 2-inch intervals. Baste ⅜ inch in from the edges. Remove the pins.

5. Machine stitch with a ½-inch seam allowance, leaving ½ inch open at the upper part of each seam. Remove the bastings. Press the seams open.

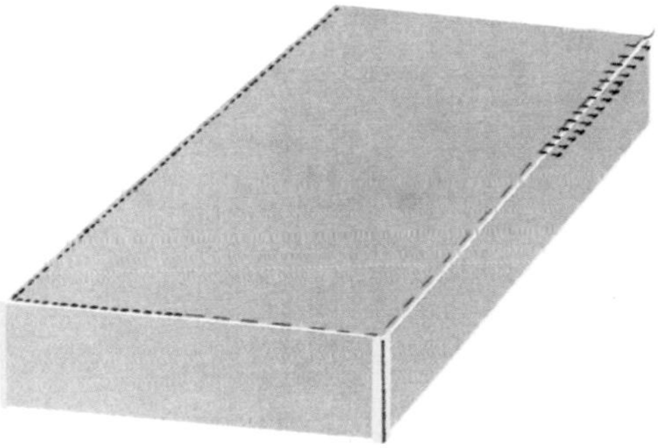

6. Place the bedskirt top wrong side up on the bare box spring and align its foot corners with the seams at the ends of the skirt foot, wrong side out. Pin the skirt foot to the skirt top and the sides of the skirt top to each of the skirt sides ½ inch in from the edges at 2-inch intervals. Baste the sides and foot to the top ⅜ inch in from the edges. Remove the pins.

7. Starting from one corner, machine stitch along one side edge, around the foot and along the other side edge with a ½-inch seam allowance. Remove the bastings. Press the seam allowances toward the skirt top.

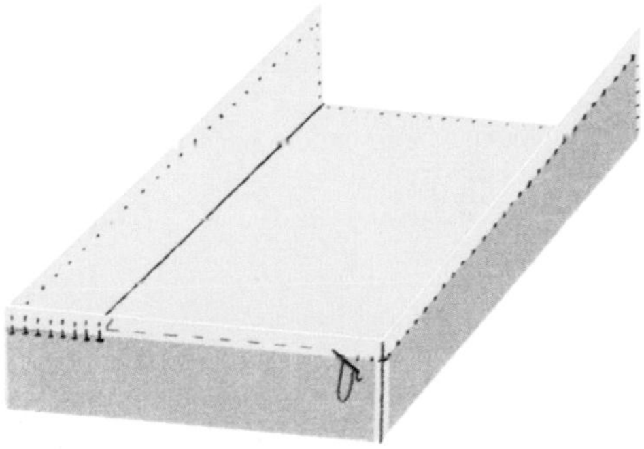

8. With the bedskirt wrong side up, turn the head end up ½ inch and press flat; then turn it up another ½ inch. Pin at 2-inch intervals. Turn the foot and sides up ½ inch and press flat; then turn them up another 2 inches. Pin at 2-inch intervals. Baste all around and remove the pins. Hem with a slip stitch. Remove bastings and press.

The Basic Bedspread

Measuring and Cutting the Bedspread

1. Cut each of the bedspread top panels 1½ inches longer than the length of the bed. If the bedspread is to go over pillows, add another 16 inches.

2. Decide on the finished width of the bedspread top center panel, subtract that figure from the bed top width, and divide the difference in half to obtain the finished width of each side panel. Add 1 inch for seam allowances to the finished width of each of the three panels to obtain the total widths, and cut.

3. Cut each side drop as long as the bedspread panels and 3 inches deeper than the height of the made-up bed.

4. Cut the foot drop 1 inch longer than the width of the made-up bed and as deep as the side drops.

Sewing the Bedspread

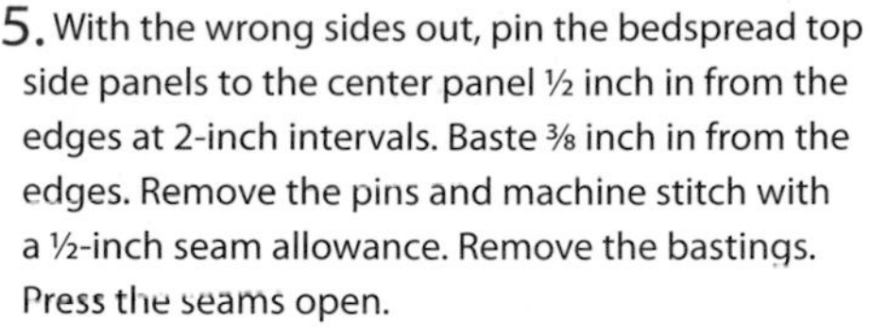

5. With the wrong sides out, pin the bedspread top side panels to the center panel ½ inch in from the edges at 2-inch intervals. Baste ⅜ inch in from the edges. Remove the pins and machine stitch with a ½-inch seam allowance. Remove the bastings. Press the seams open.

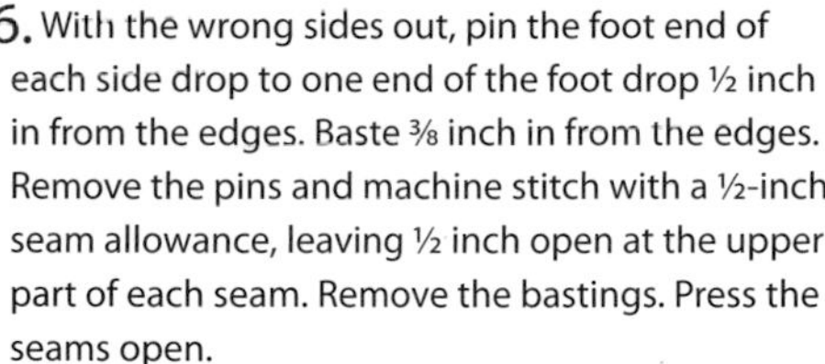

6. With the wrong sides out, pin the foot end of each side drop to one end of the foot drop ½ inch in from the edges. Baste ⅜ inch in from the edges. Remove the pins and machine stitch with a ½-inch seam allowance, leaving ½ inch open at the upper part of each seam. Remove the bastings. Press the seams open.

7. With all pieces wrong side out, place the bedspread top on the made-up bed, and align its foot corners with the seams at the end of the foot drop. Pin the top to the foot drop and then the side drops ½ inch from the edges at 2-inch intervals. Baste ⅜ inch in from the edges. Remove the pins.

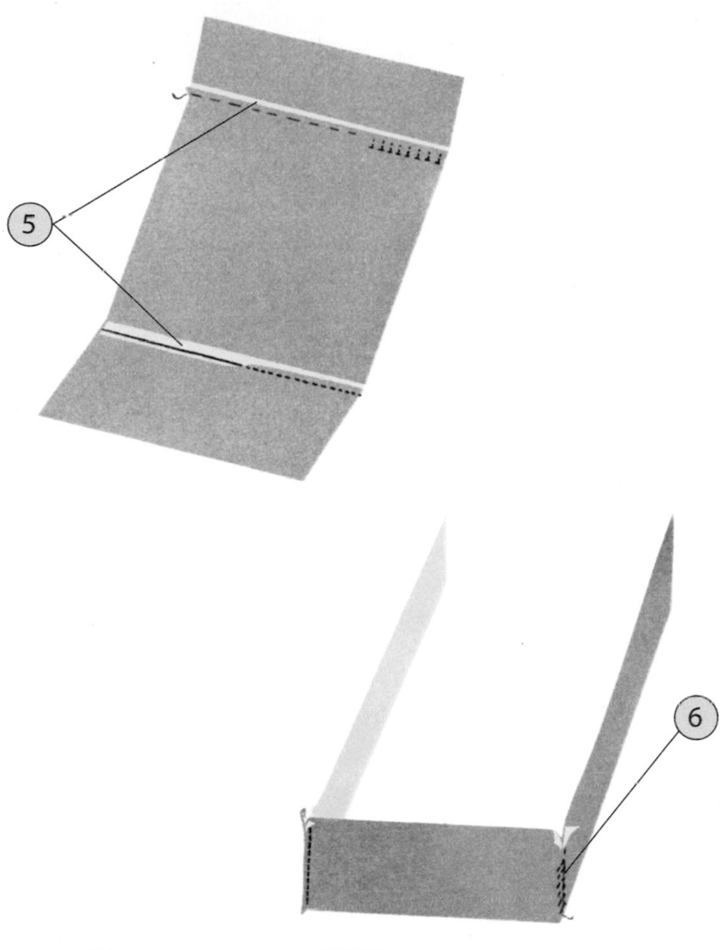

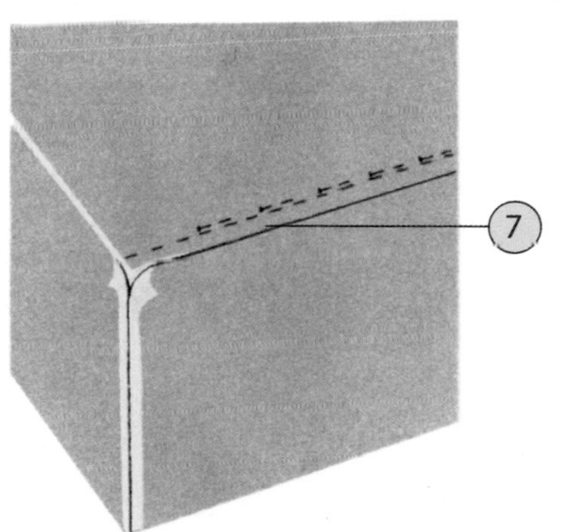

The Basic Bedspread

8. Starting from one head corner, machine stitch along one side edge, around the foot and along the other side edge with a ½-inch seam allowance. Remove the bastings made in Step 7.

9. Press the seam allowances toward the bed top.

10. Hem the edges following instructions for the bedskirt.

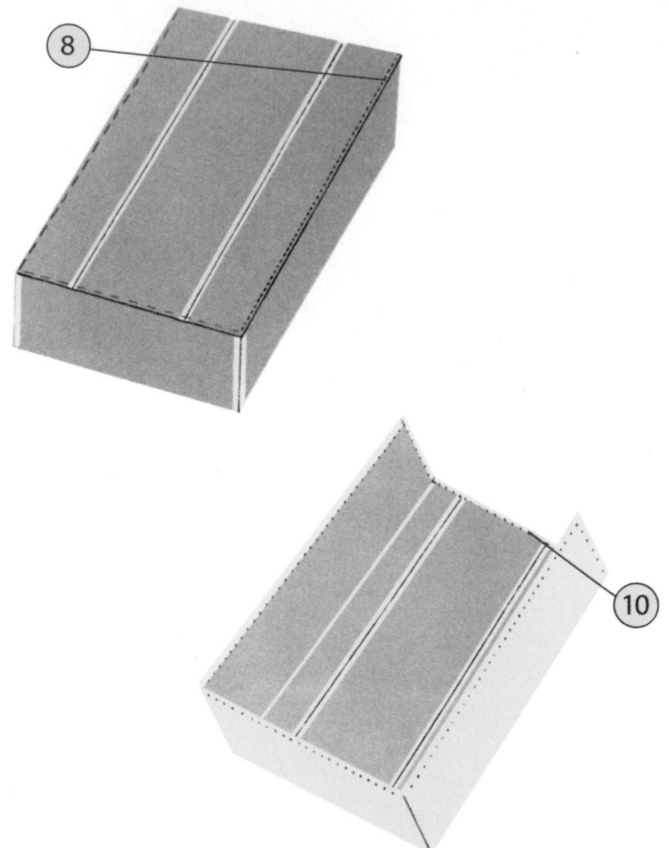

Preparing the Bedspread Lining

11. Cut three pieces from sheets ½ inch shorter than the corresponding bedspread top panel but of equal width.

12. Pin the lining side panels to the center panel ½ inch in from the edges. Baste ⅜ inch in from the edges. Remove the pins and machine stitch with a ½-inch seam allowance. Remove the bastings. Press the seams open.

13. Turn over ½ inch on all four edges. Pin at 2-inch intervals. Baste ¼ inch in from the edge. Remove the pins and press.

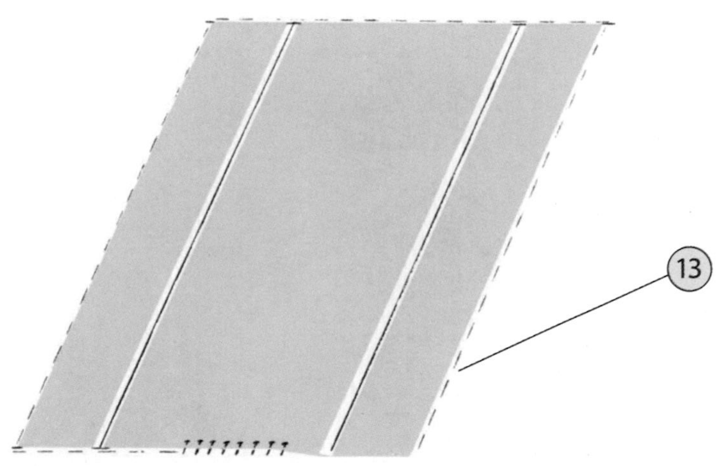

The Basic Bedspread

Sewing the Lining to the Bedspread

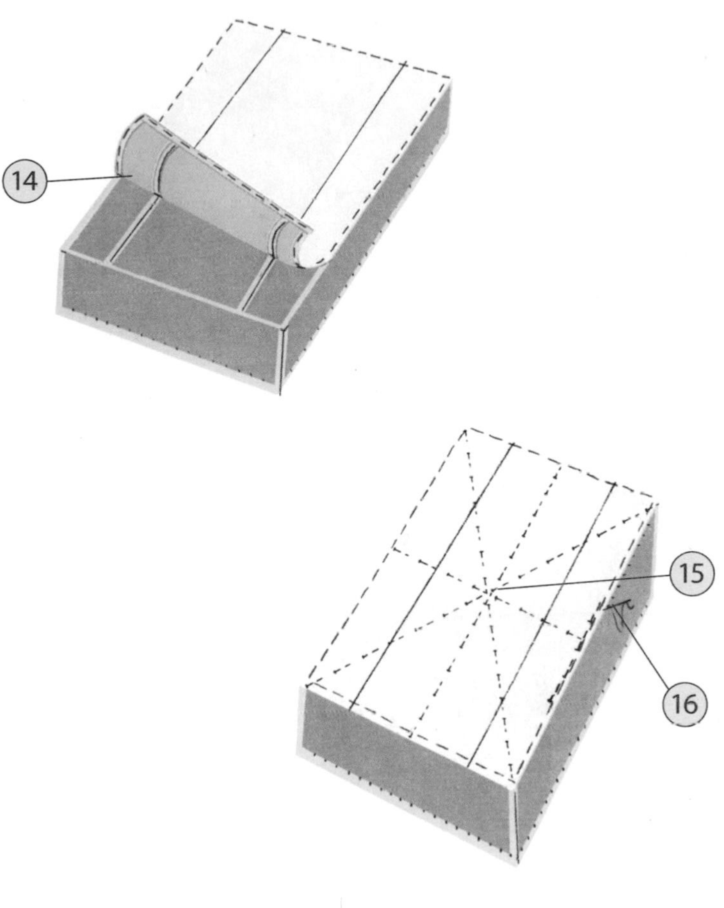

14. With the lining wrong side down and the bedspread top wrong side up, place the lining over the bedspread top, matching edges.

15. Pin the lining to the bedspread in the center and continue pinning to each corner. Then pin from the center out to the center edge of each side.

16. Pin the edges of the lining to the bedspread top ¼ inch in at 2-inch intervals. Baste ¼ inch in from the edges. Remove the pins along the edges and slip stitch on all four sides.

17. Tack the two panel seams of the lining and the bedspread top together with three stitches every 10 inches. Remove all of the remaining pins and bastings. Press.

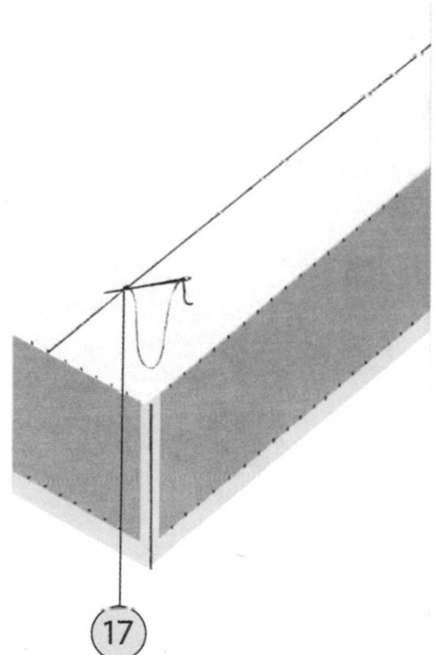

Index

Discover these other great craft books from Fox Chapel Publishing

Illustrated Guide to Sewing: Tailoring

A Complete Course on Making a Professional Suit

By the Editors at Skills Institute Press

From selecting the fabric to the final fit, learn to make a classically tailored suit with this step-by-step guide.

ISBN: 978-1-56523-511-3
$24.95 • 320 Pages

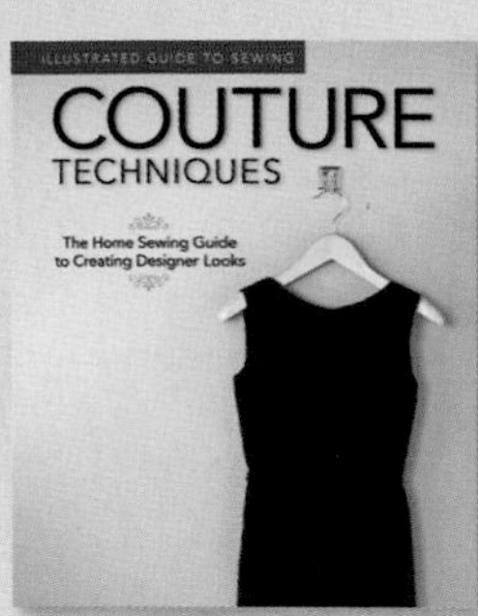

Illustrated Guide to Sewing: Couture Techniques

The Home Sewing Guide to Creating Designer Looks

By the Editors at Skills Institute Press

Create one-of-a-kind fashions that have shape, strength, and beauty with this guide to couture sewing techniques.

ISBN: 978-1-56523-534-2
$24.95 • 208 Pages

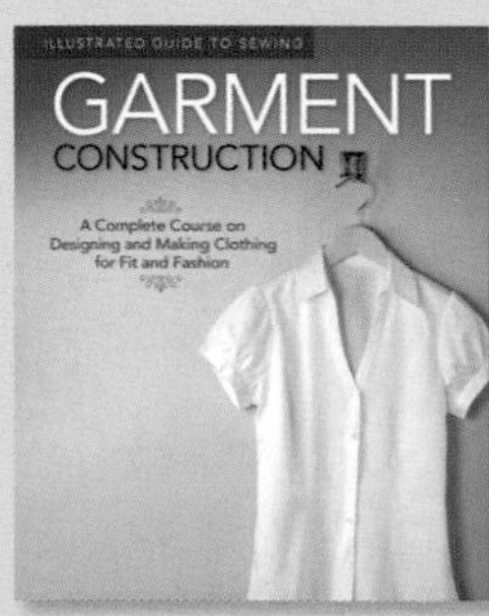

Illustrated Guide to Sewing: Garment Construction

A Complete Course on Designing and Making Clothing for Fit and Fashion

By the Editors at Skills Institute Press

Learn to make the building blocks of a great wardrobe, from the basic order of constructing a garment to trouble-shooting common fit problems.

ISBN: 978-1-56523-509-0
$24.95 • 320 Pages

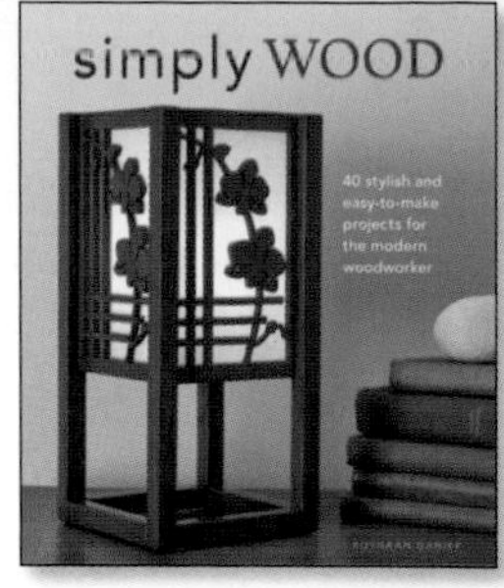

Simply Wood

40 Stylish and Easy-to-Make Projects for the Modern Woodworker

By Roshaan Ganief

Breathe new life into your scroll saw projects with unique, modern designs that will add beauty and flair to your home décor.

ISBN: 978-1-56523-440-6
$19.95 • 128 Pages

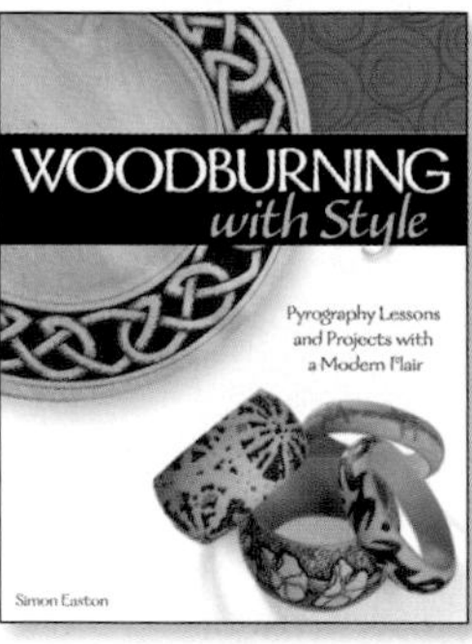

Woodburning with Style

Pyrography Lessons and Projects with a Modern Flair

By Simon Easton

This beautifully photographed, hands-on instructional guide to the art of pyrography will take you on a journey of skill-building exercises that begin at the basics and finish with stylish, gift-worthy projects.

ISBN: 978-1-56523-443-7
$24.95 • 208 Pages

Tree Craft

35 Rustic Wood Projects That Bring the Outdoors In

By Chris Lubkemann

Beautify your home with rustic accents made from twigs and branches. You'll find more than 35 eco-chic projects for a coat rack, curtain rods, candle holders, desk sets, picture frames, a table, chess set, and more.

ISBN: 978-1-56523-455-0
$19.95 • 128 Pages

Look For These Books at Your Local Bookstore or Specialty Retailer

To order direct, call **800-457-9112** or visit *www.FoxChapelPublishing.com*

By mail, please send check or money order + $4.00 per book for S&H to:
Fox Chapel Publishing, 1970 Broad Street, East Petersburg, PA 17520